THE GAME SHOW KING

THE GAME SHOW KING

A CONFESSION

CHUCK BARRIS

Carroll & Graf Publishers, Inc.
New York

First Carroll & Graf edition 1993
Second printing 1993

Carroll & Graf Publishers, Inc.
260 Fifth Avenue
New York, NY 10001

Library of Congress Cataloging-in-Publication Data

Barris, Chuck.
    The game show king : a confession / Chuck Barris.
        p.   cm.
    Includes index.
    ISBN 0-7867-0002-5: $21.95
    1. Barris, Chuck.   2. Television personalities—United States
—Biography.   3. Television producers and directors—United
States—Biography.   I. Title.
PN1992.4.B37A3   1993
791.45′028′092—dc20
    [B]   93-5953
                                                                        CIP

Manufactured in the United States of America

this book is for Red

My darling's eyes are as bright as tea,
her hair is orange as fire.
She lives inside a peanut shell,
and I love her or I'm a liar.
—Richard Kennedy

You have to go away to know about life.
　　　　　　　　　—*Ernest Villain*

PROLOGUE

I guess it all began with the Popsicle Twins. I'm fairly certain that's when I first thought of chucking it all and moving to the south of France.

When it comes to the Popsicle Twins I've got nobody to blame but myself. I auditioned and booked them. Needless to say, their first performance on the *Gong Show* was their last performance anywhere.

The *Gong Show* was a television program I created. I was also its host. The show appeared on coast-to-coast TV both in the daytime and at night. It was supposed to be a satirical spoof of your typical "stairway to the stars" talent revue. There were three celebrity judges. Each one of them could instantly terminate an act by whacking a huge gong with a large mallet. Maybe that's what the audiences liked, being able to vicariously get rid of someone they detested instantly. Maybe our audience wished life were that way. Who knows? Whatever the reason, the *Gong Show* was a massive hit for years.

I always considered the *Gong Show* the Boys Town of show business. Our creed—There's No Such Thing As A Bad Act—was indisputably debatable. The Popsicle Twins were one of those bad acts. And they weren't twins. They were two pretty teenagers; one sixteen, the other seventeen. Along with being cute, they were extremely sexy. Blond hair—a pigtail on one, two bunches on the other —blue eyes, freckles, deliciously ripe bodies under clinging tank tops, the swell of young breasts peeking out of the armholes, and high, round bottoms in very short shorts. The girls skipped out to center stage, sat down, crossed their legs yoga fashion, and to the music of "I'm In The Mood For Love," gave the greatest head you've ever seen to a couple of orange popsicles. The way those two sucked and licked and tongued those popsicles made dubious but definite television history.

Across the country, the knives and forks of our dinnertime audience were frozen between plate and mouth. Bedpans and injections were suspended in midair as wide-eyed hospital nurses and orderlies stopped dead in their tracks and watched room monitors alongside their equally dumb-struck patients. A New York police bomb squad expert lost the attention of a class of rookies learning how to defuse a trash can full of TNT. The students' eyes were riveted to the TV monitor on the wall behind the instructor's head. The sound had been turned off but you didn't need the sound to get the message. The bomb class loved the Popsicle Twins. But a United States senator's wife didn't. The senator's wife telephoned the senator and had him paged from the Senate floor. She pleaded with her husband to propose a law that would ban the *Gong Show* forever from the face of the earth. The senator's wife was a morbid harbinger of more sinister things to come.

Seconds after the program was over, the switchboards of every NBC-TV affiliated station across the country lit up like the proverbial Christmas tree. Switchboard operators couldn't handle the traffic, nor their ears the din of those hysterical callers. A tidal wave of indignation swept the country. It flooded through the corridors of NBC's headquarters in Burbank, California, and into the inner office of the company's president, Robert P. Mulholland.

Mr. Mulholland was a puritan and ferociously proprietorial toward NBC. The description of the Popsicle Twins act, the fact that it was broadcast on coast-to-coast television on *his* network, made Mulholland apoplectic. An all-points bulletin went out from the network all over Hollywood to find me post haste.

I drove to NBC with trepidation. In the best of times Robert P. Mulholland, a man known for his violent temper, was not my biggest fan. Instinct told me I would be lectured to and yelled at until Mulholland was exhausted. And then I would be dismissed wondering if I still had a show on the air. I was right on all counts.

"I want ratings, not cocksuckers!" raged Mulholland when I entered his office.

I didn't know what to say mainly because there really wasn't anything to say. No plausible explanation existed to justify exposure of

the Popsicle Twins on coast-to-coast television. Sure, they were hypnotic and diverting, but so is watching a hanging. Responsible television producers always have to remember there are kids in the audience, and nuns, and somebody's grandmother, and Baptist ministers,
nursery school teachers, Born Agains, hardline feminists, spinster
aunts; that kind of thing.

Just as I predicted, Mr. Mulholland ranted and raved until he
grew hoarse and was unable to rant any more. Drained, the president of the National Broadcasting Company sagged into his large
black leather desk chair, his face red and perspiring, his voice raw
and raspy. When he spoke, he sounded surprisingly old. He said,
"You've lost it, Chuck."

"Lost what?" I asked.

"Your fucking mind."

That night I told my wife, "Mulholland said I've lost my perspective,
or words to that effect."

"What do you think?"

"I think he's right."

It was late, after midnight, and we were in the kitchen eating
peanut-butter-and-jelly sandwiches. My wife and I solve our weight-
iest problems late at night over peanut-butter-and-jelly sandwiches.

I said, "Want to hear something strange? Last night during the
Gong Show taping I was standing on my mark waiting for a commercial break to end. It was really a wild show. I was exhausted and
sweating like a son of a bitch. The makeup lady's dabbing my forehead with Kleenex, and while she's doing that I sort of mumble to
myself, 'There must be more to life than game shows,' and the
makeup lady whispers back, 'There is.' Afterward, in my dressing
room, I got to thinking about what the makeup lady said and that
maybe she's right."

"In what way?"

"You know, all that stuff about life being short, that if you've got
your health and enough money in the bank to live happily ever after,
you should do it. And then tonight, while I was driving home from
the studio, I had this flash. Maybe we ought to try and sell the
company while the selling's good and move to the south of France."

"Really. And do what?"

"Live happily ever after."

PART I

She said, "Father Dourmant will hardly believe this. He is a French priest. He doesn't think much of Americans."
He said, "I've never met a Frenchman, secular or cleric who did."

—Michael Peterson

CHAPTER ONE

I am sitting on a bench in a park called the Place des Lices.

The park is in the small French fishing village of Saint-Tropez. The park is surrounded by outdoor cafés and shaded by large leafy trees. There's an open-air market here every Tuesday and Saturday morning. Hundreds of tents and trailers and long wooden stands materialize selling everything from cheese to fabulous antiques. Mothers push their baby carriages through the park stopping now and then to adjust their infant's hat or pop its pacifier back in its mouth. Pubescent girls slink by jiggling dangerously exposed tits and asses. Young men hoot. Old men dream.

It's a warm summer day in July and the park is filled to overflowing. Saint-Tropez is always overflowing during July and August. The streets are jammed with traffic, the park with tourists. There are lots of Americans, English, Germans, and Italians, lots of sunglasses, lots of sunburned arms lugging lots of shopping bags crammed with goodies from the village stores. I sit on my bench watching these goings-on, wiping the remnants of an ice-cream cone away from my mouth with a paper napkin, wondering if I'll play *boule* today with The Big Boys.

It's early and my friends have not yet arrived. I decide to practice throwing my *boule* balls for a while by myself. Before I can begin, my nerve endings are alerted by a couple of American tourists coming my way; a plump man in green ankle-high socks and black street shoes, and his thin, pointy-faced wife. They're both eating ice-cream cones. I think the Americans recognize me and I'm immediately uneasy. Being identified by strangers makes me uncomfortable. I become shy and hostile.

"You're American, aren't you?" says the husband.

"Hey, aren't you the guy—" says the wife, licking her cone, furrowing her eyebrows, squinting her eyes as if I'm small print.

"Do we know you?" asks the husband.

"I don't think so," I say, hardly concealing my displeasure, looking anywhere but at them. I turn my back on the pair and make myself busy taking my *boule* balls out of their sack.

"Could I bother you for a minute," says the husband, bothering me. He's going to ask me for my autograph. He better have a piece of paper and a pencil. He says, "Could you explain the game everyone's playing here in the park?"

Along with his green socks and black street shoes, the American is dressed in an bright orange nylon sweat suit. His wife is wearing a matching sweat suit, which goes with her dyed bright orange hair.

"Are these the balls?" asks the husband, grabbing one out of my hand. "They look like iron baseballs," he says to his wife.

The woman forces her lips into a tight smile. She continues to stare at me, her little pink reptilian tongue attacking her ball of ice cream, darting out swiftly and deadly, nipping chunks of sherbet. She is certain I'm hiding something from her.

"First you squat like this," I say to the husband hurriedly, wanting to get the explanation over with. I crouch down on my haunches. My knees crack painfully. I try not to wince. "In the beginning of a *boule* game somebody tosses the *cochonnet* about ten feet away from where the players are standing. That's what they call that little wooden ball over there, the one that's about the size of a marble." I point my finger in the direction of the *cochonnet*. "You roll your *boule* ball along the ground like so and . . ."

"I get it. I get it," says the husband impatiently, sucking the end of his leaking cone. "Your team tries to get more balls closer to that little wooden thing than the other team, right?"

"Yes, that's it," I answer, barely able to conceal my annoyance. The fat, out-of-shape husband irritates me. I notice his sea-of-orange wife walking away in the direction of the expensive shops across the street. I tell the husband, "Now I'm going to roll my ball and see how close I can get it to the *cochonnet*."

I roll the boule ball along the ground. It ends up fairly close to the *cochonnet*. It's a good roll. That's because I am not under any pressure. I stand up, pleased with myself.

"Can I try?" asks the American, putting the entire ball of ice cream and half the cone inside his mouth so that just the pointed end sticks out. He takes forever to hunker down. He rolls one of my *boule* balls toward the *cochonnet*. It comes much closer than mine.

Beginners' fucking luck.

I've lost interest in practicing.

I sit down again on the park bench and continue to think about things. Today I've been mulling over how similar the life of the malaria victim is to that of the expatriate. Both have recurring maladies; the malaria victim aching deliriums, the expatriate uneasy second thoughts: how one determination can—in the metaphysical snap of a finger—change your life dramatically.

It's been over five years since my wife and I were eating peanut-butter-and-jelly sandwiches in our kitchen in La La Land and I tried out my idea on her about selling the company and moving to the south of France. A few weeks later we agreed to do it and a few months later I made it happen. Just like that! I'm still shocked how fast life can change for those who can afford the luxury. One minute I'm sitting behind the chairman's desk of a TV production company in Hollywood and the next minute I'm on a park bench in a French fishing village. And what about the huge corporation I once ran. Where did it go? I made the whole company—myself included—disappear. As though I were a magician. Now you see me, now you don't. "One day," said a friend, "balloons and confetti were falling down on your head in front of twenty million TV viewers, and the next day you were gone forever."

I try to remember what prompted me to give up the entourages and excitement of national television in Hollywood for the reclusive solitude of writing and afternoons on this park bench in Saint-Tropez. In the middle of these thoughts I notice someone waving at me.

It's Henri Bruni.

Henri is my best French friend in Saint-Tropez. I've been coming here off and on since I graduated from college, and throughout all that time I've known Henri. He's my best friend because, aside from being a nice guy, he's the only one in Saint-Tropez who can understand my fractured French, and the only Frenchman I know with a sense of humor. Henri manages the Gorille bar-restaurant. He's in his middle forties, my size, with prematurely gray hair. A bad back makes Henri walk like Groucho Marx. Henri always comes to the park on his motorscooter with his daughter Emilie sitting on the back, hugging his stomach. Emilie is ten, but looks and acts nineteen. Someday she'll be a French movie star. Right now she kisses me and runs off to play with friends. Henri sits down beside me on the green bench.

Henri is licking an ice-cream cone and has brought one for me. "I saw that you were empty-handed," he says.

I don't tell Henri I just finished one. "Merci, Henri," I say.

My cone is vanilla and strawberry. A double. All of my friends know I'm into doubles now. In the beginning I would allow myself only one dip. At some point during the last few months, I changed to two dips. It wasn't long after I upgraded myself that I was busted.

"I saw you in the Place des Lices today," said my wife. "You had two scoops of ice cream."

My wife, my government, my Prime Minister. Ever vigilant. Eagle eyed. Deer eared. Her reason for being: to catch me with two scoops of ice cream, or a third chocolate-covered caramellow, or a fourth handful of salted peanuts. "I want to keep you alive" is her disclaimer.

"Yes," I confessed. "I had two scoops, but it's a French tradition. The French always have two scoops of ice cream before *boule.*"

"Last week you said one scoop was the tradition."

"I was wrong."

The first time I saw my wife was on an elevator. I joined her on the tenth floor going down. She wore a man's blue oxford button-down shirt opened at the neck, a thick brown belt with an oversize sterling silver western buckle, tight blue jeans, and fire engine-red cowboy boots. She was about a half an inch taller than me with green eyes, full lips, a cute turned-up nose, and the sexiest body I'd seen since I can't remember when. But what absolutely put me away was her incredible red hair, and her freckles. I was instantly smitten. I said, "E.M. Forster wrote that it wasn't a criminal offense to fall in love at first sight."

She said, "Excuse me?"

Red was twenty-two. I was forty-four. By the time we reached the ground floor, I proposed. God knows what she must have thought. Probably that I was just another dirty old man. She accepted two years later. My wife's name was Robin. From the moment we met I

called her Red. A few years ago she legally changed her name to
Red.

Henri listens with great interest to my story about my wife busting me with two scoops of ice cream. "Red is tough?" he asks.

"Not at all."

"She watches you very closely," he says.

"She doesn't want to lose me," I reply in my atrocious French.
"She wants to keep me around for a while. I am twenty-two years
older than she is."

"You're twenty-two years older than Red?" asks Henri, mildly
surprised.

"Yes, twenty-two years. I married her when she was a baby."

"You look more like you're *thirty*-two years older," he says.

"Heh, heh, heh, heh," goes Loulou the electrician who has joined
Henri and me on the bench. Loulou's a nice guy with an annoying
laugh. Four staccato hehs in a row. "I hope you're still able to get a
little biscuit," he adds with a leer.

"What's he mean by a little biscuit?" I ask Henri in French.

"A little hump," he answers in English.

I give my cone a mournful lick. I am momentarily horrified to
think that my life is dribbling to a close leaving me on a bench in a
French park discussing biscuit with a pair of Tropezians.

And then my heart skips a beat.

Across the way another friend, Louis Ugo, is waving his arms
trying to get my attention. He wants me to bring my *boule* balls and
come to where he and some of The Big Boys are. Earlier Louis Ugo
told me he was going to try and persuade The Big Boys to let me
play *boule* with them this afternoon. Apparently he has. Louis Ugo
continues to wave me over. He wants Loulou to come, too.

I make body motions asking: Are you sure you want me?

He nods his head yes.

So there it is. I've made a historic breakthrough. I've crossed a
major xenophobic boundary line. I'll be the first American to play
with The Big Boys; the Jackie Robinson of French *boule*.

Loulou, Henri, and I walk across the park to where The Big Boys
are. When I get there I sort of slink off to the side and take a few
deep breaths. I can't believe how nervous I've suddenly become.
Henri Bruni agrees. He says out of the side of his mouth, *"C'est
seulement un jeu."* It is only a game.

Obviously I will play with my friends Loulou and Louis Ugo. The other Big Boys won't touch me. They don't even talk to me. As far as they're concerned, I might as well be in Trenton, New Jersey.

Some Tropezians gather to watch our game. They stand in a circle kidding Louis Ugo and Loulou about playing with "l'Americain." Someone in the crowd hollers: "Hey, Louis. Hey, Loulou. This is not baseball. Let the Americains stay in the boutiques." Everyone laughs uproariously. At what? I didn't hear anybody say anything funny. But then where is it written that the French say funny things? Other than Afghans and those from Sierra Leone, the French are quite possibly the most humorless race on earth.

Louis Ugo and Loulou joke back and forth with the Tropezians, but through it all I can see the two are plainly nervous about me. I'm their responsibility, the guy they shoved down the other Big Boys' throats. I know this and I'm visibly distraught.

Louis Ugo and Loulou tell me I am going to be fine.

I nod.

"*Doucement,* Chuck, *doucement,*" they both add. Slowly, Chuck, slowly. Take your time.

A coin is flipped. Someone says, "*Pile ou face?*" Heads or tails? Louis Ugo says, "Face." Face it is. We've won the toss so we go first, which means I'll roll first. I squat and take a deep breath. *Doucement,* I whisper to myself, and then I roll my ball.

When I return home, Red says I look like a ghost.

"I played horribly," I say.

"Get a grip," she tells me. "It's only a game."

I hardly eat dinner. Later I go to my rocking chair, sit down, and stare at my crotch. I let myself be sucked into the depths of a wretched funk.

"You are being silly and childish," says Red. "And slightly deranged."

Silly, I agree. Childish, I agree. Even slightly deranged. But so what? That's how I feel and nothing I tell myself kicks me out of my mood. This surprises me. My ability to cope has somehow fallen into disrepair. My sense of values is patently out of whack. *Boule* games with the locals have become my entire reason for being. Good *boule,* good day. Bad *boule,* bad day. Bad *boule* with The Big Boys and life's not worth living. Is that what my life has come down to? It occurs to me that I might very well need psychiatric help.

"You could use a good shrink," says my wife. Red always knows what I'm thinking.

That night I sleep fitfully, replaying the afternoon's game, reliving every one of my dreadful rolls, moaning aloud at the really bad throws, the ones that went off somewhere on their own. I cannot stop myself from moaning aloud. The moans just sort of pop out.

"Ooooooooo," I howl.

"What!" asks Red, shooting straight up out of her pillow, holding herself erect by her locked elbows.

"Nothing," I whisper, and pat the top of her head. "Go back to sleep."

"You're not replaying that goddamn *boule* game are you?"

"Absolutely not," I lie. "It must be something I ate."

"Take a few Tums," she says, and settles back into her pillow.

I go to the bathroom and take a few Tums. I return to bed and lie on my back. Then on my stomach. I howl again, muffling this one in my pillow.

It's useless. I can't sleep.

I listen to the church bells ringing the hour. It's midnight. The bells finish tolling. There's a moment of quiet. A foghorn bellows sadly. My wife has fallen back to sleep. She's dreaming. She smacks her lips contentedly. Somewhere in the street a motorcycle goes by the house. A dog barks. I lie on my back staring at our bedroom ceiling with big wide Orphan Annie eyes.

My mind wanders. I think about the Ostrich and that winter night in New York City, thirty years ago.

CHAPTER TWO

I was getting ready to leave work at the ABC Television Center on West Sixty-sixth Street. I was halfway out the door of my tiny cubicle, heading for the elevator, when I noticed something depressing. The Ostrich was waving me into his office.

The Ostrich, I should explain, was my boss, Walter Armani, vice president of daytime television programs for the American Broadcasting Company. He was a stumpy man in his early forties, and nervous. (I've changed his name.) Armani had a round face, a thick neck, and beady eyes. His suit coats were baggy, his shirts too tight, his pants cuffed so short it appeared as though he was waiting for a flood. Mr. Armani was in charge of all programs on ABC's fledgling daytime television network from sign-on in the morning until the evening news. At that time there were only two half-hour game shows on ABC; one at three and one at three-thirty, so my boss wasn't in charge of much.

Which was a good thing.

An overabundance of responsibility might have caused Mr. Armani irreparable harm. The man suffered dermatological problems when confronted with trouble of any kind, particularly those relating to his department, the folks who told him about them, and most of all the culprits who created them. His attitude was: no news is good news. All of us who worked for Armani called him the Ostrich; the man who would love to be able to stick his head in the sand and not see or hear anything.

"The Ostrich is beckoning you," whispered a pretty secretary from the corner of her mouth as she passed.

"My lucky day," I mumbled.

For a vice president, the Ostrich's office was modest. It had one couch and window with a view of a brick wall. I walked up to his desk and smiled. He looked at me sternly and said, "Okay, I'm going to let you go to California, if for no other reason than to shut you up and get you out of my sight."

Mr. Armani was angry for two reasons. One was my ambition, an attribute he considered inexcusable. The second was my persistent requests to be transferred to Hollywood, a badgering I had inflicted upon him for months.

"It's where the action is," I had said over and over again. "It'll be good for the company to have a representative there."

"And good for you," Armani had groused.

Of course, good for me. If I could prove the need for an office in Hollywood, I would be the one to run it. Still, I felt our network's daytime programming department was being derelict by not having a presence on the West Coast. We weren't getting our share of the new ideas being created out there. Our two competitors, NBC and CBS, had daytime television offices in Hollywood. Why didn't we? The Ostrich ignored my pleas. So I did the unspeakable. I went over his head. I took my case to his superiors and received their permission to go.

"Nothing but trouble if you ask me," Armani said. "Personally I think you're creating a whole new basket of problems, and if there's one thing I hate it's problems."

"I know."

"A total waste of time and corporate money," added the Ostrich, handing me my expense check.

It was for seven hundred and fifty dollars. After paying for my round-trip plane ticket, hotel room, and meals, I'd be lucky if I could stay the weekend. How many Hollywood producers could I visit, how many new daytime TV ideas could I uncover in a weekend?

"Something bothering you?" asked the Ostrich, noticing the expression on my face. "Is there a problem I'm not aware of?"

"No, sir."

"I should hope not. And let me tell you this. If you ever go over my head again, write another goddamn memo to Fetter or Scherick or whoever the fuck is running things, without clearing it with me first, I'll personally see to it that you never work at a television network again. Is that clear?" The Ostrich paused, then said, "You know, maybe this idea of yours isn't that bad after all. Maybe with a little luck I'll never see you again."

The next day I left the familiar snow and slush of New York for the foreign sunshine of La La Land.

In order to conserve money, I checked into an inexpensive motel on Wilshire Boulevard in West L.A. The motel rented most of their rooms by the hour, but it was all I could afford if I wanted to stay in Los Angeles for two weeks. I immediately began telephoning the respectable television game show producers in town. I told their secretaries my name, that I was with the American Broadcasting Company, that I was looking for daytime TV properties, and if they had any to please call me back at the Del Capri Motel. Nobody called me back. Not a soul.

But then, what corporate executive would be worth calling back who stayed in a place called the Del Capri Motel? Learning this Hollywood lesson quickly, I moved. I checked into a famous posh establishment in another part of town, and took a suite that cost a hundred dollars a night. In 1962, a hundred dollars a night was a lot of money. This was going to be tricky, especially if I wanted to stay for two weeks and try to accomplish something. I only had a couple of hundred dollars left from my company expense check. The hotel room alone would wipe me out in forty-eight hours. I decided to gamble and spend my own money. So I dipped into my savings account and withdrew residuals I had recently received from a hit rock and roll record I wrote called "Palisades Park."

Palisades Park was an amusement park on the Jersey side of the Hudson River.

Every time I drove along Manhattan's West River Drive I would recite a two-liner to myself: "Each night after dark, I take a trip down to Palisades Park." One night, bored in my Forty-second Street walk-up apartment, I picked up my guitar and dashed off a song about going to Palisades Park, riding on the Ferris wheel, going through the tunnel of love, and ending up with the girl of my dreams. Not being able to read music, I sang the tune into a tape recorder accompanying myself on my Martin six-string. I sent the audio tape to two of my rock heroes of that time: Bobby Rydell and Freddie Cannon. Freddie recorded the song. It was going to be the

B side of his next record. The other side—the A side—was supposed
to be the hit. It was a song called "June, July And August."

The A side died an early death.

"Palisades Park" was a smash.

The record skyrocketed to number two on all the music charts,
which provoked an immediate summons to the chief counsel's office
of the American Broadcasting Company. The chief counsel was an
terminally mean, undersize man named Mort Weinbach. Weinbach
was never a thrill a minute to talk to under normal circumstances.
Now, punch drunk from the recent music business payola scandals
that had humiliated the three television networks, he was unbearable. The last thing he needed, especially just when everything was
calming down, was some lowlife clerk causing another scandal with a
half-ass rock and roll record. Undoubtedly Chief Counsel Weinbach
assumed I had used my position with the ABC television network
plus some under-the-table payoffs to key disc jockeys around the
country to get the record played. How else would it have risen so
high up on the charts? Certainly not on its own merits.

Minutes after I walked into Weinbach's office, I was fired.

"Why, sir?" I said, furious and frightened.

"Because."

"Because, sir? Because? What kind of answer is that, sir?"

"It's my answer and it's quite good enough."

"The hell it is, sir. I disclosed everything in lengthy corporate
memos every step of the way. I did nothing illegal. You can't fire me.
I'm not a songwriter. I can't even read music. I'm a television person. That's all I've been since I got out of college."

It was true. Television was all I knew.

My parents thought I'd never know anything. They took a dim
view of my future when the best job I could secure when I graduated from college was a position on the university's janitorial staff.

Then things got worse.

CHAPTER THREE

My father, a less than inspiring dentist in his fifties, had a stroke and died. He left us nothing. I was forced to sell his dental chairs and instruments to pay off his debts. I took what was left and invested in bad stocks, wiping out what little cash my mother might have had. My mother was beautiful and proud, and extraordinarily young-looking for her age. Humiliated and embarrassed, my mother and my kid sister were forced to move into my grandparents' cramped center city apartment. My sister regrettably dropped out of college. My mother lost her youth and beauty. Philadelphia became permanently depressing for me.

I moved to New York and got a job as a page with the National Broadcasting Company. My days were spent guiding tours through NBC headquarters at Rockefeller Center, my nights, watching the first live color television broadcasts at the NBC-TV studios in Brooklyn. Someone suggested I apply for the company's management training program. Each year NBC chose six candidates from several thousand applicants to learn every facet of corporate life. At the end of the year the candidate selected a department within NBC and made a career there for himself. It was an incredible opportunity and therefore one had to know somebody to become a candidate. I didn't know anyone. I went to the New York Public Library and looked up the board of directors of NBC's parent company, the Radio Corporation of America. I selected three board members' names and used them as my references. I was chosen as one of the six candidates. The NBC personnel department never checked.

One morning, during my training program, a clerk from the personnel department caught me feeling up a pretty young secretary behind the racks in the company's legal library. The clerk took me directly to Reuven Frank, head of NBC-TV's Evening News. I thought Mr. Frank was an odd choice as the one to fire me, but then what did I know? Mr. Frank asked if I was the trainee from Philadelphia. I said I was. He said no one in the entire company knew how to get to Grace Kelly's house in Philadelphia. He asked if I knew how to get there. I said I did. (Actually I wasn't sure.) Mr. Frank ordered me to lead the NBC News crew to her house. Grace Kelly was going to announce her engagement to a prince from Monaco. I brought the crew to the Kelly house. When we returned to New York, Mr. Frank looked at me and smiled. That's about as complimentary as he gets. Reuven and I still have lunch a half a dozen times a year.

When the management training program was over I joined daytime television sales. I had heard the quickest way to the presidency of the network was through any sales department. My boss was a hearty Irishman named John Lanigan. Lanigan liked me. He said I had the stuff good salesmen were made of. I was low man on the totem pole but I was on my way. I was also fooling around with Lanigan's sexy secretary. One night after everyone had gone, I slipped a mushy love letter under her office door. A few minutes later one came back under mine. I was thrilled she was still in her office and obviously adored me. Only the note wasn't from her. It was from the personnel department. The note explained there had been a corporate efficiency study. One conclusion of the study was that the daytime TV sales department was expendable. John Lanigan, all his account executives, all their secretaries, and I were fired. That the National Broadcasting Company had spent thousands of dollars training me for future leadership didn't seem to matter.

I bummed around New York for almost a year. Couldn't find a job to save my soul. Until the day I walked into ABC-TV for the umpteenth time and their director of daytime television, Julian Bercovici, asked me if I was still unemployed. I said I was. He said he had a job for me. I was to go to Philadelphia every day and keep an eye on Dick Clark. Why? Purely symbolic, he said. Just until this music payola business passed. Julian explained that though Dick Clark had nothing to do with payola in any way, shape, or form, the American Broadcasting Company thought it best to have someone "watch-dog" Dick's *American Bandstand* program, as a bone to the Federal Communications Commission. How long could I plan on

having this unexpected windfall of a job? Two or three weeks, a
month at most, answered Bercovici. Just until Dick's voluntary
meeting with the FCC in Washington took place, a routine compli-
ance the Commission had requested from all three networks concerning their music programs. ABC purchased a conservative suit
for me (a "watch dog" should have a conservative suit and I didn't
own one, conservative or otherwise) and sent me back to the city
from whence I had fled.

Every Monday through Friday I would board a train at Penn Station, travel to the City of Brotherly Love, watch *American Bandstand,* board a train at 30th Street Station, and return to New York. I
thought I'd despise the commute, but I loved it. One hour and forty-
five minutes, twice a day, to read and think and nap. Never again
have I been so informed on current events, so up to date on the
latest novels, so rested.

The *American Bandstand* personnel hated my guts. Clark's staff,
the TV crew, just about everyone connected with the show thought I
was a spy. Everyone except Dick. He understood why I was there.
He gave me a desk and a chair and made me feel important. Every
day at *American Bandstand* for want of something better to do, I
would write a memo to myself concerning the trivia of that afternoon: who was on the show, who canceled, what songs the performers sang, if their performances were good or bad, some meritorious
though highly fictitious feats I had accomplished, a few jokes, one or
two philosophical contemplations. When I wasn't doing that, I was
introducing myself to the various artists, chatting with them as
though I knew what I was talking about. I shook Brenda Lee's hand
and told her she had a great future in the business. She thanked me
and walked away. I had no idea she already had nine gold records.

A little more than a year later Dick went to Washington to have
his meeting with the FCC commissioners. It was the same meeting
that was supposed to have taken place fifty-five weeks before. Dick
carried over five hundred pages of my memos with him. The commissioners eyed the stack warily. There seemed to be a certain re-
luctance on their part to peruse my bales of crap. As a result, the
meeting was short and pointless. The commissioners chatted with
Dick, more like fans than commissioners, shook his hand, apologized
for inconveniencing him so, and thanked him profusely for coming.

If my hundreds of memos were not appreciated by the Federal

Communications Commissioners, they *were* by Dick Clark and the American Broadcasting Company. My quasi-bizarre diligence earned me a lifelong friendship with Dick and a permanent job with ABC-TV's daytime programming department. I was given a modest raise, a small cubicle of my own and Walter Armani, aka the Ostrich, as my boss. All things considered, it was a happy ending for me. My mother and sister had happy endings, too. My sister married a wonderful man and lived a happy life. My mother remarried an extremely rich gentleman named Bortin and lived an even happier life than my sister.

And that's brings us to just about the time I wrote "Palisades Park."

Chief Counsel Weinbach glared at me. "I don't need this. The company doesn't need this. The company doesn't need you."

I begged the chief counsel not to fire me. I said I would do anything, just please don't fire me.

"You can stay if you sign a letter that states you will never write another song again as long as you work for the American Broadcasting Company."

I signed the letter. That evening I wrote another song. I used a pseudonym. During the next five years I wrote over a dozen songs. Two of them did very well, though I shan't tell you their names. In 1962, "Palisades Park" earned me thirty thousand dollars in residuals. I bet some of that money, and a posh room in an exclusive hotel, on a better job. This time when I left my messages with the secretaries of famous game show producers, I made sure they were aware of my new address: The Beverly Hills Hotel, Bungalow 22.

Everyone called me back.

My trip was a huge success. I returned to New York with a dozen good ideas. I was rewarded with an airline ticket back to California and a promotion. This time I traveled in style. When I arrived I was given a beautiful office with three windows, drapes, a couch, a handsome plastic water decanter, and a cheerful secretary named Susanne Thurber. I also had a new title. I was now: Director of Daytime Television Programs, American Broadcasting Company, West Coast Division. The title was impressive but looked ridiculously long on my business letters. I began typing a shorter one. Duke of Daytime. My network bosses didn't find my new title funny. I was scolded severely. That reprimand turned out to be the beginning of the end of my brief corporate career.

Though I had been in Los Angeles for only a short time, I had already grown tired of my job. I loathed getting up in the morning and going to those gray ABC buildings at Prospect and Talmadge. I detested spending week after week implementing unimaginative bureaucratic orders from New York. I hated bland meals with bland people in the stiflingly boring executive dining room. And now to be brought to task so severely over a piddling matter such as retitling myself! That was plainly the last straw.

There were, however, two benefits from serving time with the American Broadcasting Company. One was learning what TV programs worked and what didn't. The other was the chance to become familiar with all the television production staffs in Hollywood. I could decide which people on those staffs were talented so I could lure them away when the time came to go out on my own. In the meantime I spent my days trying to think of a new game show idea, and looking for an omen that would tell me it was time to say bye-bye to corporate life.

One morning while throwing darts at the dart board that hung on the back of my office door, the omen appeared. My secretary Susanne Thurber rushed in to tell me some unimportant news. Had she arrived a second later I would have buried a dart in the middle of her forehead. That I didn't was the harbinger I was looking for! Some power bigger than the both of us was telling me to leave the American Broadcasting Company before I did something terrible to myself or someone else. I resigned that day.

A week later they gave me a going-away party. In the executive dining room. It was sparsely attended, just a half dozen indifferent employees happy to escape their cubicles for an hour and drink free punch. I was given gifts: a tie clip that had American Broadcasting Company inscribed on it and a company necktie to go with it. The tie was black with a scattering of gold ABC logos here and there.

"What are your plans?" asked an indifferent accountant, a plastic liner stuffed with ballpoint pens in his shirt pocket.

"I haven't any idea," I replied, "except to go to Las Vegas this weekend. Play the slots and get some sun."

"Hey! You like rodeos?"

"Very much."

"ABC Sports is covering the national rodeo championships in Las Vegas this weekend. Would you want to go?"

"Absolutely."

"Okay," said the man with the ballpoint pens, "here's what you do. When you get to Vegas, go to the fair grounds, locate the ABC remote truck, and find the director."

"Then what?"

"Just tell him who you were."

CHAPTER FOUR

My stepfather, David Bortin, was in his late eighties; kind and gentle, fragile and effeminate. He wore silk robes and ascots, and was a generous patron of the arts. My stepfather loaned me twenty thousand dollars so I wouldn't starve during the time it took me to create and sell a TV game show idea. Even though my mother warned my stepfather that I was a bum at heart, he believed in me. In return for the money, I promised my stepfather fifty percent of the profits of my future television company, forever.

"Fifty percent of nothing," scoffed my mother.

"We'll see," said my stepfather, signing the check.

I thanked my stepfather for his generosity.

"What is the name of your new idea?" he asked.

"The *Dating Game,*" I answered.

It was unlike any other game show on television. No stunts. No questions and answers. No big prizes. Just unmarried people—pretty girls and good-looking men—trying to find each other by saying whatever came into their minds. I thought it would be fun to have a bachelorette on one side of a partition unable to see three bachelors on the other side, and them unable to see her. The cute young lady would question the handsome gentlemen and then, sight unseen, using their answers as a guide, choose one of the three candidates for "an exciting night on the town" paid for by the show. I returned to my old stomping grounds, the American Broadcasting Company, and pitched the idea to its then head of daytime television, Leonard Goldberg. Goldberg liked the *Dating Game* idea and gave me seventy-five hundred dollars to mount a sample show.

I was convinced that not only would I sell the *Dating Game* but that the program would be a hit. I was also convinced that as nice and generous as my stepfather was, fifty percent of my company's profits in perpetuity was too much to give to any one man. I telephoned to renegotiate a better deal. I suggested to my stepfather that if I sold the *Dating Game* I would double his original investment and give him back forty thousand dollars rather than the twenty he loaned me. He accepted. I relished the idea that I had slid one past the old man. Later, I discovered my stepfather knew all along I was sweet-talking him out of a lot of money down the road. He didn't care. He wanted me to succeed and knew my chances were better if I wasn't strapped for cash.

Goldberg liked the sample show of the *Dating Game* but not enough to put it on the air. Instead, he put the program on "the shelf," meaning he sentenced the *Dating Game* to obscurity for the length of our contract, which was one year. At the end of that year I would get the property back. But by Hollywood standards the *Dating Game* would be finished, kaput, dead. Nobody in the business would buy a show one of the networks had already turned down.

That's the way it goes in the Land of La.

As for me, I was devastated.

I had tasted freedom. I had smelled what life was like away from The Corporation. I had felt the joy of being out on my own, of being my own boss, no longer under the thumb of a bumbling, inept martinet like the Ostrich. I could even wear whatever I liked to work; jeans, cowboy boots, sneakers, anything I wanted to. Now it seemed as though I'd have to go back to stifling suits and ties again, and boring executive dining rooms.

I returned to my cramped fifty-dollar-a-month walk-up office in the Writers Building on Little Santa Monica Boulevard. The office was this side of a jail cell, but I loved it; the plain wooden desk, the straight-back chair, the cot with its paper-thin mattress. A bathroom and pay telephone were down the hall.

I lay down on the cot.

With the exception of occasional meals and taking care of bodily functions, I stayed on that cot for the next thirty-four days and nights wondering what I was going to do with myself. It was the worst time of my life. I was broke, in debt, and out of work. The first thing I would have to figure out was how to get off that cot. The thought of returning to corporate life was beyond my comprehension. I would rather rob banks. Since I couldn't do that, what *could* I do? Little did I know the answer was just days away.

What I never considered, while staring at my office ceiling, was the stuff movies are made of. I hadn't counted on the unexpected arrival of those old geniuses, good luck and good timing. As I was contemplating the gas pipe, an unforeseen calamity was striking the American Broadcasting Company. Two new highly regarded daytime TV game shows premiered and went directly into the toilet. Replacements were needed. Fast.

Leonard Goldberg called me and said, "How quickly can you be ready to go on the air with the *Dating Game*?"

"In six weeks," I replied.

"Do it," commanded Goldberg.

"Yes, sir," I answered.

I hung up the telephone, walked into the bathroom, and threw up.

The first *Dating Game* shows we taped didn't go exactly as planned.

For some unaccountable reason the pretty and demure bachelorettes and the handsome clean-cut bachelors talked dirty to each other. They said: I'll suck yours if you suck mine. I'll tell you the size of my titties only if you tell me the size of your cock-a-doodle-do. Every other word was bang, boff, hump, diddle, dicky, twat, pussy, eat, munch, dong, and dork. Instead of questions like, "What's your favorite sandwich?" they asked each other, "What's your favorite position?" They wondered aloud whether he or she could "go the distance" or was a "quick comer"? They described the sexual feats they could perform, how many orgasms one could guarantee the other. Here's some dialogue from those first five shows.

> *PRETTY GIRL CHEERLEADER: Bachelor Number One, what nationality are you?*
> *BACHELOR NUMBER ONE: Well, my father is Welsh, and my mother is Hungarian, which makes me Well-Hung!*
> *PRETTY GIRL CHEERLEADER: Well, aren't you the clever one? Okay, Bachelor Number Three, what's the funniest thing you were ever caught doing when you thought nobody was looking?*
> *BACHELOR NUMBER THREE: I was caught with a necktie around my dick.*

GORGEOUS FASHION MODEL: Bachelor Number Three, make up a poem for me.
BACHELOR NUMBER THREE: Dollar for dollar and ounce for ounce, I'll give you pleasure 'cause I'm big where it counts.

WHOLESOME GIRL: Bachelor Number Three, what is your favorite sport?
BACHELOR NUMBER THREE: Fishing. Do you like to fish?
WHOLESOME GIRL: No, but I love bait.
BACHELOR NUMBER THREE: Would you nibble or swallow it whole?
WHOLESOME GIRL (giggling): I swallow it whole.
BACHELOR NUMBER THREE: You must have a very big mouth.
WHOLESOME GIRL (beside herself with glee): Okay, that's enough Bachelor Number Three. Bachelor Number One, I play the trombone. If I blew you what would you sound like?
BACHELOR NUMBER ONE: Ohhhh . . . ohhhh . . . ohohohOHOHO!

DORIS DAY LOOK-A-LIKE: Bachelor Number Two, what does a rabbi do on his day off?
BACHELOR NUMBER TWO: A rabbit?
DORIS DAY LOOK-A-LIKE: No. A *rabbi.*
BACHELOR NUMBER TWO: How the fuck do I know?

As a fledgling creator-producer, my first outing in the world of daytime television game shows was quickly becoming a disaster. I had produced five half hours of garbage. Totally unairable. All five shows had to be dumped. This unexpected turn of events moved me to the cusp of a nervous breakdown.

Remember, this was in 1965. The country's mood then wasn't exactly goody-goody, but neither was it as open as it is now. In those days we were prohibited by the American Broadcasting Company from saying—among other things—hell, damn, toilet, or God on the air. The tenor of the times mixed with the foul discourse on those first five shows meant certain and swift cancellation. The show's abrupt termination would provide me with the dubious distinction of having the shortest career of any game show packager in the history of television. Why all of this happened, why the program took such a

pornographic bent, was a mystery to me. I needed to do something
and I needed to do it quickly.

What I did was the result of a dream. I dreamed an FBI agent
appeared at our offices. He arrived just before that day's programs
began. He wore a Stetson hat, a spy raincoat, and carried a pair of
handcuffs. He spoke to the bachelors and bachelorettes. He told
them it was a federal offense punishable by a fine of ten thousand
dollars and up to ten years in prison to curse, or hint at anything
even faintly lewd or licentious on government-controlled airwaves.
From now on the bachelors and bachelorettes would go directly to
jail if they so much as uttered one hell or damn during the taping of
a *Dating Game* program. Of course none of that was true, but that's
what he said. And then the FBI agent unexpectedly raised a pair of
handcuffs over his head for all to see. The sight of the handcuffs
terrified the contestants. (A great touch, I thought.)

When I awoke I ran to the telephone and hired an actor friend I
knew. I told him to buy a Stetson hat, a spy raincoat, and a pair of
handcuffs. I promised to reimburse him. My friend was delighted
with the offer. He thought he was going to star in a porno film.
When he arrived and I explained what his duties would be and why,
my actor friend was visibly disappointed. But he did a great job.
Every day he convinced the bachelors and bachelorettes he was an
FBI agent and what he said was true. The contestants never uttered
a dirty word on the air again. At least not until it became fashionable
to do so. The crisis was over.

The *Dating Game* went on to become a big hit on daytime television, and make me a rich man.

CHAPTER FIVE

I am looking at the sea through the bedroom window of our three-hundred-year-old house in the old port of Saint-Tropez. It's six o'clock in the morning. Yesterday was my catastrophic *boule* game with The Big Boys. But, as the song goes, that was yesterday and yesterday's gone. Today is here and it's already warm. It isn't dark outside, but it isn't light either. I can barely see the fishing boats heading out to sea, but I can hear them tuff, tuff, tuffing as they go.

The morning hours in Saint-Tropez are my favorite. The air is fresh, the sky clear, the water flat and deep blue. It's the perfect time to take my monster off-shore racer out to sea. If you leave the port before seven o'clock you can catch the bright orange sun just rising over the mountains. Even though I've never been much on communing with nature—being a city boy I tend to be more comfortable with cement—the sight of the early-morning sun rising over the quiet sea never ceases to amaze me.

Once I clear the port, I push the engine throttles forward. A low roar comes up behind me from the monster's stern. Soon I can hear my American flag snapping in the wind, see the bow rise up in the air and feel the boat gaining momentum, faster and faster. If I look back I can watch the coastline fade in the spray of my "rooster tail" wake. I point the monster toward the horizon, and go. If I don't turn around I'll be in Corsica in four hours.

But I always turn around.

I stop the boat, turn the keys off, and listen to the quiet. A formation of ducks might fly by. A sea gull often lands on my bow. Except for an occasional sailboat in the distance, I have the world to myself. Soon everybody else will wake up and start elbowing in to share it.

But for the moment it's all mine and I love it. This feeling of serenity is one of many reasons for hanging out in this part of the world.

That's what I've been thinking about while staring at the sea from my bedroom window. That, and why am I playing sailor in the south of France and not preparing to go into my office and earn a living as I once did in the south of California?

"What's the matter?" asks my wife from somewhere deep in the middle of her pillow. Her voice is sleepy and comforting.

"I'm not sure."

"You're wondering about things, aren't you? Are you having your periodic anxiety attack over why we moved here? Or is it the one when you're feeling guilty about not going to an office every day?"

"It's the one about going into the office," I say, still looking out the window, amazed at how my wife always knows what I'm think-ing about.

"Do you want me to remind you why we came to Saint-Tropez?"

I don't answer.

So she tells me why we came to Saint-Tropez. She says, "Early, like two or three in morning, five years ago, we were sitting in the kitchen of our house in California eating peanut-butter-and-jelly sandwiches and you said, 'Honey, we ought to sell the company while the selling's good, leave Hollywood once and for all, move to the south of France, and live happily ever after.' Something like that."

I nod, remembering.

"We're living happily ever after, honey." My wife rolls over. She pulls the sheet and one of my pillows on top of her head.

"Bernard Tremaine," I mumble.

"What?" Her head's up again.

"Bernard Tremaine," I say, still staring out the window. "He was a character in an Ian McEwan book."

"No one heard much from Bernard Tremaine these days. He stayed at home and worked quietly on his book. Only family and a few old friends phoned him now."

"What about him?" asks my wife, yawning.

"Nothing."

"Please, honey," says my wife, dropping her head back down into her pillow, "get a grip."

I get dressed, kiss her cheek, and leave for the Gorille. I walk along winding streets that lead to the harbor. As I do, I feel someone's stare. It's the mean old French widow who lives on the third floor of a row house halfway between my home and the port. She's a bone-thin woman who leans out of her window every day, her skinny arms crisscrossed over a pillow lying on the window's ledge. Sometime her mean old dog leans out beside her. The old crone's always up before I am, always dressed in black and always hanging out of her window spying on the neighborhood. I always say hello to her, but she never says hello back. She never says anything back. She hates my guts. Who knows why, she just does.

This morning the ancient harpy has pushed herself further out the window's ledge than usual. Her eyes, resembling the evil slits of a water moccasin's, seem colder and more invidious than ever. Her expression is pinched, as though she's willing every muscle in her face to detest me.

I wave my hand at the malevolent hag. "Good morning," I say, smiling up at her as I always do. If she ever says good morning back to me, my knees will buckle and I will fall to the ground. As I expected, she says nothing. The widow's wrathful glare follows me under her window and down the street until I disappear around a corner. The next time I'll say, "Hi, babe," or "Hi, sugar," and see if that makes a difference.

It's a little after six-thirty in the morning. At this time of day the streets are practically empty. Two or three shopkeepers scrub the pavement in front of their stores with a wet broom. Down at the port a handful of fishermen fold their nets and clean their boats. When I arrive at the bakery I find some Tropezians already in line waiting for warm bread.

"*Bonjour,* Mister Chuck," says Madam Bonard, the bakery's fat proprietress. Mrs. Bonard is always eating her wares. So are her fat husband and two fat daughters.

"*Bonjour,*" I reply, and we kiss each other on both cheeks. I shake hands with her husband Dede and Janot the street cleaner.

"You look tired," says Madam Bonard, and winks. "You are spending too much time in bed with your beautiful wife?"

"If Monsieur Chuck wants to look rested he should spend more time in bed with you," says her husband.

Everyone in the bakery laughs.

"Perhaps l'Americain would rather be tired," says the street cleaner standing in line behind me.

Everybody laughs again. I laugh, too. It's not exactly side-splitting material, but if I don't laugh, everyone in the bakery will be hurt.

I buy bread. The bread is so good it's beyond description. The crust is crispy, the dough tastes like pound cake. I will eat the entire two-foot-long baguette unless I do something drastic. Out on the street I rip off enough bread to satisfy my hunger, look around to see that no one is watching, then toss the rest through the half-open window of a parked car. This is what I do every morning; throw half-eaten loaves of bread through the open windows of parked cars. I think I'm an enigmatic legend in the south of France: the Mysterious Bread Thrower of Saint-Tropez.

A few minutes later I arrive at the Gorille. The Gorille is a bar-restaurant that looks and sounds like what a French bar-restaurant is supposed to look and sound like: smoky, cozy, warm, and noisy. Its color is green; green canvas-backed chairs outside under a green awning. Its arch rival the Senequier is next door, on the other side of a narrow street that leads away from the port. The Senequier flies the color red; red canvas-backed chairs and a red awning. The Gorille and the Senequier are the Macys and Gimbels of Saint-Tropez. You're either a Gorille person or a Senequier person. You mate for life. There's no middle ground. If you're weaned on Gorille coffee, you'll have Gorille coffee in your stomach when they bury you. The same goes for the Senequier.

I'm a Gorille man.

The Gorille's interior is filled with half a dozen unstable tables and the worn, hard-backed chairs that go with them. Light for reading your newspaper is provided by a few 40 watt bulbs and whatever sunshine can filter through the café's dirty windows. There's a smelly john that's broken more often than it's not and a perpetually empty toilet paper spool. The bar is made of thick, smooth wood, with a brass rail running along its bottom for your foot. When I go to the Gorille I usually stand at "my place." It's at the far end of the bar against the wall, opposite the bar's entrance. I always order a café crème. The Gorille's café crème—coffee with hot milk—is delicious.

I drink it by the gallons. The French never drink it at all. They order small black espressos. The Tropeziens say that milk or cream mixed with coffee is bad for the liver. Coffee alone, fine. Milk alone, fine. Coffee and milk, death. I love when the French, who usually die at fifty from cirrhosis, tell you about livers.

"So what's new, Chuck?" asks Big Janot the dingy driver.

Since almost every man in Saint-Tropez is named Dede, Janot, Michael, or Jean François, you usually mention the person's occupation to distinguish one from the other. Big Janot the dingy driver is one of my favorite characters in Saint-Tropez. He's huge and growly, with a grand mane of pure white hair. He reminds me of an aging lion; once big-fanged and dangerous, now bluffing and toothless. I used to dislike Big Janot because I thought he didn't like me. Later I was surprised to discover that was never the case. I'm beginning to think misconceptions like that arise by my being both supersensitive and unable to speak the language well. Anyway, Big Janot has arms the size of trees. He's always wrapping those trees around my shoulders and pulling me affectionately into his chest.

"Don't worry," I tell Janot the dingy driver, "they'll break your heart in September." I'm referring, of course, to the Boston Red Sox who are presently leading the American League East.

Big Janot looks perplexed.

I explain. "It's a baseball maxim, Janot. No matter where the Red Sox are in July and August, they'll fade by the end of September. It's historical. It's a given. It happens all the time."

Big Janot doesn't understand my French. Even if he could understand my French he wouldn't know what I was talking about. And I'm sure if he could understand what I was talking about, he wouldn't give a rat's ass one way or the other. I know all of this. It just gives me sadistic pleasure to mess with Big Janot's head.

"Don't you care about the Red Sox, Janot?"

"No."

"What do you care about?"

"The wind."

He should. For forty-three years, Big Janot has been transporting tourists back and forth from chartered sailboats and yachts to the restaurants that rim the Pamplone beaches of Saint-Tropez. He uses his old battered rubber dinghy to accomplish this task. Last season during a very windy day he lost control of his boat close to shore and it overturned. Several tourists were dunked, their cameras, traveler's checks, and tote bags dropping to the bottom of the sea. Big Janot was mortified. He's been teased about that disaster ever since. Someone even stenciled *TITANIC* in big black letters on his dinghy.

I tell Big Janot, "Okay, you root for no wind and I'll root for the Red Sox."

Big Janot has a bewildered expression on his face as though he's been chatting with an orangutan. But to show no hard feelings, he laughs, whacks me on the back, and says, "L'Americain is crazy." Before I can get away, he wraps his trees around my shoulders and hugs me to his chest.

The French hug and kiss a lot. Every time you look around, men and women are hugging each other or somebody's kissing somebody else on both cheeks for hardly any reason at all. Which is odd because, unless they know you really well, they get angry if you address them in a grammatically familiar way.

Little Janot the taxi driver comes over to me. Little Janot isn't playing with a full deck but that doesn't stop any of us from liking him. Little Janot says, "Did you know, Chuck, that I have an uncle who lives in San Francisco?"

Little Janot's last name is DeBartolo. He is allegedly a distant relative—in both miles and affection—of Edward DeBartolo, the owner of the San Francisco Forty Niners. When Little Janot DeBartolo meets an American, he never fails to say, "Hello, I have an uncle who lives in San Francisco and owns the San Francisco football team." I've been a friend of Little Janot's for years. This hasn't stopped him from telling me about his uncle over and over again.

"Did I ever tell you," he says this morning, "that I have an uncle —Edward DeBartolo—who lives in San Francisco and owns the San Francisco football team?"

"Yes you have, Janot. That's really great. You must be very proud."

Little Janot smiles.

Little Janot is never without the obligatory burning cigarette hanging from his lips, his right eye shut tight from the drifting smoke, his mustache stained a burnt yellow, his teeth broken brown stumps. The French smoke as though tobacco will disappear by the end of the week. They come to restaurants with not one but two packs of cigarettes. They stack their packs next to their plate so they won't run out if the service is slow. You're not a real Frenchman unless your mustache is a burnt yellow and your teeth brown stumps like Little Janot's.

The town bell tower clangs the half hour. It's exactly seven-thirty in the morning. Outside the Gorille a pretty girl is beginning to do a strip tease on the engine hood of a Jeep.

CHAPTER SIX

The pretty girl and her friends have just closed a jet-set disco. She's undulating to thumping music. The heavy metal rock is coming from a huge portable radio nearby. The girl is slipping off her blouse. A crowd of bleary-eyed revelers is cheering and clapping. They seem thrilled by the commotion the girl's gyrations are causing. I'm not. But then I'm never thrilled by Euro-Trash; the rich playboys and playgirls from Europe and the Middle East. All summer long the Euro-Trash spill out of the discos at sunrise to dance, sing, yell, and throw up. Then they split for bed and sleep the day away. Most of the Euro-Trash men are tall and handsome with a lock of hair falling over one eye. Most of the women are blonde and gorgeous with unbelievable bodies. Sometimes I think I dislike Euro-Trash so much because way down deep, I envy them; their youth, their good looks, their up-yours attitude.

And they're just half the problem.

The other half are the Euro-Bumpkins; that horde of dull-witted polyester-clad tourists who descend upon the Côte d'Azur during the summer in locustlike numbers. This plague of creatures clog our streets and parking lots, restaurants and cafés. The boring English. The arrogant Swiss. The dense Belgiques with their terrifying red-and-white license plates that signify an accident waiting to happen. The tidy Danes in their spic-and-span mobile homes two stories high and a city-block wide, cautiously creeping along our two-lane roads at ten miles an hour. The sinister Germans on their roaring motorcycles; their bodies wrapped from head to toe in eerie black leather jumpsuits, their heads in Darth Vader motorcycle helmets with dark one-way visors.

For what seems like an eternity, I have to deal with sweat pants draped loosely over fat asses, spandex tights pulled tautly across fat asses, short shorts caught up the cracks of fat asses, ankle-high yellow socks at the end of white legs, red veiny faces sucking triple decker ice-cream cones, pockmarked teenagers whose defective teeth can barely gum sugar-covered crepes, dimwitted mothers dragging whining kids over my shoes. Oddly enough, these legions of odious people are the saviors of Saint-Tropez. They put money in the pockets of Dede Bonard the baker, and Dede Boix the butcher, and Dede Tremont the candlestick maker. They keep my friend Louis Ugo's restaurant solvent. They give Marianna, Louis Ugo's girlfriend who works at the Byblos Hotel, enough tips to cover her air fare to Orlando, Florida, in March. That's when Louis Ugo and Marianna plan to visit Disney World, take dozens of Kodacolor snapshots and make love on a Marriott Hotel water bed.

The pretty girl is still dancing on top of the Jeep. Her friends are holding hands in a big circle, skipping around her.

"Euro-Trash, what a monumental waste of time," I tell Jean Yves. Jean Yves is a roly-poly young man. He has prematurely gray hair and a mangy dog we all love named Mitterand. Jean Yves works all day, and during the summer months plays *boule* for money into the wee hours of the morning on the Place des Lices. Jean Yves is standing next to me but doesn't hear a word I've said. He's sound asleep; his head lying sideways on the bar atop his morning newspaper.

I can't stop watching the sexy girl with the bouncing bare tits stripping on the engine hood of the Jeep. Neither can Big Janot, Little Janot, Janot the gardener, Janot the mortician, Janot the notary, Janot the guardian, Janot who works at Ebel, Jean François the optician, Jean François the accountant, Jean François with the toupee, and Jean François with the full head of hair. The beautiful Ariel, sipping the espresso I just bought her, is watching, too. Right after college when I first came to Saint-Tropez, I had a big crush on Ariel. The crush lasted for years. Ariel sells fish.

I look in the bar mirror and see an American standing behind me. The American's a large, flabby man in his forties. He pushes against my back trying to get his head around my shoulders for a closer look. Finally he says, "Hey! Aren't you the guy—"

"No, I'm not the guy," I reply too quickly.

"I could swear you're the guy—"

"Nope, I'm really not."

"But you're from New York, right?"

"Wrong."

"Yeah? Where ya from?"

"Here."

The man is wearing a hot purple baseball hat, a green T-shirt chopped off at the armpits, green-and-orange flowered shorts, and sandals. The man shouts when he talks. Everyone in the bar can hear everything he says.

"You're from *here?*" questions the man, his tone of voice suggesting I'm a liar. "From Saint-Tropez? You gotta be kidding! You were born here in Saint-Tropez? Come on, you're puttin' me on, right? You're not French. You're an American, right?"

I wonder again how everyone knows that?

"You moved here, right? From the States? Five dollars says you were born in New York?"

"Wrong. I was born in Philadelphia."

"No shit! Hey, I was born in Philly, too! On Tasker Street. I was raised there. Went to Temple University. Opened my drugstore not far away on Shunk. Third and Shunk. The name's Harry Shmul. What's yours?"

I tell him my name.

"I knew it!" shouts Shmul, causing everyone to momentarily forget the girl stripping on the Jeep and look at us. Shmul is shaking his head at the wonder of it all. "You're the television producer, right, the game show king? Hey, I loved your shows!"

"Thank you."

"What were they, I forget?"

I tell Shmul some of the shows I created.

"No kidding," he says, scratching his chin thoughtfully. "Those shows were on TV a long time."

"Yes they were."

"Hey, I cannot believe this. I'm talkin' to a legend in his own time. The Game Show King! The man is standing right in front of me. Touching! We're so close we're touching. Am I right or am I right? Hey, I'll bet you made a ton of money with those game shows."

"Yeah, I made a ton of money."

"That's what you did, thought up some game shows and made a ton of money?"

"Yeah, that's what I did."

"You know," says Harry Shmul sadly, "I should have been a game show producer."

Twenty minutes later everyone has disappeared.

The pretty girl and the rest of the Euro-Trash have driven off in their sports cars to hotels and summer homes to sleep. The Tropezians have left for work. Harry Shmul has gone looking for Brigitte Bardot.

The sun is rising now. It's just above the sea wall. Morning has officially arrived. A glow begins to fill the port. The once-gray fishing village is turning yellow. Tasseled and sleepy tourists straggle to the Gorille and Senequier to drink coffee and wake up. The grown-ups carry tote bags, purses, and maps. They have foreign newspapers under their arms and cameras slung over their shoulders. Their children sit in screwed-up positions on their chairs, crayons and coloring books in front of them, blank expressions on their small faces, yawning a lot. Everyone aches from unfamiliar beds. These half-awake Euro-Bumpkins occupy the chairs and tables that once belonged to the whacked out Euro-Trash. The guard has changed.

I'm still standing at the Gorille bar. I've just finished reading my *Herald Tribune*. Henri takes a break, comes over and stands beside me. His dishrag is slung over his shoulder. He makes himself a small espresso, drops in a lump of sugar, and stirs the coffee with a very tiny spoon. Around and around goes the little spoon in the cup. I'm always astonished at the length of time the French spend stirring one lump of sugar in their cups of espresso. Maybe five minutes go by before they take a sip!

Henri says, "I see the *Dating Game* is on French television now."

"It is?"

"Yes. Every day at one in the afternoon. Even Saturday. Josette saw it Saturday." Josette is Henri's wife.

"How about that?" I say, gathering up my newspapers and writing pad, getting ready to go home to work. The news about the *Dating Game* doesn't surprise me. I've been told reruns of my show would be on French television soon. This is fine with me as long as they don't do reruns of the *Gong Show* like they're doing in Germany, and blow my cover.

Henri says, "Josette said the show she watched paid tribute to your Saint Valentine. Josette said she enjoyed the show very much. She said everyone on the program looked like they were having a wonderful time."

On my way back to our little house in the port, I recall our first St. Valentine's Day show on the *Dating Game*. None of us had a wonderful time. None of us in the company, that is. That show was an honest-to-God horror story. We used to refer to it as the St. Valentine's Day Massacre.

CHAPTER SEVEN

It all began on the first of February, 1966. That's when I received a very strange telephone call. It was from Ed Vane, the then vice president in charge of daytime programs for the American Broadcasting Company. He said, "Get a marriage."

"Sorry," I said, confused.

"We need a marriage," repeated the vice president. "We need a couple to get married on the *Dating Game* as soon as possible."

"We do?"

"Yes we do."

"How do we do that?"

"Simple. One of those pretty little girls on your show picks one of the three bachelors, they go out on one of your so-called dream dates, they fall in love, they decide to get married, and they get married."

"And they get married."

"Yes, and they get married. A marriage will do wonders for the program's ratings."

"I thought the show's ratings were good."

"They are very good, but they can always be better, and this is a way to make them better. And, the perfect time is coming up to announce a marriage. Valentine's Day! You know, Valentine's Day, romance, all that sort of thing."

Mr. Vane was referring to February 14, the date America celebrates the martyr St. Valentine's death. Lovers, and those who think or hope they're in love, celebrate St. Valentine's day by exchanging words of endearment, silly greeting cards, flowers, and boxes of candy. In my opinion, St. Valentine may be one of the better saints working the streets these days, along with St. Christopher and St. Jude.

"Well?" asked the vice president impatiently.

"Yes, get a marriage, but . . ."

"But *what?*" he said, a tinge of annoyance in his voice.

"But, I mean, how do you, as you say, get a marriage? You can't just make it happen. It has to happen on its own, doesn't it?"

"Make it happen," growled the vice president, and hung up.

I remember staring at the telephone earpiece for about three minutes, not believing what I had just heard. The vice president couldn't have been serious. Ed Vane was by and large a rational man. So what was he doing? Making a joke? "Get a marriage." Where does one "get a marriage" on a television show? One doesn't. Unless, of course, a miracle occurs. And then a funny thing happened. A miracle occurred.

The wonder of wonders arrived in the form of a long skinny inexperienced *Dating Game* production assistant named Jonathan Debin. He burst into my office yelling, "Wait until you hear this!"

"Wait until I hear what?" I muttered, still holding the phone in the air.

"We have our first *Dating Game* marriage!"

"We have our first *what?* We have a marriage?"

"Well, we do and we don't. The couple isn't married yet, but they're going to be in the next week or so."

I couldn't believe my good fortune. We were actually going to "get a marriage." I told Debin to fetch me the couple's forms.

All of our game show contestants filled out forms that gave us basic information regarding their backgrounds, hobbies, likes and dislikes, favorite movie stars, things they like to do on a date. We also used the forms to record how we rated the prospective contestant; their appearance, whether they were introverted or extroverted, how they performed during the audition. In order to prevent contestants from understanding what we wrote about them, we devised a code. The code included some of the following symbols: NW (no way), PITA (pain in the ass), PTL (partly the look), GAFFY (faggy), DAAR (dumb as a rock), TW (the worst), ROJO (red hair), and someone with a pockmarked face was given a VOPE (Victim Of Pizza Explosion). We would also grade them A, B, and C, and numerically on a 1 to 4 basis, with 4 being the best. A typical notation at the top of a contestant form might read B1/PITA/ROJO, who would not be as good as a C4/PTL.

Debin returned with the couple's forms. The forms revealed two interesting people. She was a model, he a race car driver. On the telephone she told me they wanted to be married as soon as the race car driver's mother arrived in LA from Greece. That would be in two weeks.

"Great," I told the model. "We'll announce your marriage on the air at the end of our Valentine's Day show. You and your husband will make an appearance on stage and we'll give you lots of prizes. We'll be half lying, of course, since we pretape our programs a week ahead of time. You won't be legally married when we actually do the show, but you will be by the time the show airs."

"Swell," said the model with surprisingly little enthusiasm.

"I hope the two of you are as happy as you've made us."

"Yeah, we're very happy," she replied. She didn't sound very happy.

"Now don't go changing your minds on us," I said jokingly but not jokingly. "We could all be in a lot of trouble if you did."

"Don't worry," said the model, "by the time the program's on TV we'll be hitched. I promise."

We taped our Valentine's Day special a week before Valentine's Day. And what a special it was. I approved things that sent us thousands of dollars over budget. My business manager was worried. The network budget director had a fit. I didn't care. We did Valentine's Day on the *Dating Game* like it was never done before on coast-to-coast television. The two bachelorettes were dressed in red-and-white evening gowns and wore beautiful corsages made of red-and-white gardenias. The six bachelors appeared in elegant black tie and tails. At the end of the program we brought the newlyweds (to-be) onstage. When the couple entered, white flower petals fell like snow from above. They walked down a red carpet that led to an arbor of red roses. Huge red hearts punctured with Cupid's arrows hung from invisible wires near and far. Frank Sinatra's record of "Love and Marriage" filled the studio. Standing stage right was a pretty model. She held airline tickets to Hawaii in one hand, hotel reservations in the other. Surrounding the model were his and her luggage and his and her matching motor scooters.

The race car driver's jaw went slack, surprise and delight filling his face. The model appeared confused. They hugged and kissed. The studio audience loved it. We caught shots of women sighing and wiping their eyes with hankies. Valentine's Day on the *Dating Game* was a grand success. The vice president was thrilled. He said the program was worth all the money we spent on it.

The next thing happened a week later, three days before Valentine's Day. I was taking a hot bath, soaking out the week's stress and strain, when the telephone rang. The telephone was on a wicker stand next to the tub. I was always fearful of the receiver falling into the bathwater and electrocuting me, but I never moved the phone. Convenience defeating intelligence once again. I said hello and someone on my staff said, "Are you seated?"

I said that I was more than seated and asked what was up.

"The Valentine's Day couple."

"What about them?" I asked.

"They're not getting married."

That night was the first time I howled in my sleep.

My staff and I spent the next day and into the night plotting and planning, going over our options. Shortly after midnight I realized what the couple was doing.

"They're blackmailing me," I told my people. "They know we spent a fortune on the Valentine's Day show and they know it can't air unless they're married. They also know that we'll probably be happy to pay them ten, twenty, who knows, thirty thousand dollars so that we don't have to eat the show. What's thirty thousand dollars to us when zillions are at stake?"

"Scumbags," "Dirty rats," "Sons-of-bitches," growled numerous devoted and dog-tired staff members.

"Okay," I said to my secretary, "get that model, who looks more like a hooker than a model to me, on the phone."

A minute later the model picked up her telephone receiver and said, "Hello?"

I said, "What do you want?"

"Ten thousand dollars would make it worth our while," she replied.

I was relieved. It could have been worse.

"Each," she added.

"Okay," I said, "but only, I repeat only if you adhere to my plan."

"Adhere?"

"Follow."

"And if we don't?" she asked.

"Then I'll destroy the Valentine's Day show, sue the two of you for the gifts we gave you, air a rerun, and tell the two of you to go fuck yourselves."

She asked me what the plan was.

I told the model the three of us would fly across the border to Mexico the next morning and the two of them would get married as fast as I could find someone to do the job. When the license was in my sweaty little palm, they would get their check for twenty thousand dollars.

Twelve hours later we were in Tijuana, a dung heap of a town. There was garbage in the streets, bone-thin dogs pissing on dusty truck tires, and a red-hot sun baking the hair into my head. Some half-drunk Mexican clergyman said some quasi-religious gobbledegook and pronounced the model and race car driver man and wife. An old woman with a kind face and gnarly arthritic fingers typed up the license. As it came out of the typewriter, the model reached for the piece of paper, but I beat her to it and stuffed the document into my pocket. Then I gave the race car driver their twenty-thousand-dollar check.

"You two know this is blackmail," I said.

"Tough titties," replied the model.

"It ain't no skin off your fucking nose," said her new husband.

Maybe it was Tijuana, but the new husband looked seedier than ever. His face seemed thinner, the dark circles under his bloodshot eyes blacker. His unwashed hair had been dyed and streaked blond on top but the roots were still brown. His flowered sport shirt and baggy trousers gave him the appearance of a sleazy zoot suiter from the fifties. His new wife was destined to become a fat cow.

I told the newlyweds I could report them to the police.

"You won't," said the model. "You know why you won't? You won't because the show we did is too goddamn important to you. And to your boss, the faggot vice president who was fucking thrilled to pieces."

I told the model that the vice president just happened to have a wife and five sons.

"Yeah, so what?" said the race car driver. "That doesn't mean a fucking thing."

The model turned to evaluate her rat's-nest hairdo in a chipped wall mirror. Still looking in the mirror, her fingers poking at the sticky do, she said, "I just want you to know, smart-ass, that I'm not a model. I only said I was to get on your stupid show. I'm really a hooker."

"And I'm an elevator operator not a fucking race car driver," said her greaseball husband, flashing me a stupid so-there smile and waving the twenty-thousand-dollar check in my face.

The hooker said, "We'll give you a call and let you know when we'll come by to pick up the luggage and the motor scooters."

Then the two walked out the door, slamming it behind them.

I looked at the old woman still sitting behind her typewriter, her gnarly arthritic fingers lying in her lap. I shrugged my shoulders. "What's a guy to do?" I asked.

"Cancel the check," she said, smiling.

Which I did by telephone five minutes later.

CHAPTER EIGHT

On my way back to our little home on the sea I am once again spellbound by the colors of Saint-Tropez. The orange-and-yellow row houses. The splash of red-and-green flowers in the window boxes. The short clothes lines that loop from window to window filled with pink and blue underwear, and purple-striped children's socks. My neighborhood in Saint-Tropez often reminds me of a motion picture set in Hollywood. Sometimes I think if I step behind the facade of homes and shops I'll discover these buildings are nothing more than brightly painted pictures on large wooden flats.

I round a corner and see the mean old French widow. She's leaning out of her window as always, her evil little eyes watching me coming down the street. As I get closer, I smile and give her a jaunty wave. She doesn't smile or wave back.

I wish I could speak to the mean old hag. I would love to ask her exactly what her problem is. But I cannot speak French, not well. I walk about the village like a mute, or worse, invisible. I might as well not be seen. What good is it that I am? I am unable to express myself, tell someone to fuck off, ask a *boule* player on the Place des Lices to get his act together and start playing, or the next minute make him laugh. No one in this town knows my personality. They haven't a clue if I'm funny or learned or sensitive. For all the good my French does me, I might as well be Helen Keller. When I leave a French friend's house, after a delicious home-cooked meal, do I say, "That was absolutely delicious. The best broiled chicken I've had in years. And those creamy mashed potatoes! They're almost as good as Musso & Frank's in Hollywood. Almost, but not quite." No, I can't come close to saying that. What I say is, "Yummmmm," and rub my stomach like a fool.

I unlock and push open the heavy front door of our house. Inside it's cool and quiet. I'm a bit late getting back, but it's still early in the morning. My wife is sleeping and so is our watchdog Buddy. I go to my office on the second floor. I open the shutters of the windows that face the sea, and those that overlook a tiny park in a cul de sac. The minuscule park has one bench and two old trees.

I can tell by simply smelling the air that it's going to be a flat sea. It's important to know if the sea is flat or not. The flatter the sea the better it is for the monster. When the sea is smooth my boat flies across the water. When the sea's rough with waves, I can throw my back out. The first thing I do every morning is check the water from our bedroom window. If it's flat I'm excited. It means that sometime during the day I'll be able to take a hell of a boat ride. I'll usually wake my wife and tell her, "The water's flat, honey!"

Often in New York, first thing in the morning, I'll go look at the toilet bowl in our bathroom, come back to the bedroom, wake my wife, and announce, "The water's flat, honey."

She doesn't think that's funny.

Anyway, it's time to go to work. I sit down at my big wooden desk. I turn on my desk lamp and audio cassette machine. The overture from a Verdi opera begins. A light sea breeze coming through the window fills the room with fresh air. I wait while my computer warms up.

In front of my window a group of excited swallows fly about, chattering away, appearing then disappearing down the narrow alley that leads to the old stone pier and the sea. This morning the sky and the water are almost identical in color; an intense blue-white. Elegant yachts and sailboats travel past my window. In the distance, on the other side of the bay, I see the small town of Ste. Maxime. The magnificent view delights me. I telephone my sister in Philadelphia. I want to share this exquisite moment with her.

"I'll take the declining American city any day," she says. "Too much beauty makes me sleepy."

"Makes you sleepy?"

"Just remember, the French sent Dreyfus to Devil's Island."

"What's that have to do with anything?"

"Just tell me this. Can you get good pancakes in Saint-Tropez? Or pumpkin pie? Or soft pretzels?"

"There's more to life than soft pretzels."

"Don't forget creamed spinach? Can you get good creamed spinach like they make at Horn & Hardarts? Or Bookbinder's fried oysters? Of course you can't. And how about the fascist, right-wing asshole politician Le Pen?"

"What about him?"

"The creep makes 'em come in their pants."

"Yes, but . . ."

"You know what they say about the French. When God created France He was embarrassed because He made the country too beautiful. So He created the French people to even things up. Got to go now. Bye bye."

In a way, my sister's right.

The French people aren't all that bad, but they do get on your nerves. Eventually they make you nuts. Like my uncle Charlie Blenzig from Pelham Park. If you wait long enough, my uncle Charlie will get on your nerves, then make you nuts. That's because he does annoying things. Like the French do.

The French delivery man will stop his truck in front of your car on narrow little streets and then deliver parcels for the next twenty minutes, constantly glowering at you for appearing inconvenienced. (A dog's usually sitting in the truck's front seat, glowering, too.) French women zip their Renaults and Peugeots into the parking space you've been waiting five minutes for, chuckling to themselves at your outrage.

Another thing. Frenchmen never change their clothes. My friend Lucien, who plays *boule* with me, either has twenty black-and-white-striped T-shirts or he wears the same one every day. And Frenchmen don't bathe, at least most of the Parisian taxi drivers don't. A major rule to remember when in Paris is crack a window as soon as you step into a taxi, especially on a rainy day.

And how about the French personality; at least as it applies to Americans? The way sales girls think they're doing you a big favor if they decide to wait on you. The way waiters exhibit their disappointment you're not eating somewhere else. The way the French believe they're giving you an enormous compliment if, after years of ignoring you, they finally say good morning.

But then the French love dogs, so how bad can they be?

Anyway, three hours have passed and I'm bored with sitting at my desk.

I stand, stretch, and walk across the room. I lean out a window like the mean old widow and stare at the sea. While in this hypnotic state, I recall my trauma concerning John P. Grissom. I have no idea why. More and more my mind is behaving in a most bizarre fashion. How strange to muse about a man as distasteful as John P. Grissom on such a beautiful French morning. I wonder what prompted me? Whatever the reason, I persevere. I roll back the years to the morning Ruth Goldberg sounded the alarm. Ignoring the elevator, she had run up several flights of stairs and down the corridor barging into my office with a look of horror on her face.

"What's the matter, Ruthie?" I asked.

Ruthie put her hand on her chest. She was unable to speak. She took a few seconds to catch her breath.

And then she told me.

CHAPTER NINE

"John Grissom is trying out for the *Dating Game*," she gasped.

John P. Grissom was a forty-year-old, tall, bone-thin writer of eclectic newspaper columns. The columns were usually hidden in over one-hundred-seventy dailies' back pages. His tedious creations covered everything from new inventions to new television programs. Actually John P. Grissom was not the man's name. I have changed the name of the man for reasons you will understand later. Suffice it to say that this devious and evil man, this emaciated and pompous cigar-chomping slug, hated everything, hated television most of all. And in all of television, Grissom detested daytime television in particular and game shows specifically. The anorexic sloth's greatest joy was the news of a new game show debuting. John P. Grissom could then indulge his perverse pleasure in decimating the program. He was known in game show land as The Exterminator. The Exterminator was obviously performing undercover work in our offices prior to reviewing the *Dating Game*. He would then write a despicable critique, gleefully look forward to the swift decrease in my program's audience his review would cause, followed by the show's inevitable death. The Exterminator would have struck again.

"What shall we do?" repeated Ruthie, anxiously gnawing on a cuticle.

Ruth Goldberg was my talent coordinator. She booked our celebrity guests and contestants. Ruthie and I were two of the "older" members of my company. We were in our late thirties. Ruthie and I acted as surrogate mama and papa to the youths who made up most of my production staff. Ruthie was prone to lecturing me, but it didn't matter. I loved her from the first day we met.

"We have to do something," Ruthie said. "We can't leave that weasel to his own devices."

I told Ruthie that was exactly what we were going to do.

"What?" she asked.

"Leave the weasel to his own devices."

"Are you mad?" she said, beginning a lecture. "That's the dumbest thing I ever heard. I can't believe you're just going to sit there and let that loathsome oaf pass himself off as a prospective contestant so that he can trash our show. You go to the reception room right now and tell that awful man we know who he is and that we're going to close down our contestant operation and send everybody home unless he leaves. God knows the terrible things being bandied about in that room by those damn kooks who come to audition. The Exterminator will overhear plenty. Those jerky nymphets waiting to try out will give him all sorts of juicy tidbits for his horrid little column. No, it's a self-destructive decision to let him stay and I won't allow it."

"Let him be," I snapped, my eyes turning to icy slits. My employees always tended to agree with me when my eyes turned to icy slits. Except Ruthie.

"At least let me warn our staff," she continued angrily. "Let me tell them who he is and what he does, and to watch what they say."

Which she did whether I approved or not.

Sneaky John P. Grissom slithered routinely through the contestant operation. He didn't do very well. On his contestant form was stamped the words: TISH BGI, which is BIG SHIT spelled inside out.

"He's really awful," said my contestant coordinator, Ronnie Kuvakas, a tassel-haired twenty-year-old who looked fourteen. His job was to evaluate all the noncelebrities who tried out for the show. Ronnie had seen Grissom audition.

"I know," I said.

"He's a loathsome piece of garbage," Ronnie added for good measure.

"I know," I repeated.

"So what do you want me to do with him?"

"Book him."

"I don't believe you," he wailed, appalled.

"The man's an idiot," groused Ruthie Goldberg. I wasn't sure if she was talking about me or The Exterminator.

To Ruthie and Ronnie's dismay, John P. Grissom—mudraker, womanizer, boozer, destroyer of television programs—appeared on the *Dating Game*. The girl on that particular show was adorable. Two of her bachelors were nice-looking and outspoken. The third bachelor, Charlie Dickens, aka John P. Grissom, was the consummate horse's ass; an insufferable fop who thought he was irresistible. He sat there on his stool, a dead cigar butt clenched between yellow teeth and smirking lips. His blue-and-white-striped bow tie hung loosely from his gaunt neck, and his brown herringbone sport coat was a size too big for his wishbone-thin shoulders. Grissom's clothes appeared to be draped on a Third World coat tree. When queried, John P. Grissom pontificated one long, arrogant, pretentious, and self-important answer after the other. The odious lech was rejected, naturally, for a nice guy—Bachelor Number Two—sitting on the critic's right. The repugnant journalist appeared miffed and was observed looking off to the side pouting. As he left the stage, Grissom could be heard sniveling to himself, "Tom Selleck and Burt Reynolds weren't chosen, either, Selleck several times." Grissom was right about that, if it was any consolation to the lowlife creep.

And there the story would have ended if only I hadn't had another idea. The notion entered my mind the day after the program was taped, the morning The Exterminator surfaced. He arrived at our offices all smug and self-satisfied, gloating as only John P. Grissom could at how he tricked us into thinking he was a contestant. After he announced who he was, he stood back and awaited our surprise, which we all feigned admirably, I thought, especially me.

"No kidding!" I gasped. "You're John Grissom and not just plain Bachelor Number Three? Honest to God? Holy mackerel! Go know."

John P. Grissom made himself comfortable in a chair by my desk. I didn't offer him the chair, but he made himself comfortable in it anyway. He adjusted his bony ass, then positioned his tape recorder near my mouth. He fetched a cigar from his sport coat pocket and lit the stogy with a match. When at last the cigar was burning nicely, Grissom held the extinguished match aloft until someone came forth with an ashtray. Ready at last to proceed, John P. Grissom said, "I have some last-minute wrap-up questions for you. I hope you don't mind."

No, I told the skinny fuck, I didn't mind.

Grissom grunted a response and was about to begin when I said, "John, before we start, I've got an idea I'd like you to think about."

Out of the corner of my eye, I saw Ruthie Goldberg bristle. She was finger-signaling me, thumbs down: No. No. No. She didn't want me to say what I was going to say, even though she had no idea what I was going to say. But I told Grissom anyway.

"You played one side of the partition, John, the side the three bachelors sit behind. But if you're going to do a story on the *Dating Game,* I think you should experience both sides of the equation. You should do another show sitting where the girl sits. Then you'll have the complete picture. You'll find out what it feels like talking to three pretty young ladies you can't see. You'll also experience the agony of making a choice and how, for good or bad, you have to live with that choice for an entire evening," adding lasciviously, "if you know what I mean?"

The Exterminator gasped with surprise and joy. His cigar butt fell to the floor. He couldn't believe his good fortune. Forgetting about his so-called "wrap-up questions," Grissom, the ultimate ham, a horny skirt-chaser who would hump a snake with a hairlip, hurriedly stashed his tape recorder back in its case, took my hand into his damp palm, shook it limply, and said, "A simply splendid idea."

And then he left.

When I was sure he was gone, I shouted, "Great!," clapping my hands with delight.

"Ridiculous," said Ruthie, scowling.

"Outrageous," snapped my contestant coordinator.

Ruthie sighed and sniffed, "Now I guess you'll want me to book three gorgeous movie starlets for that bozo to talk to?"

"Wrong."

"Wrong? Okay what do I do?"

"Book three hookers."

"Three hookers? Why three hookers?"

"If we're going to go down in flames we may as well have a little fun doing it."

Ruthie booked three hookers.

*   *   *

They were pretty young women, but definitely hookers.

We taped the program a week later, and it was great. The call girls were terrific. They never gave The Exterminator a chance to be dull or tedious. Their earthy answers completely befuddled the bore. He seemed a beat behind for the entire show.

Now came the part of my plan that caused me some misgivings. John P. Grissom was about to come face-to-face with our bimbos. Was it obvious they were prostitutes? Would he see through my little travesty and be furious? Would he think we were making sport of him? Would the results of this bit of fun and games cause a backlash? Would we end up worse off than if Grissom had simply written his original critique? Was it wise to fuck with The Exterminator?

When Grissom saw the two call girls he didn't choose swivel-hip around the partition, he actually groaned aloud and then went visibly weak in the knees. I thought for a minute he might collapse from disappointment. Naturally, either one of those sexy trollops would have provided him with the evening of a lifetime. You could hear Grissom muttering, "Damn, damn, damn."

When the hooker he did choose appeared, The Exterminator's face turned red. I thought he might be having a coronary on national TV. Grissom would become the only person I ever knew who almost died of happiness. The idiot did an embarrassing jig on stage, and then ended his dance by jumping into the air and clicking his heels. When the show's host, Jim Lange, told the couple they were going to spend four days—and nights!—on a lush Caribbean island, John P. Grissom jumped up in the air and clicked his heels again. She giggled demurely behind her hand as though she had just left the convent that morning. I couldn't wait for Grissom and the girl to leave, which they did, carrying themselves as though they were the Duke and Duchess of Windsor. They waved good-bye to the studio audience and disappeared. For all intents and purposes, that was that. But it wasn't. This little morality tale had an astonishing ending.

When The Exterminator and The Hooker returned from the Caribbean, Grissom telephoned me. "I just wanted to thank you," he said cheerfully. "It was the trip of a lifetime. I don't think we ever got out of bed." The Exterminator cackled mischievously. "Oh, and one more thing," he added.

"What's that?"

"We're getting married."

I recall dropping the telephone.

The marriage of The Exterminator and The Hooker took place on the back lawn of the journalist's home.

A violin player dressed in a tuxedo sauntered about playing Mendelssohn's "The Wedding March from the Midsummer Night's Dream" over and over again. The gushing couple were joined in holy matrimony under an arbor of white roses. A colleague, whose name I've conveniently forgotten, was Grissom's best man.

The Hooker's maid of honor was a different story altogether.

She was a nineteen-year-old call girl named Cherry Garcia. I'll never forget that girl (or the name) as long as I live. Cherry told all of us proudly that she was Miss Hollywood Call Girl of 1968. She also removed her dentures and showed us how she had all her teeth pulled so she would be eligible for Miss Best Head of 1969. All a guy had to do that afternoon was flash a twenty-dollar bill and Cherry's uppers and lowers were in her purse lickety split. If anyone almost gave away the trick I had played on John P. Grissom, it was The Hooker's maid of honor: Unforgettable Cherry Garcia, with her tits and ass hanging out of her virginal white minidress and her in-and-out false teeth.

After the ceremony, everyone lined up to congratulate the couple. When it was my turn to kiss the bride, she whispered delicately into my ear, "You better keep your goddamn mouth shut if you know what's fucking good for you."

I promised her my lips were sealed.

When Mr. and Mrs. Grissom returned from their honeymoon, John wrote his critique of the *Dating Game*. It was an upbeat and favorable review, a big departure from The Exterminator's usual style. His critique closed by saying, "The *Dating Game* should be around for a long long time."

It was.

CHAPTER TEN

It's late afternoon in Saint-Tropez and I'm still at my desk. I'm tired of writing. I listen to the sounds of the village from my office window. The din is familiar to me. It makes me feel secure. The splashing waves against the rocks. The occasional motorcycle whizzing past. A rattling delivery truck. A family of tourists jabbering to each other as they walk below my window.

The church bells sound the hour. It's four o'clock. Time to get ready to play *boule*. I close the shutters and leave my study.

Downstairs, Teetee, our cute French cook, is putting away groceries in her kitchen. Something is simmering on the stove that smells good. In Teetee's kitchen something is always simmering on the stove that smells good. I sneak behind Teetee and tickle her. The plate she's holding drops into the sink and breaks.

"Fanks a lot," she says.

The French cannot pronounce "th." They say "f" instead. Fick, not thick. Fanks, not thanks.

I tell T-Burgers, "I'm sorry."

She shrugs her shoulders without turning around.

There's no one quite like our French cook. Her name is Tita Mercurio. We call her Teetee, Burgers, sometimes T-Burgers, mostly UCM—the Ultimate Cooking Machine. Teetee's in her early thirties and as pretty as any college beauty queen. My wife and I think Teetee is the best cook in the south of France. We aren't the only ones who think this way. On at least three occasions friends of ours have tried to steal the UCM away from us. Two of these so-called friends made offers in my presence, immediately after swallowing a mouthful of her incredible pie crust.

"I can't believe you just did that," I told Ed Snider, owner of the Philadelphia Flyers hockey team, the last culprit to do so.

"Do what?" he asked, reaching for another slice of T's pear pie.

"Try to hire my cook, right in front of me, here at my dinner table."

"She's that good," he said.

Teetee the Ultimate Cooking Machine.

"Are you hungry? Want somefing to eat?" she asks me cheerfully, the anger from my tickling her all gone now, her back still to me. She's picking up the pieces of broken plate from the sink.

I tell her I'm not hungry.

She says, "It's Cathy's birfday today."

Cathy is Teetee's sister-in-law. I think Cathy Mercurio could have been a French movie star. Her husband, Teetee's brother Jean François, could have been one too. And Cathy's brother, George. They all resemble those young, great-looking people who inhabited the early French films of Godard, Lelouche, and Truffaut: leading men whose handsome faces I envied years ago, leading ladies I married in my dreams.

"Does Red know it's Cathy's birthday?" I ask. "Did she buy Cathy a present?"

"I fink so," she says.

I go to the hall closet and collect my *boule* balls. They're in a small blue canvas bag.

"Are you going to play wif The Big Boys again?" hollers the UCM from the kitchen.

"I don't think so," I yell back. "Not after my less than brilliant debut the other day. I've got to work my way back up the ladder. It's not going to be easy."

And it's not. I think about that and wonder why I even care. Was this the goal I had in mind when I started out in life; to be, at sixty-two years of age, accepted by The Big Boys of Saint-Tropez as one of their regular *boule* players? Must I be competitive until the day I die? Even now, exiled as I am here in Saint-Tropez, I continue to want to be a doer? How about just being a relaxer? A taster? A snoozer? A reader? A hugger? A bum?

Teetee comes out of the kitchen and says to me, "Don't worry, you'll be playing wif The Big Boys again. You'll be a regular. You can count on it." And then she says, "Give me five and show me firty-two."

That's our little saying. It means give me a handshake (give me five fingers) and a smile (show me thirty-two teeth). I give her a handshake and a smile. Technically I can't ask her to do the same. I can't tell her to show me thirty-two. Teetee doesn't have thirty-two teeth. That's because, next to Eskimos and Ugandans, the French have the worst teeth in the world. Mention the word floss and the French think you're talking about a girl. So I say, "Show me twenty-eight," which is about all the teeth the young girl has left. (Thank God the ones that are gone are in the back of her mouth.)

The Ultimate Cooking Machine shakes my hand, smiles, and goes back to her kitchen.

"Bye, Teetee Burgers," I shout as I leave.

"Bye, Chuck," she yells from the kitchen. "Don't forget to concentrate. Fink before you shoot."

The afternoon's *boule* game is uneventful.

I team up with two identical twin brothers named Jean Claude and Jean François Moreu. The twins' family owns a restaurant on Pamplone Beach called Les Jumeaux: The Twins. I can't tell the twins apart. I always slur the second half of their name. So does everyone else in town. The twins and I play three guys from Ste. Maxime, the town across the bay. I never like playing guys from Ste. Maxime. Tropezians and Ste. Maximers don't get along. It's a big time disgrace if you lose to a team from Ste. Maxime. That's more pressure than I like to bear.

We beat the guys from Ste. Maxime in the first game, 13–8, but they squeak past us in the revenge game, 13–12. I'm sorry we lose. If we had won, the twins and I could have gone home. Now we're required to play a third and deciding game. Not a thrilling proposition. I know the Ste. Maxime guys can win if they try. Makes me wish I didn't come to the Place des Lices this afternoon. As it turns out, we come from behind and take the last one 13–11.

Afterward I go to the Café Des Arts and have a drink with the twins, Henri Bruni, Janot the ex-mailman, Fat Phillipe who owns the town tennis shop, Bruno Soncini the electrician, and Gigi the retired fisherman who always wears the New York Giants baseball cap I gave him. When everyone's drink arrives we smack glasses.

"Salute!" we all say.

Music is coming out of wall speakers in the Café des Arts. I find myself listening to "Mr. Businessman" by Ray Stevens. I'm startled. What a peculiar song to hear in 1991 in this fishing village bar in the south of France. "Mr. Businessman" was a big hit in the sixties. It was my company's adopted theme song. We played a forty-five of it every Friday morning before our staff meeting. I used to play the record to get my employees in a happy mood. You did things like that in the sixties.

> *Did you see your children growing up today*
> *And did you hear the music of their laughter*
> *As they set about to play?*
> *Did you catch the fragrance*
> *Of those roses in your garden*
> *Did the morning sunlight warm your soul*
> *And brighten up your day?*

The good old sixties. Free love, birth control pills, the Beatles, marijuana. My mind slips away from the noisy French bar and returns to a cold February night at film director Hal Ashby's apartment in New York. Over twenty years ago. My first introduction to sweet Mary Juana.

As usual, I was in The Apple selling a new game show idea.

Exhausted from jet lag and sales pitches, I was in desperate need of rest and rehabilitation. The evening I was about to enjoy would, by all rights, accomplish all that. It had the makings of greatness. I was going to be with my good friend Ashby, he was going to introduce me to the world of extraterrestrial delights by way of the finest grass this side of Bogotá, and last but far from least, I had a hot date I had been looking forward to for a month.

The evening didn't quite turn out that way.

The hot date and I, and a few others, sat around Hal's living room smoking grass and eating Milky Ways. I loved the Milky Ways but was extremely disappointed with the marijuana experience. Quite frankly I didn't think there was a whole lot to it. It seemed an inordinate amount of time was spent making the joint (packing, rolling, licking, etc.), adjusting the roach on its annoying little clip and then passing it around the room, exposing everyone there to every-

one else's germs. Worse than that, I experienced nothing the least
bit extraterrestrial, no fantastic "high" I had heard so much about,
just an insatiable craving for more Milky Ways. Inhaling the weed
only made me cough. It also diverted my attention from figuring out
how to get my hot date back to my place and into bed.

Later, in the wee hours of the morning, the two of us stood on the
corner of Third Avenue and Twenty-eighth Street trying to hail a taxi
before we froze to death. The temperature was in the single digits
and cabs were nowhere to be found. My date and I were stranded in
the street for what seemed like an eternity waving our arms frantically at nothing. When a taxi finally stopped I was met at its door by
another man who appeared out of the night and claimed the cab was
his. An argument ensued; some pushing and shoving took place. My
date suggested I let the man have the taxi, we would find another.
Absolutely not, I growled. This was my cab. Even though the jerk-
off with the big mouth was a head taller than I, if he wanted to fight
for the taxi I'd be more than happy to oblige. But first, in order to
allow myself more freedom of movement and to prevent my fine
dark-blue cashmere overcoat from getting dirty or damaged, I decided to fold the coat carefully and place it on top of the cab's trunk.

Fortunately I have a certain expertise regarding the folding of
suits and coats. It was a knack I learned while working on school
holidays at my grandfather's depressing men's clothing store. I was a
boxer; the one who folded the merchandise neatly and placed it in a
box for the customer. The boxing of a suit coat or overcoat requires
the following procedure: Slipping your arms into the coat's sleeves,
bringing your fingertips together, then bending the coat backward
and inside out along its center seam. With a snappy twist of the
hands (this was the tricky part), the coat became neatly halved and
folded so that later when it was removed from the box it would be
creaseless. I followed this same time honored technique while folding my dark-blue cashmere overcoat.

Unfortunately my body movements had suddenly been reduced to
slow motion. I was taken with sudden seizures of laughing. Putting
my hands through the coat's sleeves made me cackle until tears
came to my eyes. Every time I touched my fingertips I was reduced
to uncontrollable giggling. The mere thought of performing my
snappy twist made me laugh so hard I ended up doubled over and
holding my sides. Each step had to be repeated and repeated. Moan-

ing from my aching ribs, I finally finished. I turned and placed the coat carefully on the taxi's trunk. The overcoat fell to the slushy street. There wasn't any taxi trunk. There wasn't any taxi. It had left five minutes ago with the big-mouthed jerk, and my hot date.

My trip to New York was not a total waste. I sold my new game show idea to the American Broadcasting Company. It was called the *Newlywed Game.*

CHAPTER ELEVEN

HOST: What will your husband say the length of his inseam is?
WIFE: Seven inches.

The *Newlywed Game* attempted to determine which of four newly wedded couples—all married less than a year—knew each other best. It was 1966, and even though the times they were a-changin', we still couldn't mention the word "sex" or say "making love" on our television programs. Not at the jittery American Broadcasting Company. Instead of making love we said "making whoopee" or used the expression "whoopee session." Even with those absurd handicaps, the *Newlywed Game* worked like magic.

HOST: What household chore did your wife say you do exactly the same way as you do when "making whoopee"?
HUSBAND: Wash the dishes.
HOST: Your wife said take out the garbage.
HUSBAND: Take out the garbage?
WIFE: Yeah. You just do it. There's nothing fancy about it. You just put it in and put it out.

HOST: What one fact made your last "whoopee session" uniquely different from all the others you've had?
WIFE: It was unique because it was in the hallway on a newspaper.
HUSBAND: Oh, God, think of our son!
WIFE: What son?

HOST: Where did your wife say you had your most unusual "whoopee session"?

HUSBAND: In the sink.
HOST: I'm sorry. Your wife said in the butt.
HUSBAND: Damn, I almost said that.

HOST: Where will your husband say your worst "whoopee ses-
sion" usually takes place?
WIFE: In the bathtub.
HOST: In the bathtub?
WIFE: Yes. Because the water always makes his peeny shrivel up.

While the newly wedded wives were off stage in a soundproof
booth, we asked the four husbands questions about their married
lives. The husbands would answer the questions, each one hoping
his wife would match his answer when she returned to the stage.
Then for round two the situation was reversed; the husbands were
sent to the soundproof booth, and we asked a new set of questions to
the wives. When a couple matched answers, they received points.
The couple with the most points at the end of the show would win a
washing machine, or something equally exotic.

HOST: What will your husband say annoyed you most during your
last romantic interlude?
WIFE: When he stuck it in my ear.

The intriguing thing about the show's prize was, it was something
all four couples always wanted very much. So when the program's
host told the winning pair what they would receive—"You've just
won this beautiful washer-dryer!" "This complete bedroom set!"
"This power lawn mower!'"—the couple went bonkers. No matter
how angry the husband and wife had been with each other, when
they heard what their prize was they kissed and hugged and carried
on like you wouldn't believe. Conversely, the three losing couples,
upon discovering what they might have won, appeared devastated.
Why was that? How did we get such consistently incredible reactions? The simple answer, a secret no one ever figured out, was this:
We asked all the *Newlywed* contestants to write down on their appli-
cation forms the one prize they would most like to win. Then we
merely put the four couples who wanted the same prize on the same
show.

HOST: Who will your wife say is your favorite classical composer?
HUSBAND: Neil Sedaka.

We were often accused of prompting the *Newlywed Game* contestants or writing answers for them. I can tell you right now, we didn't. Why would we? We could never have written anything as funny as the words that fell spontaneously from the mouths of those young couples. Who could have created the following exchange?

HOST: What will your husband say is his least favorite condiment on his wiener?
WIFE #1: Mustard.
WIFE #2: Ketchup.
WIFE #3: Ketchup.
WIFE #4: Ben Gay.

The *Newlywed Game* was another huge daytime success.

A few months after the *Newlywed Game* went on the air, at eight o'clock on a Wednesday morning, Leonard Goldberg telephoned my office in Hollywood. He was calling from New York.

"I knew I'd catch you in," he said.

It was the same Leonard Goldberg who, as head of ABC daytime television, put the *Dating Game* on the air. In the meantime Mr. Goldberg had been promoted to chief of all programs—day and night—for the network. Leonard told me their new Tammy Grimes nighttime hour was a disaster. I said I was sorry to hear that, which of course I wasn't. He said he was going to have to cancel the program right away. My pulse quickened. Goldberg explained that he desperately needed something to fill the empty hour, to "hold the line, as it were" until a permanent replacement could be found. My chest felt as if it were in a vise. I could hardly breath. Goldberg said, "I'd love to use your two half hours, the *Dating Game* and *Newlywed Game.*"

My heart skipped a beat. The first two game shows ever to be on prime-time television!

"Except . . ." said Goldberg mournfully, pausing.

"Except?"

". . . your shows have problems."

My heart sputtered and fell to earth. I knew it was too good to be true. So why was he calling?

"What kind of problems?" I asked, my voice cracking with disappointment.

"They're not nighttime, if you know what I mean."

I didn't know what he meant. "If you mean they're not as expensive, then you're right," I offered quietly. "But if you mean they're not as entertaining, then you're—"

"On second thought they may very well be," mumbled Goldberg, thinking aloud, ignoring my presence on the other end of the line.

"Be what?"

"We can give bigger prizes on the nighttime *Newlywed Game*," he said to himself. "Maybe yachts, a small house, his and her Jaguars." Then, as if waking from a trance, realizing I was around somewhere, Goldberg said, "Perhaps I shouldn't have called, didn't want to from the start, but then the *Dating Game* was my choice and it's done so well. Just thought I'd touch base with you, pick your brain. I really don't hold out much hope for your shows going prime time, but then—"

"But then what?"

"But then you never know. What do you think about that idea?"

"What idea?"

"Giving big prizes on the *Newlywed Game*."

"I hate to say this," I said. "I know I'm cutting my own throat, but that won't work. Now the *Newlywed Game* is fun. It's played for laughs. True, the couples get mad if one or the other misses a question, but they won't kill each other. You don't kill your husband or your wife over a washer-dryer. But put a yacht up there and you've got an entirely new show. The fun will turn to violence. What you'll have is the *Death Game*."

"Okay," said Goldberg. "I see your point. Perhaps the *Newlywed Game* can make it on its own. Without changes. But the *Dating Game*, now that's a different story."

"In what way?"

"I don't know. All I know is, something's wrong with the *Dating Game*. It's not nighttime. Not the way it is now. Something's missing. I can't put my finger on the problem. Maybe you can. I'll give you forty-eight hours to try and figure it out. If you can find a way to give the *Dating Game* nighttime quality, I'll put both the *Dating*

Game and the *Newlywed Game* on the air in two weeks, Saturday night, eight to nine. If you can't, what the hell? At least I got the blood flowing through your veins. Call me the day after tomorrow. Friday morning. Same time."

If you can find a way to give the *Dating Game* nighttime quality.

How does one define nighttime quality?

During the first twenty-four of my forty-eight hours I couldn't think of a thing. Neither could I eat or sleep. During hours twenty-five through forty-five I visited churches and temples, the more intelligent members of my family, good friends, and a few enemies; the houses of worship for revelation, the people for inspiration. I asked the same questions over and over again. How can I change the *Dating Game* to make it a nighttime contender? What can I change? We pick the prettiest girls we can find, and the most handsome or funniest bachelors. The girls asked the best questions they were capable of creating. What else is there? That's the show.

Neither the buildings nor the people had any answers.

As a last resort I sought out my old mentor and hero, Reuven Frank. Mr. Frank was now the intelligent and clear-thinking boss of the network's entire news operation, wise in the ways of television. What better man to ask advice? I was sure Reuven would give me the answer. He gave me nothing. All Reuven wanted to know was how come the winning *Newlywed* couples got so excited over a goddamn washing machine. "It's seems you give them exactly what they want. How do you do that? How do you get lucky like that every day?" I told Reuven it was a secret, thanked him, said good-bye, and hung up the telephone.

On the forty-seventh hour I retreated to my office to watch the sun rise and begin prepping myself for the inevitable heartache to come. A golden opportunity down the drain without so much as a tiny creative suggestion from me. And now my time had all but run out. I was to call Leonard Goldberg in New York at eight o'clock. I checked my wristwatch for the millionth time. It was exactly seven-fifteen. My secretary, Loretta Strickland, walked in a few minutes later with two black coffees in Styrofoam cups and sat down opposite me on the other side of my desk. She smiled weakly. I did the same back to her and took the coffee she offered.

"Thanks."

"You're welcome," she said. "He's an ass."

"Who is?"

"Goldberg."

"No he's not."

"The show's fine the way it is," said Loretta. "You can't fix something that's not broken. I mean, what can you possibly change?"

"Please," I said, holding up my hand. Any more thinking and my head would explode.

"We select the prettiest girls," said Loretta into her Styrofoam cup. "The handsomest men. We ask the best questions. Send the dates to the best restaurants. I mean—"

Prettiest girls. Handsomest men. Best questions.

"And what else, Loretta?"

"I'm sorry?"

"You said prettiest girls, handsomest men, best questions. What was the last thing you said?"

"Best restaurants."

"Best restaurants. Best restaurants. That's it, Loretta!" I yelled. "That. Is. It!"

CHAPTER TWELVE

I climbed up on my desk, did a little jig, jumped off the other side, and hugged Loretta so hard I disfigured her beehive hair-do she got up at dawn to coif. Fifteen minutes later, I telephoned Leonard Goldberg with the solution to our *Dating Game* problem.

"Which is exactly what?" said Goldberg, not in one of his better moods.

"The *Dating Game* is romance, isn't it?" I asked. "That's what the program's all about. And what's one of the most important ways we make the show romantic? We send the winning couples to the most romantic restaurants we can find in and around Los Angeles. Mainly because that's all we can afford to do."

"Get to the point."

"On the nighttime version of the *Dating Game*, instead of sending the winning couples to local restaurants as their prize, we'll send them to the most romantic cities in the world! Paris, Rome, Venice, Vienna, Madrid, Rio de Janeiro, Casablanca. We'll have a bigger budget for our nighttime show and that's what we'll spend it on; a better payoff, nighttime quality dates! What do you think?"

"I think there'll be a shit storm if we send these young kids off to foreign cities all by themselves. The girls will come back pregnant and the two of us will have lawsuits coming out of our ears."

"I'll send a chaperon," I said nervously, making everything up as I went along. "I'll send an employee of mine with every date. Who better to watch out for the interests of both my program and your network than one of my faithful employees?"

"Most of your faithful employees are kids themselves."

"I'll send the older ones. A chaperon will have to be twenty-one years or older."

There was a monstrous pause on the other end of the telephone. "What do you think?" I asked again, holding my breath.

"You have two weeks to get those programs ready for air," replied Mr. Goldberg.

Halfway through the first year of our nighttime *Dating Game* program I ran out of romantic cities.

Winning couples were now visiting Reykjavik, Poznan, Vanersborg, Riga, Cherkassy, Uskudar, Lagos, Fairbanks, Quito, Tunis, and Estonia's questionably sentimental Lake Pelpus. The chaperons, most of whom had never been outside of the state of California, who would turn giddy with excitement when I would tell them where they were off to, soon became jaded world travelers. On one occasion I flipped open the office door of *Newlywed Game* producer Mike Metzger, stuck my head in, and said, "You're going to Morocco!"

"Which part?" he asked sullenly.

The good news was, we didn't have one catastrophe. Considering the numbers of dates we shipped out and the places they went to, we were lucky to escape unscratched. Russia, China, Africa, Tibet, down the Nile, up the Amazon, and never any serious problems. We did, however, have minor ones.

The guide on our romantic Amazon river trip, while showing the *Dating Game* couple what not to do—"Do not trail your hand in the river like this. A piranha, the predatory fresh water fish of the family Characidae, can come along and nip off your thumb"—had his thumb nipped off by a piranha. The guide sued the show. In a crowded elevator in a romantic downtown Kampala hotel, an angry girl pulled three large clumps of hair from the head of her *Dating Game* date. The stricken bachelor sued the show. In romantic Kata Kinabala, Malaysia, our male chaperon, Gene Banks (age fifty-two), and the *Dating Game* couple (the girl age eighteen, the boy age nineteen) were photographed frolicking in the surf naked as jaybirds. The picture found its way into several international newspapers. During dinner in romantic Brisbane, Australia, the *Dating Game* bachelor dropped several sleeping pills into the chaperon's cocktail. Our eagle-eyed chaperon, Trixie Dejonge, quickly switched glasses and twenty minutes later the bachelor was sleeping comfortably in his mashed potatoes. The bachelor sued the show. In senti-

mental Kurdistan, while having lunch in a restaurant still under construction, a *Dating Game* pair and their chaperon had a workman fall
through the ceiling over their heads and land in the center of their
dining table. The corsage in the bachelorette's hair was bent over
from weight of plaster dust. The couple were both lawyers, albeit
rather dumb ones. Neither sued the show. In the Sistine Chapel, in
romantic Rome, our *Dating Game* chaperon, Jimmy Comorre, was
standing on the left side of a bench waiting for a glimpse of the Pope.
Three nuns stood on the right side. Tired of waiting, Jimmy stepped
down from the bench and the three nuns slid off the other end,
landing in a pile on the floor. Fortunately no one was hurt and
nobody sued.

By now, Chuck Barris Productions had doubled in size.

Most of the new men and women I hired never had resumes. It
didn't matter. I went by instinct; searching for bright, ambitious,
hungry high school dropouts and college students with vivid imagi-
nations and great personalities. I think my intuition, at least in those
days, was magical. The magic worked both ways. I gave talented
people an opportunity to be connected with hit television programs,
make good money, and earn show credits. In return, these young
creative minds gave me exciting, inventive, sometimes visionary and
always professionally executed television programs. I also worked
them like dogs and they never complained.

The freedom that prevailed created a spirit in our halls that was
almost tangible. It was truly one for all and all for one. We were a
commune rather than a corporation, preferring our fellow compan-
ions to the companionship of others. We worked together and social-
ized together; in the offices during the day, in the studios at night, in
restaurants and bars when the new day began. We wore the company coat of arms on baseball caps, windbreakers, and carryalls
wherever we went. A jealous competitor was overheard grousing,
"They look like a retarded softball team," to which someone quickly
added, "Marching all the way to the bank."

Life magazine did a feature on my company. The story described
us as a cult of barefoot and bra-less hippies living in eccentrically
furnished offices running around Hollywood making hit TV shows. I
was quoted in the piece as saying, "As long as my employees excel in

their jobs, they can wear anything they want and decorate their offices any way they chose to."

There was a group picture of all of us.

We looked like a Beatles album cover.

But then everyone in Hollywood looked like the Beatles. It was the late sixties. Some said the best of times. Neither recession nor nutrition was anything to worry about. Dairy was good for your bones and meat for the blood. Caffeine got you going in the morning and scotch calmed you down at night. Pancakes, eggs, bacon, toast, and butter were as necessary for breakfast as cake, cookies, and candy were to quench your craving for sweets after smoking marijuana. Kosher hot dogs were as American as apple pie and ice cream. Cigarettes were only a little bad, cholesterol existed but we didn't care about it and AIDS didn't exist at all. Birth control pills wouldn't give you cancer and you didn't have to use a condom to get laid. Sex was in, restraints were out. Even foot-in-mouth lovers like myself scored now and then.

It was also the worst of times. Some called them frightening years. Vietnam threw a dark cloud over everything. Airports were filled with tearful farewells, sea ports with depressing troop ships. Urban riots and political assassinations, angry protestors and violent marches, billy clubs and tear gas canisters were ruining the land. Free love and its partner, the soaring population explosion, were ruining the world . . . and my company staff meetings. These meaningful weekly conferences were interrupted more and more by wailing infants and screeching mothers; a six-week-old prune wrapped in a pink blanket who had grown hungry, or a young female production assistant yelping because her teething newborn bit her nipple. "Hey," I would bark, "if you can't keep your kids quiet, nurse them out in the hall. I've got important things to say here and I can't hear myself think."

Every Friday morning I would close our switchboard and jam the entire company into my office. We'd start the festivities with some folk music played by the CBP Stompers, our in-house band. After the concert I would relate the latest news concerning our company —good and bad—to the throng squeezed into the couches and armchairs, girls doubled up on the laps of boys, fifteen or twenty more sitting on the rug, others less fortunate standing in the hall. Now and then during these Friday staff meetings various workers were brought up on charges, tried before the company, found guilty or not and punished accordingly. Often the indictments were frivolous: failure to share a pizza with a starving associate, losing a company jacket, leaving work early to help deliver a roommate's baby without telling anyone, going to the bathroom ahead of a more senior member of the company, forgetting to bring the boss a coffee ice-cream cone from Baskin-Robbins. Once in a while the allegations were more serious.

Like the time one of my employees, Mike Ogiens, threw me out of his house.

CHAPTER THIRTEEN

Mike Ogiens was a trusted employee who had risen through the ranks from Chinese Bandit—the lowest form of life, a contestant phoner, similar to a West Point plebe—to a show producer.

Mike was living with an airline stewardess named Tricia, pretty but tough, in a West Hollywood apartment. One Halloween the two decided to throw a costume party. Mike invited me to come. I was living in Malibu at the time. The thought of driving all the way into the city for a goddamn costume party was far from thrilling. Mike begged. He said it would "make the evening" if his boss could attend his, and Tricia's, first important soiree. So I agreed to come. (How could I not?) Of course I didn't wear a costume. Never did in my life. Nor did I intend to stay very long.

Fifteen minutes after my date and I arrived, a white-faced Ogiens called me out onto his apartment terrace. Once there, Mike slid the sliding glass door shut, turned, and said, "I'm going to have to ask you to leave."

"Why?"

"You're the only one here without a costume."

"Oh."

"It's not fair," he added.

While Mike sputtered on, I noticed tough Tricia peering around a curtain to see if my ejection was going well. When our eyes met, she pulled her head back.

"No problem," I told the sweating Ogiens, and I meant it. I was happy to be able to flee so quickly, without the usual excuses or having to slip out the back, Jack.

I drove away cackling with glee at the absurdity of it all, how I would be back in Malibu far earlier than expected. That was Friday night. When I woke up Saturday morning I wasn't cackling. I was furious. I was certain my fury would abate by Sunday. It didn't. On Monday I was standing in front of the company elevator at eight o'clock in the morning. I didn't want to miss Ogiens when he arrived. And when he did, when the elevator doors opened to reveal the culprit, I pointed my finger at him and said, "You're fired."

Late that night, when everyone else had gone, Mike returned. He knew I'd be in my office. He stayed in the doorframe, afraid to come any farther, and pleaded his case. It was the girlfriend's fault. He never should have listened to her. It was a foolish mistake. It would never happen again. When I didn't change my mind, Ogiens asked if he could be tried in absentia at our next Friday staff meeting. I agreed that he could.

My defender at the Friday meeting told the gathering, "You would expect an employee to put out their best linen and silverware when his or her boss came to dinner. Offer your boss your best chair, your best wine. Not kick your boss out the door. Not even if it was your fondest wish. Stupidity is what I call it, dangerous stupidity." The company agreed. Ogien's dismissal was upheld unanimously, colored perhaps by my pretrial statement that anyone voting for his return would likewise be fired.

Several months later Ogiens phoned to ask if I would write him a letter of recommendation. Of course I would, and did. I wrote that young Ogiens was a loyal, diligent, and competent worker. I closed by saying: "If, however, he ever invites you to a Halloween party, you better wear a costume."

Mike Ogiens went on to become a vice president at the Columbia Broadcasting System.

It might have been confusing times for some, but it was heady times for me. I sold two more game shows in the late sixties: *Dream Girls,* a parody based on the country's obsession with beauty pageants, and *Family Game,* the natural evolution from *Dating Game* and *Newlywed Game.* All four of my programs were broadcast Monday through Friday on national television. *Dating Game* and *Newlywed Game* were also seen at night. My company was producing twenty-two half hours of game shows a week, fifty-two weeks a year—more television half hours than any other entertainment company in America. With that amount of work we all knew we would have steady jobs for a while. Now we could trade our junk heap of a car in for a better one, buy some new clothes, find a nicer apartment, and finally get our teeth fixed. In those days my employees' mouths were so full of Novocain they had to say things twice before I could understood them.

The late sixties and early seventies might very well have been the best period of my life. No matter how long I labored or how late I went to sleep, I woke up raring to go. It was energizing being a success. I savored this feeling of power, secretly delighted in having an entourage, enjoyed the fawning head waiters, and most of all the ability to make wishes come true. This was accomplished most of the time by way of an enchanted audio cassette recorder I carried in my pants pocket.

The enchanted recorder was like the bottle you trip over on the beach that has a genie trapped inside. The genie would grant you three wishes. My enchanted recorder was open-ended. I could wish for as many things as I wanted; the latest Harley Davidson motorcycle, a brand-new bright orange Pontiac Firebird I saw in a showroom window, an interesting Parker pen, a date with a certain girl. I simply told the enchanted audio-cassette recorder of these things, laid it down on my secretary's desk, and voilà! the next day there it was! The Harley in my garage, the Pontiac in my parking place, the pen on my desk, the date waiting that evening at the restaurant. I liked that.

During this time of newfound wealth and power I tried projecting an image of modesty and unassuming charm, but in truth I failed. I'm certain I acted cocky and self-centered. I didn't want to, but I'm sure I did. It was difficult not to. It was a time of immense good luck, good fortune, and good health. It was also a time of wonder. One morning over breakfast I said to David Gotterer, my business manager, "I can't believe what's happening to me. I have four network television shows on the air, two on in prime time, a business that's grossing two million dollars a year, and no end in sight! I don't believe it. I have to keep pinching myself to make sure I'm not dreaming."

"First thing every morning," suggested my business manager, "remind yourself of your enviable state. Say to yourself: 'Chuck, you are a very lucky boy.' "

Later that day I had a medal made to wear on a chain around my neck. The medal says: Chuck You Are A Very Lucky Boy. (I'm wearing it right now.) A few weeks later I took the medal to St. Patrick's Cathedral in New York. I dipped the medal in holy water. I'm not Catholic, but I didn't think it would hurt. Shortly after my visit to the cathedral my company grew bigger and more powerful. I would sell two more game shows: *How's Your Mother-In-Law* and *Three's a Crowd*. We would go from twenty-two to twenty-seven half hours a week. I would use a motorcycle to ride around Hollywood at night checking the tapings of seven different shows on television lots and in theaters, and our contestant operations in various hotels and office buildings.

At first I played down our growth, was almost embarrassed by it. My company's rapid metamorphosis from bare foot and bra-less to profit and loss statements and efficiency reports bothered me. I told everyone the whole thing was a drag. Makes me feel uncomfortable, I said.

"We've become something you never wanted us to become," complained Ruthie Goldberg one night after everyone had gone.

"What's that, Ruthie?"

"We've become corporate."

Of course she was right. But if I was disillusioned I didn't stay that way for long. In 1968 I took my company public.

We became Barris Industries.

At first my minuscule knowledge of Wall Street frightened me. I was uncomfortable and insecure in the company of brokers and analysts, stocks and bonds, balance sheets and annual reports, lawyers and accountants. As a result, I hid behind a screen of frivolousness and eccentricity. My first board of directors meeting—held in the impressive conference room of our New York law firm—appeared to be something out of Woodstock. Half of those seated around the conference-room table wore Nehru jackets and gave the peace sign when they said hello. They were my fellow workers. Outwardly I reveled in the shock my troops had created throughout those staid Park Avenue offices. Inwardly I had a gnawing sensation I was making a big mistake.

Which brings me to my first annual stockholders' meeting, an event that began badly and went downhill from there. The attire I insisted on wearing—a torn flight jacket, white T-shirt, Levi's and sneakers—quietly embarrassed me. And then came that deceptively bland first question. "What's the stock selling for today?" asked a middle-aged mother, her pretty daughter sitting next to her.

"I'm not sure," I replied jauntily, "but I'll find out for you as soon as the meetings over."

"You're not sure?" gasped the horrified stockholder. "You're not sure? You're the president and chief executive office of this company and you don't know what the stock is selling for?"

I was mortified, my blush covering every exposed part of my body. For the rest of my corporate life I never entered another stockholders' meeting without knowing the exact price of the stock. Unfortunately no one ever asked again.

But if at first I was insecure and frightened by the world of high finance, I got over it. It didn't take long to comprehend that I was going about this public thing all wrong. Far from being a drag, owning a public company could mean possessing a money machine. I became convinced that a man with a creative mind, who knew exactly what he was talking about, had a flair for the hipper dipper, a dash of the carnival barker, a touch of the elixir salesman, a man with those qualities could make a fortune on Wall Street. Mike Todd would have been perfect. They would have stood in line trying to give Mike money.

It also became clear to me that not all the stockbrokers and stock analysts—dressed to the nines in their gray Armani suits and bright yellow foulard ties—were the financial geniuses they professed to be. The more familiar I became with them, the more fallible they appeared. Not the majority by any means, but a larger number than I originally suspected. I noticed how some heretofore intimidating dealmakers missed an offer's nuances, didn't thoroughly comprehend a proposition's potential risks or rewards, were gravely lacking in good old street smarts. It wasn't unusual to hear about a smart CEO running circles around a whole posse of investment bankers. Nor was it uncommon for company presidents to know more about their businesses than the leverage buyout big shots on the other side of the negotiating table. And why shouldn't they know more? It made sense. Still, there were many who could play the game well. I wanted some of them on my team.

By our second board meeting all my fellow workers resplendent in their hippie garb and peace signs had been replaced by intelligent financiers and astute businessmen in suits and ties.

"Not only has the company changed," complained my old comrade in arms, Ruthie Goldberg, "but you've changed, too."

"I know," I replied. "It's because I've come to a couple of important conclusions during the last six months."

"Oh? And what might they be?"

"One is, the stock market's really just one big game show."

"And the other?"

"We're good at game shows."

CHAPTER FOURTEEN

Saint-Tropez has one very small movie theater with only a few dozen seats. The theater is on the Place des Lices and exhibits movies only on weekends and only during "the season." Occasionally the local schools use the movie theater for their plays and Christmas pageants. The movie's concession stand consists of an orange-and-red popcorn machine that sells either salted or sugared popcorn. The bill of fare is mostly old American movies. The movies are always dubbed in French. I go to the movies in Saint-Tropez as much as I can. Since I've already seen most of the pictures back in the States I generally know approximately what the actors are saying. I hear how it sounds in French. It helps me learn the language. Plus I love movies.

"Have you ever made one?" asks Henri one Sunday afternoon as the two of us and Henri's daughter Emilie leave the theater. We have just seen *Bambi*. I learned two new French words.

"Almost once," I answer. "And yes, on another occasion."

My ill-fated career in films began with a phone call I made to Dick Shepherd, at the time a powerful agent in one of Hollywood's biggest talent agencies.

I told Dick I wanted to buy the motion picture rights to a Larry Collins-Dominique Lapierre best-seller, *Or I'll Dress You In Mourning*. "I think that can be arranged," he said, and made an appointment for me with the writers' representative; a pudgy, squat man named Irving "Swifty" Lazar. Mr. Lazar looked exactly like an aging Mr. Magoo. In those days Swifty considered himself the most influential and best talent agent that ever existed. Probably still does. After I got to know Mr. Lazar I didn't like him at all. On the other hand, he detested me at first sight. This is the way he described me to others: "He has hair like a Fuzzy-Wuzzy, wears torn jeans and sneakers, and talks with a cigar butt in his mouth."

Because of Mr. Lazar's responsibility to his clients Collins and Lapierre, and because I had lots of money, Mr. Lazar was required to meet with me. When we talked it was as if each word he spoke gagged him as it came out of his mouth. He said, "You can have the rights to the book but there's a problem. The bullfighter, El Cordobés."

"What about him?"

"El Cordobés has final control."

"Meaning what?"

"Meaning you must have El Cordobés's approval before you can make a film of *Or I'll Dress You In Mourning*. I told Collins and Lapierre they were foolish to let the bullfighter have the final say regarding who could or couldn't make a film of their book. Simply asinine. Collins and Lapierre told me El Cordobés wouldn't be a problem. I predicted the opposite. I said the bullfighter would be a big problem. He fights bulls. How smart can he be? I promise you getting the bullfighter's permission won't be easy."

"Why?"

"Because it won't," snapped Mr. Lazar impatiently, and promptly ended the meeting.

I wrote out a check for the motion picture rights of the best-seller and left the repulsive man's office. Not long after that I embarked on a crusade to obtain written permission from a bullfighter so that I could make a motion picture of his life, an odyssey I shall never forget.

Or I'll Dress You In Mourning is the story of Manuel Benitez, an illiterate Spanish peasant who became one of the world's richest and most glorious matadors. The wonderful book tells the tale of this man's courage and tenacity against almost insurmountable odds, especially in Franco's fascist Spain.

I traveled first to Saint-Tropez to meet the book's authors. Larry Collins met me at Nice Airport. It was hard not to notice the astonished expression on his face. Was it my fuzzy hair, my torn jeans and sneakers, my cigar, the unexpected revelation that I didn't look anything like Sam Spiegel or any other Hollywood producer Collins knew? We drove to Saint-Tropez where I was introduced to Larry's writing partner, Dominique Lapierre. Lapierre also appeared a bit taken aback when we met. "Can't judge a book by its cover," I said, shaking Lapierre's hand, convinced my childish warning had just lost the last ounce of stature I may have had. Now, twenty-five years later, the three of us still talk about that first meeting. Later, while a short plane ride away Russia was invading Czechoslovakia, Collins, Lapierre, and I were sailing in the gulf of Saint-Tropez, enjoying caviar and white wine, discussing the book and how a motion picture might be made of it.

That night we went to dinner in the port. The restaurant, L'ascale, was a favorite of the international celebrities who arrived in Saint-Tropez during July and August. In front of L'ascale, crowds of tourists held at bay by ropes were jumping into the air hoping to see a movie star, a rock star, a film director, someone of importance, over the heads of other tourists. Photographers snapped pictures as Larry, Larry's wife, Nadia, Dominique, and I entered L'ascale. Radio Nice interviewed us at our table during dinner. Flashbulbs exploded when the two best-selling authors and the alleged important film producer from Hollywood—the one with the fuzzy hair and sneakers —departed the restaurant. Numerous autograph seekers made driving away difficult.

The next night Collins and Lapierre had plans. I was on my own. I wandered back to L'ascale and stood behind the ropes with the other tourists. I jumped into the air trying to see the important people arriving for dinner over the heads of those in front of me.

From Saint-Tropez I journeyed to Spain to meet the bullfighter. Though I couldn't speak a word of Spanish and El Cordobés not a word of English, we became immediate friends. He was street smart, warm, and friendly, but definitely not impressive. The man was shorter and thinner than me. How impressive could he be? Why all the clamor, I mused, the adoration for this skinny, unpretentious man known throughout the Spanish-speaking world as El Cordobés, The Maestro?

More impressive than the matador was his huge ranch named Villobos. Only one other ranch stood as high above the Spanish plains as his and that was the governor's. It was with great pride El Cordobés showed me his herds of fighting bulls grazing on his thousands of hectares, the three Rolls-Royces and four Mercedes in an extra large garage, and the bullfighter's newest race horse which he had brought into his living room for my inspection.

The next day I flew with Dominique Lapierre in El Cordobés's private plane to Madrid to see him fight. El Cordobés was the pilot, learning how to fly, being taught by a former pilot in the Spanish Air Force who sat at the matador's right. As we approached Madrid Airport the voices I heard from the plane's radio seemed to grow louder and more shrill. I asked Dominique what all the excitement was about. Dominique told me the tower was instructing all the commercial airline pilots to keep their planes at least a hundred miles away from the airport for the next fifteen minutes.

That afternoon, I saw El Cordobés enter Madrid's municipal stadium in his Suit of Lights. The sight of him dressed as he was, the expression on his face, his stance, his attitude; a spirit that exuded calm and courage, the entire tableau was simply extraordinary. Now I knew why this bullfighter was worshiped and adored, why they called him The Maestro. The man as matador had a remarkable charisma, an attraction to both men and women only a handful of performers will ever have. He also had an injured right shoulder, the result of a recent wound he suffered from a bull's horn. Now when it was time for the kill, El Cordobés had to work harder. With his weak shoulder, and in the short amount of time at his disposal, it had become difficult—and dangerous—to push his sword through the iron-thick neck muscles just below the bull's shoulder blades. But he eventually succeeded. And in the twilight of that day The Maestro bowed to the cheers of the standing-room-only stadium.

Later that same evening, Dominique Lapierre returned to Saint-Tropez and I rode with El Cordobés in his Mercedes to Seville, where he would fight next. Also in the car was El Cordobés's best friend, a tough guy with a crippled leg named Paco Ruiz. As we drove, the three of us ate some fresh ham that Manolo sliced from the large ham bone he always kept in the trunks of his cars. El Cordobés felt secure with a huge ham in the trunk of his car. It was a habit left over from the days when Manuel Benitez's destitute family almost starved to death.

While it was still dark, Paco pulled over to the side of the highway and stopped the car. We left the Mercedes and walked across the road to a grassy field on the other side. There we slept until morning. Manolo, for that was what El Cordobés's friends called him, found nothing unusual about stopping whenever he felt like it to sleep along the side of the road if he was tired. "Once a peasant, always a peasant," I think is what Manolo said before he fell asleep. At dawn, when I opened my eyes, I discovered we were surrounded by fifty or sixty locals: peasants, farmers, children on the way to school, laborers on their way to work. Everyone stood quietly in awe of their sleeping hero, content to simply stare at The Maestro.

For one year I met Manolo in different places all over Spain, Mexico, and South America. Everywhere we went Paco Ruiz was always by his side, as was Manolo's fiancée. El Cordobés had a fiancée in every Spanish city we visited. Each fiancée was chaste, pubescent, and beautiful, and each was absolutely convinced she was El Cordobés's only fiancée. Oddly enough, each fiancée invariably had two sisters, one for Paco and one for me. The sisters were neither beautiful, pubescent, nor chaste.

And in all of the cities we traveled to, I always asked El Cordobés the same question, nicely and with great tact: Manolo, will you give me your written permission to make a motion picture of your life as written in the book, *Or I'll Dress You In Mourning?* It will be a spectacular motion picture and you will be even more famous than you are now. And in all the cities we visited, Manolo always gave me the same answers, nicely and with tact: Only for a million dollars and only if I play myself.

Which was out of the question.

How could a Spanish peasant who couldn't speak a word of English play the lead in an multimillion-dollar American movie? Paul Newman, yes. Manuel Benitez, absolutely not.

Matters were made so frustrating because with the glaring exception of El Cordobés, everyone else was in place. The respected Marty Ritt would direct. Academy Award winners Irving Ravitch and Harriet Frank would write the script. And Martin Baum, head of ABC Films, would pay twenty million dollars, a lavish budget in 1968, to have the picture made and distributed. Jack Valenti, president of the Motion Picture Producers Association, was pleased with this joint venture between our country and Spain. Valenti promised his full cooperation. I was that close to breaking into movies. Big Time. But not close enough. I had to have El Cordobés's written permission, and I didn't have it.

"Send Medavoy," said an anxious Dick Shepherd, smelling the

multimillion-dollar deal, tasting it. "Medavoy's hip, smart, a great negotiator, and he can speak fluent Spanish."

So a young agent named Mike Medavoy accompanied me to Mexico City where The Maestro was going to perform. Mike Medavoy was a rolling dynamo. One just knew by looking at the pudgy red-haired, red-cheeked, freckle-faced lad that he was going to be someone to reckon with in La La Land when he grew up.

Following the bullfight, Medavoy and I were invited to dinner with El Cordobés. The Maestro was sending his limousine for us. In the limousine would be Paco Ruiz, El Cordobés, El Cordobés's Mexico City fiancée, and sisters for Paco and me. Medavoy and I were to meet the limousine in fifteen minutes in the parking lot under the hotel so that we could disappear into the night unnoticed. While waiting for the limo, Medavoy and I had a drink in the hotel bar.

"What seems to be the basic problem here?" asked Medavoy, using his forefinger to spread the salt evenly around the rim of his margarita cocktail glass.

"El Cordobés and I can't communicate," I told Medavoy. "Not about the important things. Since I can't speak Spanish I can't explain the reasons Manolo, El Cordobés, is making a big mistake in not agreeing to let us make this film."

"I presume you've appealed to his pocketbook and his ego. Told this guy about all the additional fame and fortune he'll receive if Hollywood makes a big-ticket picture based on his life."

I said I had.

"Put your finger on the deal breaker as you see it," asked Medavoy.

"El Cordobés won't agree unless he can play himself."

Medavoy sent the last sip of his first margarita down the hatch, ordered another, then turned to me and said, "This is going to be a piece of cake."

CHAPTER FIFTEEN

The limousine took us to a small restaurant somewhere in the outskirts of Mexico City. All of us walked through the kitchen and up a flight of stairs to a private dining room. Inside the room a mariachi band was playing a spirited version of "Guadalajara" near a long dinner table crammed with delicious Mexican food. We all took our seats. I sat across from Manolo and between the matador's two prospective Mexico City sisters-in-law, Paco's date on my left, mine on my right. My sister was a mere seventeen years old, unusually young for a sister, with the face of a sad horse and a body bursting with hormones. As soon as we were seated, my sister laid her dainty fingers on my crotch.

"What's he want?" asked Manolo, indicating with his eyes Mike Medavoy at the other end of the table.

"Wants you to sign the paper?" I answered in the mixture of pantomine and sign language the two of us had developed.

"Do I get a million dollars and play myself?"

"You get the million dollars but you don't play yourself."

"Then forget it," concluded The Maestro, adding, "Seems like an asshole."

"Could be."

"What should we do with him?" finger-signed El Cordobés, a mischievous glint in his eyes. "Have fun with him or let him be?"

Since Medavoy's piece-of-cake trip was doomed to failure, who cared what happened to Medavoy. "Suit yourself," I answered.

So while the young Spanish convent student on my right, sister of The Maestro's intended, slipped her hand inside my fly, El Cordobés had the devoted Paco Ruiz slip some Spanish hinky-dinky into Medavoy's sixth tequila. The evening proceeded pleasantly. I was graciously fondled throughout the meal and jerked off for dessert. We were all entertained after dinner by the refreshing young talent agent from Hollywood. I must say Medavoy's awkward two-step dance was rather funny, the way he swayed from side to side, then with swift short choppy steps, ran around in tight little circles, particularly dressed as he was in his white shirt-sleeves, light-blue boxer shorts, red garters, high black socks, and black shoes. But it was the lampshade on his head that made the frolic memorable. Like the cherry on a sundae.

When the cigar smoke eventually cleared and the sun came up the next morning, nothing had changed. Young Medavoy was safely strapped into his Aero Mexican plane seat flying toward Hollywood, four aspirins in his stomach and a double Bloody Mary in his hand, and I was walking around Mexico City with an unsigned contract in my left trouser pocket wondering what to do next.

Several months later, almost a year since my adventure with the bullfighter began, El Cordobés and I arrived in Córdoba, Spain. I came to Córdoba vowing this city would be my last stop. By now I'd had it with *Or I'll Dress You In Mourning*. My patience and energy were running on empty. If I didn't get Manolo's signature on the contract while I was in Córdoba, I would drop the project.

The Maestro was returning to his hometown, the city from whence he took his name, to fight in front of his friends and neighbors. The homecoming celebration would take place in the magnificent stadium the town had constructed in his honor. Not being a bullfight aficionado, I cannot speak with authority regarding the sport. But being a sports fan, and knowing a good sporting event when I see one, I can say the third bull I saw Manolo fight in Córdoba that late afternoon was a contest I'll never forget. With the afternoon light diminishing dangerously in favor of the bull, and the crowd screaming, *"Morto Toro! Morto Toro!"* over and over again, El Cordobés struck with flair and daring. Down on one knee, eye to eye with the furious animal, Manolo suddenly stood and plunged his sword deep into the bull's heavily muscled neck. As the animal dropped to his front knees, then his hind knees, then over on his side, the jampacked stadium rose stood and cheered The Maestro. While Manolo triumphantly circled the arena, the girl I was with— an attractive heiress and friend of my sister from Philadelphia—said, "Disgusting."

As a traveling companion, the young lady I had asked to accompany me to Córdoba had been a poor choice. And when Manolo tossed the bull's bloody ear into her lap—the height of a compliment, I'm told—my traveling companion screeched with horror, then swooned. "Oh, God, get me out of here," she moaned the moment her senses returned. My unremitting concern about getting the contract signed at the cost of paying suitable attention to the heiress, coupled with the spectacle I had dragged her to, was apparently too much. This barbaric ear thing, bull blood on her brand-new silk blazer, the blazer called Toro Toro she had purchased at Hermès in New York just for her trip to Spain. Revolting. Me, the ear, Córdoba, the entire afternoon had been totally revolting. And now this wretched bloody ear. A few minutes later the heiress fled the stadium, the city, and the country. In her haste to depart, she took my airplane ticket with her.

"Don't worry about your plane ticket," finger-signed and pantomimed Manolo. "Tomorrow you fly with me to Málaga and watch me fight there. Or are you afraid to fly with me?" Manolo had just received his pilot's license, a source of immense pride to the illiterate matador. To celebrate the accomplishment, Manolo purchased a shiny new twin-engine Cessna; orange with blue trim. "El Cordobés" was painted on both sides of the fuselage in bright red script. "You are good luck," continued Manolo. "If you fly with me to Málaga, I will sign your movie contract."

I couldn't believe what I was hearing. Such a surprise. So unexpected. But that was Manolo's style.

"Without you playing yourself?" I asked, hardly able to contain myself.

"Yes. Let Paul Newman fight the bulls. I will be curious to see how good he is."

"Where shall we sign the movie contract?" I asked, excited but still somewhat skeptical.

"In the cockpit," answered El Cordobés.

"In the cockpit? Of your plane? When?"

"When we land in Málaga," answered Manolo, then he grinned and walked away.

The next morning at six I met El Cordobés's chauffeur in my hotel lobby. He drove me to a small military airfield. There, at one end of the field stood The Maestro's new Cessna. Inside the plane was El

Cordobés studying maps of his route south to Málaga. I climbed into the cockpit and sat in the co-pilot's seat. The bullfighter was busy with the serious responsibility of navigation. Using rulers of various sizes and calibrations, Manolo planned our trip. I knew full well much of what he was doing was more for my benefit than his and had little to do with getting us to Málaga. Nevertheless I looked earnestly over his shoulder as he hoped I would. When Manolo finished he turned to me and smiled—Manolo had a great smile— and then he pointed to my pants pocket where he knew the contract lay folded for almost a year.

"Remember," he said, "when we land."

"When we land," I repeated.

To show my appreciation I gave my friend something he had been admiring as long as he knew me, an inexpensive high-tech chronograph wristwatch. El Cordobés was astonished at first, and then touched. He gave me his wristwatch in return. I said it wasn't necessary. He insisted. It was a gold Patek Philippe. A month later I would take the wristwatch to Patek Philippe in Paris and have it appraised. I was told it was worth over ten thousand dollars.

Now it was time to go. We buckled our seat belts. El Cordobés accepted final instructions from the antiquated control tower. We both gave the thumbs-up sign to the matador's chauffeur and Paco Ruiz standing side by side in front of the Mercedes. The bullfighter winked at me, release his foot break, revved the engines, and we commenced to roll across the rocky airfield.

At first I didn't know what it was. As we came closer I could see it was a military truck. A dozen or so soldiers were working nearby, clearing the field of extra large rocks, throwing the rocks into the truck. The truck was directly in our path. We were closing in on it at a very rapid rate of speed. I was so sure Manolo saw the truck, I said nothing. Yet he continued to head straight for it. But then that's the kind of guy he was; it was The Maestro's nature. He was a daredevil, a tease, a big flirt with women, a practical joker with men. Obviously Manolo was merely attempting to scare the living daylights out of those soldiers and then veer off at the last minute when the joke was over. Only we didn't veer off. I turned to see what Manolo was doing. He was busy checking his dials, making absolutely sure everything was correct.

That's when we crashed.

*   *   *

"Then what happened?" asks Emilie. The three of us—Emilie, Henri, and myself—are sitting on a bench in the Place des Lices eating our usual afternoon ice-cream cones.

Then what happened?

There was silence. It was so quiet I could hear the locusts cricketing in the grass. As the dust disappeared I realized the plane's nose was buried in the ground under the overturned truck; its tail straight up in the air. Manolo and I looked at each other to see if we were hurt. We weren't. Neither one of us considered the possibility that the aircraft's full gas tanks might explode.

Then Manolo began to howl.

He howled and howled for what seemed like forever, though it was probably only a minute or two. All the time he was howling, the matador pounded the plane's steering wheel with his fists, ridding his body of the rage and frustration as best he could. Poor man, I recall thinking. Poor, embarrassed man. Humiliated in front of a friend he wanted so much to impress.

And then the wailing and pounding stopped, and El Cordobés never spoke of the accident again.

"Did he sign the contract?" asks Henri.

"Yes, just before the Iberia airliner touched down in Málaga. He wrote a tidy but small Manuel Benitez, something he also had just learned to master. We shook hands and my adventure was over."

"Did you make the film?" asks Emilie.

"No, we never made the film. The Spanish government changed their minds. Franco was still in power and he said no."

"Did you ever make a film?" asks Emilie.

"Yes. *The Gong Show Movie.* But that's another story."

The three of us sit quietly for a few minutes.

"What ever happened to the redheaded, freckle-faced agent who went with you to Mexico City?" asks Henri as we leave the Place des Lices.

"He is now the head of a major motion picture studio."

CHAPTER SIXTEEN

"I don't like it."

"What!" I gasped, sitting up.

I had just concluded what I thought was one hell of a sales pitch for my newest game show idea. I was slumped back all cocky and self-satisfied in the massive leather couch of Mr. Edwin T. Vane, the vice president of daytime programs for ABC-TV. I had expected Mr. Vane to leap across his desk begging me to let him have my new idea. After all, the man had four of my hits on his network as we spoke.

"You don't like it?" I whined. "What do you mean, you don't like it?"

"I don't like it. It's potentially unwholesome and dangerous."

Ed Vane was a straight-arrow kind of a guy. He parted his hair, wore three-piece suits, and went to church every Sunday with his family. If he thought an idea potentially unwholesome and dangerous, chances were he was right.

"Aw, come on . . ." I sniveled, deflated and confused.

"You know as well as I do, Chuck, there are two things in America you can't make fun of. The flag and mothers. And a mother-in-law is somebody's mother."

"But," I argued, "if audience identification is key to the success of a game show, then mothers-in-law are made to order. They're so identifiable it's ridiculous. Just like dating and marriage. You don't have to date to know what dating's like. You don't have to be married to know what marriage is like. And you don't have to . . ."

". . . have a mother-in-law," interrupted Mr. Vane, "to know what having one's like. But that's not the point, Chuck. Game shows tend to make fun of people, and you cannot make fun of a mother-in-law, who in effect is, as I said, someone's mother. You absolutely cannot."

"We won't," I promised.

"I don't believe you."

"Believe me, we won't."

He believed me.

He shouldn't have.

How's Your Mother-In-Law? took place in a courtroom setting.

A son or daughter-in-law would address a jury composed of five members selected from the studio audience. The son- or daughter-in-law would tell the jury of an allegedly unfair practice, trait, or deed the villainous mother-in-law had inflicted upon him or her. Like the son-in-law who was always forced to strip to the waist in the hallway of his mother-in-law's apartment. The mother-in-law would then spray deodorant under the lad's arms before he was permitted to continue into the living room.

After a commercial break, the mother-in-law would defend her actions. ("He never bathed. What was I to do?") A comic, playing a lawyer complete with white wig and black robe, would address the jury on the son-in-law's behalf. ("Talk about embarrassing and humiliating situations.") A second comic/lawyer would do the same for the accused mother-in-law. ("How would you like that stinky thing" —pointing to the son-in-law—"sitting next to you at dinner?") The jury would decide whether the mother-in-law was within her rights to do what she did. If she was, she would win a prize. If she wasn't, the son-in-law would win a prize.

How's Your Mother-In-Law? played on ABC's daytime television network every day, Monday through Friday. Mr. Vane and I watched the first week's shows with trepidation. To our vast relief, the Monday and Tuesday half hours were a great success. They were funny, engaging, and amusing.

"I won't say I told you so," I said to Mr. Vane as we left the studio Tuesday evening.

The vice president smiled, in this case pleased to be wrong. "Very entertaining shows," he told me, patting my back. "Very entertaining."

Unfortunately he patted my back too soon. The Wednesday,

Thursday, and Friday shows were anything but entertaining. They were embarrassing. On second thought, make that humiliating.

It started with the first mother-in-law on Wednesday. She was a round, jolly woman with a great big smile. She was smiling when she walked on stage and smiling when she took her seat. She was smiling throughout her introduction and still smiling long after her introduction was over. I should have been concerned about all that smiling, but I wasn't concentrating. I had allowed myself to be distracted by other matters as I watched the show in the control room; pleased with the way things were going, happy that I had personally selected the smiling mother-in-law, glad to be alive. And then I instinctively began to sense danger was in the air. I became concerned, then panic-stricken. Why was I panic-stricken, I wondered? The answer came to me a little late, but it came nonetheless. The round, jolly woman who never stopped smiling was petrified. Her plaster-of-Paris grin was a smokescreen to camouflage her terror. She was, as we used to say, "BLT on toast." Big League Trouble. The lady was going to be sick, or maybe worse.

Of course I was right. Minutes later the lady fainted dead away. Very slowly, almost as if in slow motion, she slid off her seat and onto the floor like a slinky. She ended up spread-eagled on the stage, her dress pushed up to her waist, fat thighs over stocking tops, big baggy bloomers, an awesome girdle, all there for twenty million viewers to see.

"Cut away from the poor woman!" screamed Mr Vane, sitting at the other end of the control room.

"Get a little closer," I whispered into my director's ear.

The director, paralyzed by the turn of events, was unable to do my bidding. Instead he sat transfixed, staring as I was at the monitors.

The next thing I remember seeing were two stagehands—one holding the woman's arms, the other holding her legs—lugging the unconscious mother-in-law away. The woman's head was bobbing up and down as she went by, banging lightly on the floor. Her tongue hung out of her mouth like an exhausted dog. Her dress moved up to her armpits.

"This is not a good sign," said Mr. Vane.

No it wasn't. And if Wednesday's program was bad, Thursday's was worse, and Friday's was—how shall I say it—it was when we came undone.

* * *

The sound was an intermittent reverberation, a staccato rat-tat-tat.

We picked up the annoying reverberations on our high-intensity microphones. It was a mysterious noise that aggravated everyone. For a while nobody could locate the source of the irritating rat-tat-tat. It wasn't until we were deep into Friday's show that we realized it was coming from one of our mothers-in-law.

"What's she doing?" asked a concerned Mr. Vane.

"She's suffering from flatulence," I replied.

"She's what?"

"She's farting."

"That's not a good sign," said the vice president.

I agreed. It certainly wasn't.

On it went. Rat-tat-tat. Rat-tat-tat. And then much to our dismay she moved the decibel count up a notch or two, manufacturing long, loud raspberries.

During the commercial break I went to the stage to talk to the woman. Her name—changed here for proprietary reasons—will be Mrs. Florence Volcheck. Mrs. Volcheck was a kind and pleasant person, shy and retiring, the sort of lady who would be more at home in an apron by a bowl of cookie batter than on a TV game show stage.

I whispered, "Are you okay, Mrs. Volcheck?"

"Not really," she whispered back.

"Oh?" I whispered.

"I'm sorry," she whispered, "but I'm afraid I have a problem."

"And what might that be?" I whispered.

"Uncontrollable gas," she whispered.

"I see," I whispered.

I was about to say something, but she let one go and I had to step back and wait a few seconds.

"Sorry," she whispered.

"Not at all. Is there anything I can get you that might help your problem?" I whispered, trying not to breathe.

"I'm sorry," she whispered, farting again and blushing, "I don't think so. When this happens there's not much I can do about it."

"You're sure there's nothing I can get?" I whispered. "Tums? Beano?"

"Positive," she whispered, shooting off three little ones as she spoke.

"Well, hang in there, Mrs. Volcheck," I whispered. I patted her wrinkled hand and left, thrilled to be able to breathe through my nose again.

The show continued. A few minutes later Mrs. Volcheck's comic/lawyer, the pallor in his cheeks turning gray, proceeded to do what we cautioned the comics never to do. He attacked the poor defenseless mother-in-law. He used her as the butt of his rather extensive repertoire of fart jokes. The studio audience roared with laughter. I thought the comic was very funny, too, but I knew the show had taken a disastrous turn. The vice president agreed.

"This is exactly what I warned you about," pouted Mr. Vane. "These comics will be our undoing. A comic out of material is one of the most dangerous animals on earth."

Mr. Vane was certainly right about that.

The comics were booked on the show for a week at a time, Monday through Friday. That was about three days too many for a comedian to have to depend on extemporaneous material. Sooner or later, around Wednesday or Thursday, the comic would run out of jokes, come up empty. Then, in desperation, the now-panicked comic would turn on one of the best targets for humor known to man; a mother-in-law.

"So Mrs. Volcheck here has a little problem," said her comic/lawyer, his arm around the woman's shoulders. "She farts a lot. Hey, it's not a laughing matter. As a matter of fact Mrs. Volcheck here went to see her doctor about the problem, didn't you, Mrs. V? She told the doctor she couldn't stop breaking wind. Farted everywhere. In stores, in church, at family get-togethers. Isn't that right, Mrs. Volcheck? So the doctor told Mrs. Volcheck to take her clothes off, climb up on the examination table, lie on her side, and pull her knees up to her chin. Then the doctor left the room. He returned a few minutes later holding a long pole with a large iron hook on its end.

" 'What are you going to do with that?' shrieked Mrs. Volcheck."

" 'Open the window,' said the doctor.' "

How's Your Mother-In-Law? was canceled three weeks later.

CHAPTER SEVENTEEN

On July 14, 1789, a mob of Parisians stormed a jail called the Bastille. The Bastille was a hated penitentiary used for arbitrary and secret imprisonment by the French Crown. The mob of peasants went to the Bastille to find stores of ammunition they could use for their uprising. They didn't find any ammunition, just seven pathetic prisoners. Anticlimactic as it was, the storming of the Bastille marked the beginning of the French Revolution. Bastille Day is now a national holiday in France, the equivalent of our Fourth of July. Both nations celebrate their independence with parades and fireworks.

Every Bastille Day, I charter a yacht. Red and I take a dozen friends and sail from Saint-Tropez to Cannes to see that city's marvelous fireworks display. The fireworks begin at ten o'clock in the evening. Our yacht departs Saint-Tropez at about ten in the morning, arriving at an island near Cannes around noon. We drop anchor, swim and play for a few hours, then dinghy to the island and eat lunch at a restaurant called Chez Frederick. Chez Frederick has the best broiled lobster in the world. For a Philadelphian who was brought up in Bookbinder's seafood restaurant, saying Chez Frederick's lobster is the best in the world is quite a statement. But it is. The lobster is brought to you on a huge silver serving dish. It's taken from a bed of crisp and simmering fried onion rings and delivered to your plate dripping goblets of butter. My veins start clogging up the minute I see the serving dish coming toward our table.

After lunch we all return to the yacht bloated from too much food and drink. Some read, some nap, some sit around chewing antacid tablets. Around five or six at night all the boats start sailing over to Cannes Harbor to jockey for good places facing the shore, and drop anchor. During the next few hours, while everyone waits for the fireworks to start, we trade desserts with other sailboats and motor yachts near by. The goodies are delivered from one boat to another by various crew members in their ships' tenders.

About now, Cannes Harbor begins to resemble the World War II port of Dunkirk. There's a flotilla of vessels bobbing up and down on the water for miles around; everything from beat-up two-oared row-boats to magnificent Arabian yachts. While the sun disappears be-hind the hills of Cannes, disco music can be heard from the larger ships; guitars, clapping hands, singing and general carousing from everywhere else. Customs agents and police race around the harbor in their big rubber Zodiacs ostensibly maintaining law and order. They manage, as they go, to collect a bounty of gifts in the form of bottles of wine and tasty morsels handed down to them by the flo-tilla's accumulation of incredibly beautiful women.

As day turns to night, the Cannes skyline begins to glitter. Lights of homes and automobiles in the port and up in the hills start to blink and twinkle as though it were heaven here on earth. Now and then a renegade rocket will fly through the air and explode, lonely in the vast black sky. This will invariably cause someone to yell, "It's starting! It's starting!" But it's not. It's just a false alarm.

At ten o'clock sharp, the overture begins; recorded music piped out to sea. Everyone busies themselves finding the right seat with the best view. Children are gathered up, dogs cuddled so they won't be frightened. Wives sit on husbands' laps. Lovers slide closer to each other. Treats are stacked up to eat during the performance. Cameras are adjusted. A lot of, "Hurry up, hurry up. Now it's really starting." And then the fireworks begin.

Bright red-and-white sunflowers explode overhead. Millions of green-and-yellow stars rocket past us low in the sky, stop, and then fall to earth, extinguishing themselves just above our heads. Erup-tions here and there send brigades of multicolored flares into the air to light the harbor as though it were day, and then fall to earth on little parachutes. Small pops, and then grand clusters of orange, green, red, white, and blue lights form a brilliant canopy above the boats. "Oohs," and "Ahhhs" abound, and "Wow!" and "Holy mack-erel!" The end of the evening's entertainment is signaled by a gigan-tic pyrotechnic display of lights and sounds, the grand finale, a mem-orable sight. At its conclusion, the entire armada cheers. They do this by blowing their ships' horns—big horns, little horns, bells, claxons, sirens, alarms, buzzers; anything that makes a noise—giving the city of Cannes a seafaring standing ovation.

Afterward we sail back to Saint-Tropez arriving at one or two in the morning. Bastille Day is always a long day, but a good one. Most of the time our trip to Cannes is enjoyable. Nothing drastic happens. However, there are exceptions. Like the time baseball star Rusty Staub and Senator Ted Kennedy came along.

But I'm getting ahead of myself.

Let's go back to the day before my sixtieth birthday.

I knew my wife was up to something, but I didn't know what it was. Telltale clues began appearing everywhere. The most blatant one occurred the night before the big day. That's when I was asked by a friend to meet him at nine o'clock the next morning in a ship's garage in the old port. He said he wanted me to "see a new paint job on his sailboat." See a new paint job, my ass. It was a surprise party of some sort. I detest surprise parties, but not wanting to disappoint Red, I went along with the gag. The following morning, just as I thought, the person I met took me nowhere near a ship's garage. I must admit to a certain confusion, however, when he led me toward the boat slips. Berthed in one of the slips was my wife's surprise; a spectacular three-ton, thirty-three-foot-long speedboat. Across the racer's windshield was a big white banner with red letters that read: Happy Birthday Chuck.

I was stunned.

It was a Riva, an ageless beauty, the classic Italian racing boat of the Mediterranean. Its wood exterior was covered with twenty coats of varnish. It shone so brightly in the morning light that I was forced to shade my eyes. The boat's interior was covered with rich, thick, cream-colored leather. The bow had a pair of gleaming stainless-steel hatches on top, and below was a comfortable bunk that could sleep two. The Riva was wired with a stereo radio and audio cassette system, a jack for my guitar, and four waterproof speakers. Two 300 horsepower inboard engines growled in neutral, waiting anxiously to be taken out to sea. It wasn't a new boat. The Riva was twenty years old, rare, mint, and timeless.

"It's been refurbished to the max and it's rarin' to go," said Patrick Mercurio, my racing instructor. He smiled.

I nodded.

Patrick Mercurio. The man Red had hired to teach me how to drive a three-ton high-powered monster over a gigantic sea at seventy or eighty miles an hour. Me, a product of center city Philadelphia and New York. The only water I ever played in was at the beach in Atlantic City, New Jersey. It didn't matter. I loved the idea. Red knew I would.

"You know what I think, honey?" she said by way of explanation for her novel gift. "I think you need a little buzz. I don't want you to waddle up on me." She used the word "waddle" in a strange context. She probably meant get old, wither, shrink.

I told her I wouldn't waddle up on her.

She said, "Believe me, honey, this boat will change your life."

"I'm sure it will," I replied, still dazed.

And it did.

I immediately stopped writing. I became a wharf bum, Red a wharf widow. I carried a picture of the Riva in my wallet next to my wife's. From the time Patrick smiled at me until I could drive the Riva with confidence, I lived with my instructor and my boat.

Patrick's short and stocky with blond hair and a big infectious grin. He's the brother of our cook. He's also a offshore racing champion, born to be on a boat, any kind of boat. He's been hanging around them since he was a baby; navigating, pulling sails, running up and down rigging as though they were the pavement in front of his house. Patrick's toes are now prehensile, like a monkey's. He can hold on to a boat's sides with only his feet. He can even teach a city boy like me in love with cement, how to sail.

Patrick showed me ways to tame the monster, to make it obey my every wish. He did this by taking me and my boat to sea every day, and some nights, for almost a year. I raced up and down the Riviera gaining confidence and experience. I survived the fear of sudden storms and high winds. Patrick taught me how to park my monster in slips and docks of all sizes and depths. He showed me the way to steer my Riva under the low and narrow stone bridges that arch over in-land canals, and through rocky channels. We searched for rough waters and when we found them rode the tops of waves ten feet high, as if the monster was a surfboard. Out at sea, Patrick gave me the courage and skill to hold my wooden Riva close enough to a heaving sailboat to actually pass supplies—and on one occasion my wife—from one boat to the other without either ship slowing down. And perhaps most important, the two of us acting as a team could retrieve a baseball cap that blew into the water faster than any other pair in the Mediterranean.

Soon I began asking Patrick when I would be ready. Meaning, when did Patrick think I could go out to sea alone.

"You'll know when I buy you an ice-cream cone," he always answered.

When that day arrived, Patrick stood on the boat's bow and I navigated him right up to a pier near an ice-cream parlor. I jockeyed the monster in close enough to allow Patrick to jump off my bow onto the pier. Then I hovered nearby until he returned. When he did, I guided the monster to the pier again and held it steady while Patrick, balancing two ice-cream cones, tiptoed back to me along the bow to the cockpit. I carried the exercise off just fine. He gave me my ice-cream cone. I was ready.

My first time out alone, I crashed.

Twice.

CHAPTER EIGHTEEN

All because of a goddamn rubber boat bumper.

The lady who lost the bumper was Madam Lizbeth Schiff-Dupee of East Hampton, London, and Saint-Tropez. She used to be just plain Liz Schiff from Arizona. Then she married Paul Dupee who owns the homes in East Hampton, London, and Saint-Tropez. Both Paul and Lizbeth are attractive and fortyish. He is, among other things, a gentleman, a nice guy, and part owner of the Boston Celtics. She is, among other things, a lady, extraordinarily phony and pompous, but rarely dull. Our short-lived friendship began after I rescued her goddamn bumper.

"Remember this. You must be a gentleman on the sea at all times."

Patrick's father had drummed that rule into my head over and over again. A lady in distress due to an errant bumper was obviously an opportunity to be "a gentleman on the sea."

The goddamn bumper had fallen off Madam Lizbeth Schiff-Dupee's junior-size Riva as she was motoring into port. I had been following her closely and could see she was in a major dither. Whether it was her inability to attach her bumpers to their cleats and drive her boat at the same time (not a good practice), or whether her mind was elsewhere, say dealing with the portentous dilemma of the evening's dinner party seating arrangement, Madam Lizbeth Schiff-Dupee was a mass of anger and frustration. When the bumper came loose and floated away, the lady threw her arms up to the sky and let out a horrendous wail.

"Never fear," I hollered in a gentlemanly fashion.

She didn't hear me.

So I waved to let her know I would take care of everything.

She gave me a thin-lipped smile.

By the time I turned the monster around, the goddamn bumper had floated over to the sea wall and was bobbing up and down against it. With great élan, I wiggled the monster between a pile of evil-looking rocks and a battle-scarred ferryboat. People were filing onto the ferry. Those already on board peered down at me over the ship's bow. They watched with noticeable indifference as I tried to position my monster so that I might fetch the floating bumper. It didn't take me long to realize, as I wedged myself betwixt rocks and ferry, that I was in big trouble. I was where I shouldn't have been, and now that I was in, it was going to be a bitch getting out. And I still hadn't gathered up Madam Lizbeth Schiff-Dupee's goddamn bumper.

A fisherman came to my rescue. He climbed down to where the sea smacked up against the rocks, grabbed the bumper, and tossed it into the stern of my boat. I thanked the man without looking at him. My eyes were riveted instead on the jagged rocks behind me and the unmovable ferry's bow in front of me. I kept turning my head back and forth between the two as if I were watching a tennis match. I couldn't remain in that precarious position forever. I had to go. With a cavalier salute to the apathetic crowd that had gathered along the rocks and to the indifferent spectators on the ferry, I threw the boat's gears forward and smashed into the ferry's cast-iron bow! The collision's thunk startled the ferry passengers. They were no longer indifferent. They looked down at me in awe. Embarrassed, I gave the passengers a carefree that's-life shrug, saluted them once again, threw the boat's gears into reverse, and smashed into the rocks behind me! That brought a derisive cheer from the assembly gathered there.

When I returned to my slip, Patrick, his brother Jean François, and their father Moineau were waiting for me. The Mercurio men examined my boat's two sizable gashes. Moineau Mercurio glowered. He was visibly displeased, and a displeased Moineau is not a good thing. He is one bad-tempered hombre, unless he's your friend. Then he's the best friend you could ever have. Still, if there's one thing the lean, mean Moineau cannot tolerate, it's a stupid ship's captain. Before I could explain that I was simply following the rules of conduct he taught me, Moineau growled, "You did a very dumb thing. You just risked a hundred thousand dollars worth of boat for a ten-dollar bumper."

And then he walked away.

His two sons followed in his wake.

For everything bad, as they say, there's always something good. From my embarrassing and amateurish experience in the harbor came a great name for my boat.

Bam Bam.

It is now Bastille Day, one year later.

We're all having lunch at the restaurant Chez Frederick on an island near the city of Cannes. Out in the channel in front of us is my speedboat *Bam Bam.* It's tethered to the stern of *Obsession,* the yacht I've chartered for the occasion. Among our guests are our good friends Larry and Nadia Collins. The Collinses live in Saint-Tropez and have for years. Larry had asked weeks before if his old buddy Ted Kennedy, the senator from Massachusetts, and Kennedy's girlfriend could join us on Bastille Day aboard *Obsession.* The senator and his girlfriend were going to be staying with the Collins family for the holiday weekend.

The senator's never been a favorite of mine. On the other hand, I admired his brothers very much. I voted for John when he ran for President, and I would have voted for Robert, too. Ted's a different story altogether. To me, the youngest Kennedy brother is a brilliant senator. Away from the Senate he's a dunce. I do feel a certain compassion for the Kennedy family. They have suffered implausible tragedies. Still, having the senator with us would cause three monumental problems.

"Name them," demanded the Redhead.

"First, the senator and his girlfriend are strangers to us. I'm not enthusiastic about outsiders under my roof be it land or sea. You know that better than anyone. Everybody with us on the yacht are good friends. When you anticipate being stuck together in close quarters for sixteen hours, you better be with friends. So the part about not knowing the senator or his girlfriend really bothers me. Second, I'm going to have to bring *Bam Bam* along to fetch the senator. As a result, I'll miss the ride to Cannes with you and all our friends on *Obsession.* Third, since Kennedy's arriving in Cannes

Harbor at three in the afternoon, I'll have to interrupt my lobster lunch to go pick him up."

"And fourth," said my wife, "if you say no, Larry and Nadia won't be able to come with us, and how would that make you feel? It wouldn't be the same without them."

"No problem," I told Larry, later that day. "Of course the senator and his girlfriend can come. It'll be an honor to have him join us." But now that the time has arrived when I have to actually fetch the senator, I'm not thrilled.

Being forced to leave my lobster and butter-soaked onion rings annoys me greatly. Taking my anger out on my food, I break lobster claws violently, spraying lobster gook on enough people sitting near me to warrant a reprimand from the Redhead. She leans over and whispers in my ear, "Grow up. You're making a real pain in the ass of yourself. Besides, Larry and Nadia are going to realize you're annoyed about having to collect the senator and they're going to feel awful."

Twenty minutes later *Bam Bam*'s tied to a sea wall in the Cannes Harbor. Larry, Patrick, and yours truly are waiting for Kennedy's limo to arrive. It's unbearably hot in the midday sun.

"No time for Englishmen to be out," I mutter snidely, mangling a line from Noël Coward.

Larry smiles.

Patrick doesn't understand.

"You know, Patrick," I say, killing time, "I'd like to sell this old boat and get a brand-new *Bam Bam.* I love a Riva so much I'd like to be its owner from the day it was born."

"I know how you feel," says Patrick.

"Did you know this boat's had five owners?"

"Yes, I know it's had five owners."

"It's twenty years old, for Christ sake! It's got gashes dings and dents, a leaky bilge and God knows what else. Look at the wood around the driver's seat. It's rotted. One of these days I'm going to be sitting up here and suddenly—poof!—I'm going to crash right down through the deck and end up in bilge water."

"That could happen," says Patrick, nodding.

"A new Riva's going to cost me two hundred thousand dollars, right?"

"Right."

"So I'm going to have to sell this one before I can buy a new one. Unfortunately that's not going to be easy, not in the condition this boat's in."

"You're right," says Patrick, "it's not going to be easy."

And just like that, Senator Kennedy's limousines appears.

Two shiny black automobiles pull up to the curb above us, their tires fairly screeching to a halt. Limousine doors swing open. Kennedy, fat and red-faced and dressed in a business suit, shirt, and tie, is the first to step onto the dock. Next is his tall, sexy young date, a fashionably dressed girl wearing a bright red blouse, a tight black skirt and fuck-me pumps, followed by the rest of the hangers-on from the other limousine. Kennedy slaps the shoulders of his driver and the other members of the entourage bellowing farewells to one and all. To my friend Collins, standing alone in the back of *Bam Bam*, the senator booms an enthusiastic greeting. All the while, large and heavy pieces of luggage are being handed down to me and Patrick with instructions where to place them and how they should be arranged. And then the senator does something I had to see to believe. He walks onto my boat in his filthy street shoes, leaving monstrous black sole prints across *Bam Bam*'s beautiful leather seats.

"Jesus!" gasps Patrick Mercurio.

"I thought the guy knew better," I grouse to Patrick. "Didn't he grow up in Hyannis Port, or somewhere by the sea? Weren't the Kennedys sailors?"

And then, before Patrick and I can stop her, the senator's girlfriend in the fuck-me pumps steps aboard. Fuck-me pumps are those pointy-toed dress shoes that have six-inch-long, razor-thin stiletto-like daggers for heels. Can you imagine what these weapons can do to soft leather upholstery? The girlfriend proceeds to saunter across the boat's cushions as if she's just been crowned Miss America and she's doing her walk down the runway.

"Put 'em through a wave," growls Patrick in my ear. "Drench 'em."

It's a tempting idea, but I don't do it.

"You must be a gentleman on the sea at all times," I tell Patrick. "Isn't that what your father taught me?"

I deliver the senator and his girlfriend to the yacht *Obsession* dry as the Mojave Desert. When we arrive, Patrick and I strain every muscle in our bodies holding the three-ton speedboat close to the yacht so the trio can climb safely off *Bam Bam* and onto *Obsession,* a job made doubly difficult by the mildly turbulent seas. First the girl, then Larry, and then Kennedy. As the senator goes up the yacht's ladder he gives my shoulder a patronizing pat and says, "Nice driving, Skipper." The man obviously thinks I am some sort of water-taxi hack. This misconception of Kennedy's has what appears to be the tacit approval of my good friend Collins. He doesn't correct the senator. He hasn't even properly introduced me. Right then I construct the following scenario: Collins has decided to scam his friend the senator into thinking he chartered the speedboat *Bam Bam* and the yacht *Obsession* to entertain his old buddy from Massachusetts. I'm probably wrong—ol' Lar's just a tad absent-minded now and then—but at this moment that's what I'm thinking. As Kennedy goes up *Obsession*'s ladder, I pull on his pant leg. The senator stops and looks down at me.

"My name's Chuck Barris, Senator," I yell up to him.

Kennedy says, "Nice meeting you, fella," and attempts to continue up the ladder.

I hold on to his pant leg.

"I don't know if you're aware of this or not, Senator, but you just stepped off my speedboat and onto my yacht."

The senator is momentarily taken aback. But only for a moment. "Of course I knew that, Chuck," he replies, "and beautiful boats they are."

Patrick and I take the *Bammer* to my friend Myrna "Yahoo" Snider's magnificent sailing yacht *Sintra.* We borrow some upholstery cleaner from Yahoo and scrub the black sole marks and fuck-me pump scratches out of the boat's leather. When we return to *Obsession,* I tether *Bam Bam* to its stern by a long thick rope and rejoin the festivities aboard the yacht. Later I return to the yacht's stern to check *Bam Bam* and see if she's still nice and secure. Not only is the boat secure, but two people are in the back, humping.

It's the senator and his girlfriend.

CHAPTER NINETEEN

On closer examination Kennedy and the girl aren't humping. They just look like they are.

The senator is wearing his bathing suit and the girl's wearing hers. The couple are kissing and hugging and rubbing up and down like a couple of high school kids. If their being on *Bam Bam* without my permission is not enough to infuriate me, then the next thing I see most definitely is. I notice one of *Obsession*'s crew is on his way out to *Bam Bam* in a rubber dinghy with a magnum of champagne and sticky hors d'oeuvres for the senator and the little lady to nibble on, and spill all over my boat.

"What are those two doing in *Bam Bam*?" I howl to no one in particular.

"Easy, honey," says the Redhead, materializing at my side with Patrick. "The senator's our guest, so be nice. Besides, what's so terrible? They're only necking. Now admit it, isn't this a great day? Do you see how everyone's enjoying themselves?"

"So he's a guest, so what? I didn't give him permission to roll around the back of my boat like it was a fraternity house couch. And who the hell told that guy in the dinghy to bring Kennedy the magnum of champagne and the munchies?"

"Help!" yells someone.

"Ted asked for some champagne so we sent him a bottle of champagne," says the Redhead calmly. "Have you eaten anything? The boat's provided the most delicious food you ever tasted. Let me get you a platter."

"Did he ask for a magnum?"

"He asked for champagne," explains the Redhead. "Have you noticed how nice the crew is? They're bending over backward to be nice to everyone."

"Help!" yells someone.

"You didn't have to bring him a magnum."

"Big deal, so we gave him a magnum," says my wife. "So what? It's not going to change your lifestyle, is it?"

"Help!" yells someone.

I tell Patrick to make sure no more food or drink goes out to *Bam Bam*.

"You got it," he says.

"Help!" yells someone.

"Is someone yelling help?" I ask.

"I think so," answers Red.

Over on the left, in the water, Rusty Staub is flapping his arms up and down.

"Help!" he yells again.

"Rusty's such a great guy," says Red, "always up, always having a good time. Look at him down there behaving like a silly goose."

"Help," yells Rusty.

Actually Rusty's not behaving like a silly goose.

Rusty's drowning.

Patrick realizes this and dives off the side of the ship.

Rusty Staub was one of the best baseball players who ever worked the major leagues. He's a big, strong, heavyset guy with huge arms and legs, and, as of late, a rather sizable paunch. After retiring from the game a few years back, Rusty stopped growing stronger. Instead he grew wider. Much wider. Rusty loves to eat, which he does often and well. And after eating, he loves to nap. Once, following an enormous lunch, Rusty fell asleep in a wicker lounge on the terrace of our house in the vineyards above Saint-Tropez. From up in my office, I could see parts of Rusty down on the terrace; mainly his bare legs crossed one over the other. For five hours nothing on Rusty Staub moved. At least not from the knees down. By the end of the fifth hour I was sure Rusty had suffered a heart attack from being wider, and died. In my house. On my wicker lounge. I dashed downstairs and out to the terrace. I studied Rusty up close and saw nothing move anywhere! I knelt down and placed my ear on his chest. Rusty said, "What are you doing?"

Red and I look over the side of the yacht *Obsession* and watch swimmers from all directions converge on the sinking Staub. Crew members from three different boats are bringing rubber dinghies to the disaster area. They all get there in time to save Rusty.

Of course the real problem's just beginning; a dilemma comparable to lugging a panic-stricken whale into a small dinghy. Three hundred pounds of bones, blubber, organs, blood, salad, wine, lobster, fried onions, bread, butter, several slices of pecan pie, and half a bucket of saltwater. How do you get this ton of ball player out of the sea without the bug-eyed and uncommonly strong Staub taking you with him when he finally sinks like an anchor to the bottom of the Med? Somehow, out of all the volunteers, Patrick solves the problem. He manages some way or other to hoist the bloated baseball hero into a dinghy.

Red says, "That was almost Rusty's last gurgle."

"Good title for a movie," says my friend Robert Downey who has joined us. "Rusty's Last Gurgle."

"I'm so embarrassed," says Rusty later, while devouring half a watermelon and two pounds of salted pretzels. "I made such a fool of myself."

We all agree that he did.

Meanwhile the paparazzi have arrived; the sensation-seeking photographers with their cameras and telephoto lenses. They're circling the tethered *Bam Bam* in small outboard motorboats while the blissfully distracted senator and his inamorata French-kiss their brains out. The converging paparazzi resemble a pack of wild dogs closing in on wounded prey. Kennedy is too busy to hear the outboard motors, the clicking lenses, or see the paparazzis' smiling faces.

"They've found Kennedy!" someone says on board *Obsession.*

"He wanted to be found," says someone else.

The next day pictures of *Bam Bam* are on the front pages of newspapers all over the world.

Banner headlines scream: BACK IN DEEP WATER AGAIN, EH, TEDDY? and, INCORRIGIBLE TED: SUN AND FUN ABOARD A SPEEDBOAT CALLED BAM BAM. Double-page spreads in most of the journals. Some in color, too.

Weeks later groups of tourists are still crowding around *Bam Bam*'s slip trying to get a glimpse of the fabled floating motel. Letters are flooding into the Mercurio Yacht Company from boat enthusiasts all over the world who want to buy old *Bam Bam*. A wealthy German offers slightly more than what we originally paid for the boat. I can barely hide my glee. I'll now be able to buy a new *Bam Bam*. I take the German's check and shake his hand with deep, abiding sincerity.

But old *Bam Bam* isn't pleased with our divorce. In fact, she's pissed and let's everyone know about it in no uncertain terms. On the German's maiden voyage, one engine stalled, the ship-to-shore telephone shortcircuited, and the poor man and his seat fell through the boat's rotting floor into the bilge.

CHAPTER TWENTY

This morning I recall the time a chimpanzee played with his balls on the *Dating Game*.

I am reminded of that celebrated occasion by the presence of an organ-grinder man in the Place des Lices. He is turning the wooden handle of his bright yellow organ, making it play music. The man is dressed in a maroon Turkish cap, a multicolored vest over his bare chest, and baggy green pantaloons. He has a monkey, dressed in the exact same outfit. The monkey, attached to one of the organ's wheels by a long chain, is dancing to the music, holding out a copper cup in his little hand, begging for coins. The organ grinder's monkey resembles the Marquis Chimp who appeared on the *Dating Game* and fondled his nuts for the entire show. This was all the result of one of my highly questionable "great ideas."

On this particular *Dating Game* program I decided to substitute a famous trio of monkeys—the Marquis Chimps—for the handsome bachelors. The bachelors would be off stage responding to the girl's questions. The chimpanzees—dressed up in suits and ties—would be sitting on stage in the bachelors' chairs. Because of the partition, the girl wouldn't know who she was talking to. It would appear as though she was trying to spend a night on the town with a monkey. I thought the idea might evoke an interesting half hour. As it turned out the show was more than interesting. It was historic.

Just before we began, the monkeys' trainer gave each chimp a handful of M&M's—those little chocolate-covered candies—to keep them occupied, calm them down. The Marquis Chimps adored M&M's. One of the chimps, Bachelor Number Two, accidentally dropped his M&M's. The poor creature's eyes widened in alarm. He grabbed his crotch with both hands and yanked it from one side to the other and up and down, trying to find his candy. When the stage lights came up and the show began, millions of Americans saw a pretty girl about to have a discussion with three chimpanzees, one of whom was obviously a sex maniac. I must admit it certainly looked that way. What else would you say about a monkey that had bulging eyes and was pulling his testicles every which way?

"Monkey Number Two's masturbating!" screamed our uptight Calvinistic director, Bill Carruthers, seated in the control room. "Get that camera off his crotch. Pan up, for God's sake! Pan up!"

Standing behind him, I shouted back, "Like hell you will! You keep that camera right on the chimp's nuts, and stay there!"

As the show proceeded, the first chimpanzee unscrewed one of the two iron knobs from the top of his chair and threw it into the audience. The knob hit a gentleman's forehead raising a little blue lump just above his eyebrow. The second Marquis Chimp gave up searching for the errant M&M's and concentrated on discovering different ways to play with himself. The method he seemed to delight in most was to gently pluck his gonads as though they were harp strings, causing the chimp to roll his eyes and screech like a damn fool. The third monkey, the one the young girl chose as her escort for a night on the town, ran around the partition and bit her leg.

The organ grinder and his monkey leave the park, and so do I. I walk down to the port and meet Henri at the dock. It's Saturday, Henri Bruni's day off. The two of us are going to spend the morning fishing.

It's a gray day, no sun, and the water's flat calm.

We're part of a small herd of boats all gathered around a large cement marker stuck in the sea. The marker warns sailors of shallow waters between it and the shore.

Henri says, "Josette tells me your program the *Gong Show* is playing now on German television."

I know this and I'm not pleased.

"Josette's cousin who lives in Munich sent her a newspaper clipping in the mail. It is a television critique. Neither Josette nor I understand German, but Josette's cousin does. She says the review is not, I guess you say, flattering."

Except for John P. Grissom, I never received a flattering TV review in my life.

"Here," says Henri, handing me the newspaper clipping, "for your scrap heap."

"Scrap book," I tell him.

I scan the German review. I see the word *dreck* next to my name. That doesn't bode well.

We sit quietly for a while, fishing. I pour Henri and myself a cup of hot coffee from my thermos. The coffee smells good. I stare at my fishing line and recall the *Gong Show;* those defiant, crazy years, the beginning of our corporate breakdown. Mine, too. I muse how I might have been the only American male who ever had a midlife crisis on national television. How did that all begin? I can't seem to remember. It's all so vague.

And then I do.

"It started with Lyn Bolin," I blurt out.

"Is Lyn Bolin a man or a woman?" asks Henri Bruni, reeling in a small fish.

I think Lyn Bolin was the first female vice president of network television programs in the history of the industry.

I disliked Lyn Bolin intensely, and she me. But we needed each other. I needed to be on NBC-TV. She needed hit game shows.

"What have you got for me?" she asked one afternoon when I came to call.

"A reverse talent show," I answered. "Instead of a lot of good acts and a few bad ones, we have a lot of bad ones and a few good ones."

"Why?"

"Because when we went out looking for good acts, we only found bad ones."

"So now, correct me if I'm wrong, so now you want to do a daily half hour daytime television show that showcases a lot of bad acts?"

"Right."

"I don't believe you."

"That's not all. We'll have a trio of celebrities on the show who have the right to get rid of the act anytime they want to."

"How?" asked the lady vice president.

"By hitting a huge gong. I call the idea . . ."

"Wait! Don't tell me! Let me guess. The *Gong Game*, right?"

"Close," I replied. "The *Gong Show*."

"Before I put a penny into this hare-brained idea of yours," said Bolin, "I want to see a live run-through."

So we did a live run-through.

The run-through took place in an rehearsal hall on the NBC-TV lot in Burbank, California. We had a bad one-man band. We had a dog act in which the dog didn't do a thing. We had a man with a rather large baboon. I had no idea what the baboon did. (The man said it was a surprise.) We had a lousy folk singer and a half-ass tap dancer. I was setting all of these people on their marks, giving them their order of appearance, how to get on and get off the stage, when I heard this enormous commotion behind me. I turned and saw Lyn Bolin surrounded by an entourage of male game show producers. They were all sitting in the grandstand talking loudly, hooting and laughing at one another's latest bon mot. I couldn't concentrate. I walked over to where the group was seated and asked if they would please hold the noise down a bit so I could finish our rehearsal. And then I went back to my acts.

The next thing I knew, Lyn Bolin was practically standing inside my right ear.

She said, "Don't you ever fucking give me instructions again. Especially on an NBC stage and especially in front of my producers. Do you fucking hear what I just said?"

"I'll give you fucking instructions any time you and your goddamn producers make it impossible for me to do my job."

"You do and you'll never fucking work on the NBC lot again as long as I'm around."

I said, "Up yours, Lyn."

Bolin glared at me for what seemed an eternity, then turned and left the rehearsal hall, her entourage of sycophant male producers trailing behind her.

We had no other choice but to do the same. My *Gong Show* acts packed up to leave, the NBC crew capped their cameras, my staff gathered up their papers and ballpoint pens, and the baboon bit his trainer on the neck.

"That was the surprise," said the trainer. "He was going to bite me on the neck."

"I see," I said. For some reason, I always did.

"There's more," said the trainer.

"Like what?"

"I bite him back."

CHAPTER TWENTY-ONE

As Ms. Bolin promised, I never worked for NBC daytime television again as long as she was vice president.

As a result, nothing happened to the *Gong Show*. I didn't want to take the idea elsewhere and admit that NBC passed on it. I would have to wait until Bolin was fired. It happened to all network programming executives sooner or later. It was only a matter of time. And then (hopefully) her assistant, Madeline David, would take over. Madeline loved the *Gong Show* idea.

So I waited.

In the meantime I went on with my life.

I created and produced a half a dozen game show pilots for the three television networks, none of which got on the air: *Game Game, Cop Out, Music Game, Spoof.*

One show—the *Parent Game*—came close.

The *Parent Game* was yet another spinoff of the successful *Newlywed Game.* Instead of husbands trying to match answers with wives and wives with husbands, parents attempted to guess how their kids would reply to personal dilemmas while their children postulated what their parents might say. Other than working with children— not exactly my idea of a rollicking good time—the *Parent Game* was fun to do and quite entertaining. The show was amusing, embarrassing, startlingly extemporaneous, and highly identifiable. The *Parent Game* had all the qualities of another hit game show.

The head of daytime programs for NBC-TV paid me two hundred thousand dollars to do a sample pilot of the *Parent Game.* The executive's name was Budd Grant. Budd was a nice guy. Budd loved the *Parent Game* pilot so much he ran onto the studio floor when the pilot show was over and kissed my forehead. "Unofficially," he whispered in my ear, "you're on the air." Consequently I went ahead and performed the traditional announcement to my employees.

The traditional announcement entailed calling everyone together, explaining that I had just heard from the network, pausing for the required dramatic effect, then either putting my thumb down signifying no sale or pouring a hidden can of beer over my head, meaning we were on the air! The beer would invoke a whooping cheer from all present; lots of hugs and kisses and dancing in the halls for a half hour or so. True, over the years the beer-pouring had become so frequent that my news of the more than likely *Parent Game* sale elicited a rather blasé cheer, little hugging, and no dancing. Such is success.

Soon word filtered back to our offices that the *Parent Game* would be on the NBC schedule at eleven in the morning. And so began the process of hiring a new show staff, making intra-company promotions, setting up a contestant operation.

And then the most bizarre chain of events took place.

The National Broadcasting Company suddenly sent a pair of ex-FBI agents—one short and young, one tall and old—to investigate my company, and me. I presumed this was NBC policy due to the game show scandals (Charles Van Doren, the *$64,000 Question*, *Twenty-One*) that had shaken the network some years back. I went along with the probe as pleasantly as I could. We obviously had nothing to hide.

Of course the ex-FBI men were immediately taken aback by my office. It resembled a subversive pawnshop. Three TV sets, an upright piano, a full set of drums and cymbals, various other musical instruments, *Dating Game* and *Newlywed Game* show flags hanging from standard flagpoles, and the most bizarre collections of artifacts you've ever seen. This colorful harvest of junk was the result of unsolicited souvenirs from the "romantic cities" the *Dating Game* chaperons and couples had traveled to. They brought the keepsakes back from all over the world hoping their gift to me would be the most unusual I had ever received. As a result my office was festooned with rows of painted bells from India, poisoned arrows from Africa, stuffed gila monsters from the Galapagos Islands, native swords from Bali, balls and chains, daggers, whips, and manacles, petrified monkey balls from Tibet, peace signs, the Manhattan skyline at night rolling by on a wall over one of my couches, a dried alligator from Brazil, a necklace of horses' teeth, bottled black widow spiders mounted on fake twigs, pornographic statues from Ceylon, and a stuffed boa constrictor that hung like a roller coaster. There was also an X-ray of my lungs hanging in a baroque frame behind my desk. If the ex-FBI investigators didn't have a jaundiced impression of me before they were escorted into my office, they certainly did shortly thereafter. The agents talked to me and my employees for a few days, then disappeared as suddenly as they came.

Finally the Friday arrived when the official telegram confirming the sale of *Parent Game* to the network was to arrive. We never got it. And then late that afternoon we heard we were dropped from the NBC schedule. And here's the strangest thing of all: We could never find out why. Budd Grant refused to return my telephone calls. Vice presidents and other top corporate officials were unreachable.

"I knew I should never have trusted a man who spelled his first name with two d's," I told my sales manager.

"What are we going to do?"

I asked him what all the local television stations across the country were showing their audiences when they weren't airing programs from the networks.

"*Lassie, Lone Ranger,* the *Three Stooges, Rin Tin Tin,* other reruns."

"Reruns? That's all the local stations show, reruns? Nothing brand new, no first-run programs made just for them?"

"No."

"So let's sell them *Parent Game.* I'll buy the pilot back from NBC."

"I don't understand," said my sales manager. What he lacked in imagination he made up in tenacious salesmanship.

I persisted, a little slower this time. "We're all ready to go with *Parent Game,* right? We have our show staff in place, a contestant operation going, and when we have the pilot back we'll have a sample program to show the stations."

"You mean go to the local stations and try to replace cheap reruns with an expensive first-run program? Are you crazy? The station managers will never go for it. They'll laugh in my face."

"Don't be so sure. We'll make *Parent Game* as inexpensively as possible. We'll film five shows a night, two nights in a row. We'll grind out ten shows a week. That'll keep the cost of production very low. You'll sell *Parent Game* to one television station in every market in America. You'll be giving the local program operator a half-hour game show made just for him! With just two stipulations: The stations must sign fifty-two week contracts and agree to pay us every week even if they don't air the show."

"You're crazy," said my sales manager, lighting his third cigarette in a row. After it was lit, he said, "What'll we use for a rate card?"

"We'll make one up."

And we did. We sold *Parent Game* to over one hundred cities. The show reached seventy percent of all the television sets in the United States. The first year, *Parent Game* grossed a million dollars. That was twice as much as any of our network shows ever made, if the show was lucky enough to stay on the air a full year without being canceled. We kept this new form of television sales a secret for almost five years. During that time my company produced new first-run shows for local TV stations and earned a fortune in return. Eventually all my competitors found out what we were doing and the honeymoon was over. But I had started something that revolutionized the business. Today, first-run syndicated television is a multibillion-dollar industry.

"A blessing in disguise," said my sales manager many years later, reminiscing about the *Parent Game*'s beginnings.

And it wasn't until many years later that we finally found out why NBC never aired the *Parent Game* in the first place.

One of the two ex-FBI agents, the short young one, had reported back to the network that we "fixed" the *Dating Game* show. He said we created the bachelorettes' questions and the bachelors' answers. He insisted our program was "rigged" (a red flag word in the television industry) meaning we selected the winning couple before the program was produced. The network fled the *Parent Game* scene, leaving a trail of memos behind ordering everyone at NBC never to deal with me or my company again.

Of course the short ex-FBI agent was lying.

We never preselected a couple beforehand nor did we ever force questions or answers on anyone. That's not the way it worked. It worked as follows: The girl asking the questions would come to our offices a week or so before her show was filmed to meet with our *Dating Game* staff writers; two young imaginative guys specializing in boy-girl questions. The prospective bachelorette would suggest various topics, subjects, and directions she wanted to explore. The two writers would assist her wherever they could. If a question the girl constructed was too bland, the boys would help add spice to it. If the question was too dirty, the boys would sanitize it. Only one rule was enforced. Before leaving, the girl had to be comfortable with all the questions she was going to ask the bachelors.

At first glance the job these young, single guys had—spending their entire working day with gorgeous girls—might sound more frivolous than significant, a position the two writers should have been paying me to perform. Quite the contrary. The job was both taxing and dangerous. The boys never got a break. We ran those girls through one after the other, nonstop. The hours were long, with no days off. For weeks on end the two writers were sequestered with the sexiest, most delicious young females in Hollywood; a Mecca for every would-be starlet, model, budding actress, and porn aspirant running loose in the world. There was never a shortage of *Dating Game* girls. They were always parading in and out of our corporate headquarters wearing outrageous outfits for their interviews, their incredible breasts hardly contained in blouses and T-shirts, sporting short shorts and miniskirts that barely hid their panties when they crossed and recrossed their long legs. Month after month these voluptuous creatures sat with the two writers, flirting and giggling, telling their most intimate secrets, a few breaking the poor writers' hearts, some rewarding them with a late-night quickie, all of them leaving a mixture of fragrant perfumes and warped principles long after they had departed. I suppose one might say the position was too good, and in there lies the rub. It would eventually drive the *Dating Game* question writers batty. Six to eight months was about as long as they lasted. Then, physically and emotionally spent, it was off to Vermont to blow spit bubbles under a spreading chestnut tree or up the California coast where you might find one sitting crosslegged on a Carmel street corner wiggling his lips up and down with a forefinger.

So why did the short young ex-FBI agent lie?

Because he had once tried out for the *Dating Game,* and had been rejected. The code at the top of his contestant form read: C2/PTL/ VOPE. A not-so-hot, only half-decent-looking guy with bad skin.

CHAPTER TWENTY-TWO

During the time of the *Parent Game* crisis I created and produced an evening variety program called *Operation Entertainment.*

I got the idea for *Operation Entertainment* from the shows Bob Hope used to perform at various military establishments around the world. We did the same thing only we never left the country. We would go to an Army, Navy, or Air Force base, set up a stage, order out thousands of troops to be our audience, and film a couple of one-hour *Operation Entertainment* programs. We had a major celebrity as our weekly host or hostess, big-name acts, and a twenty-eight piece orchestra.

Operation Entertainment was a better than average prime time variety show and stayed on the network for a year. But it was a tough program to do. Remote situations always are. Once you leave the studio you're faced with technical problems, weather problems, logistical problems. As difficult as *O.E.* was, it also provided us with some memories that are hilarious only in retrospect. Like the time we were going to reunite a marine, who was stationed in Vietnam, with his mother at Camp Pendleton, in California. I can't recall who that week's celebrity host was, but I do remember him standing at center stage with his arm around this pudgy mom with a name I'll never forget: Mrs. Beatrice "Call Me Honey" Dropp. Honey Dropp was from Lexington, Kentucky.

The show's celebrity host asked Mrs. Dropp if she had any children.

She said she had one son.

"What's your son's name?"

"Marine Private First Class Raymond C. Dropp," said Mrs. Dropp proudly.

"Thank God. I was afraid you were going to say Cough," said the clever host, winking at the television camera to make sure the viewing audience didn't miss his cute play on words. "Tell me, Mrs. Dropp—"

"Call me Honey."

"Tell me, Honey, have you heard from your son lately?"

"No I haven't," she answered, never taking her eyes off the super star host's arm, amazed that it was around her shoulders. "He's in Vietnam. It's hard to stay in touch with him. I get a letter once and a while."

"Correct me if I'm wrong, Mrs. Dropp—"

"Call me Honey."

"Correct me if I'm wrong, Honey, but isn't it your birthday this week?"

"Yes it is," she answered, hiding her head in the palms of her hands, blushing. "How'd you know that?"

"A little birdie told me," said the host, smiling badly.

"Oh, my," giggled Mrs. Dropp.

"Tell me, Mrs. Dropp, Honey, what would you do if I brought your son out here on this stage to give you a big birthday hug?"

"I'd die."

I was in the control room of a videotape remote truck not far away from the stage. At the exact moment Mrs. Dropp said, "I'd die," I listened on my intercom to an emergency telephone call from our stage manager to the director. The stage manager, speaking in a cup-mouthed whisper, said, "The marine who's ready to go out on the stage to meet his mother just told me the woman standing out there is not his mother."

"He said what!" yelled Carruthers. My high-strung director was seated in front of me, conducting the program from a row of monitors on the wall, as if he was Arturo Toscanini.

"The marine says that's not his mother out there," repeated the stage manager, still whispering.

"Oh my God, you've got to be kidding!" yelled the director.

"I'm not kidding."

I said into my headset mouthpiece as calmly as I could, "Do you have Private First Class Raymond C. Dropp from Lexington, Kentucky, standing beside you?"

"Yeah. He says he's Private First Class Raymond C. Dropp from

Lexington, Kentucky, all right, but he says that's not his mother out there on the stage. He says it must be some other Raymond C. Dropp's mother. What'll I do?"

"There can't be two Raymond C. Dropps from Lexington, Kentucky, in the Army!" whined my dangerously rattled director to his stage manager. "This guy's jerkin' your string."

"I really don't think he is," replied the stage manager's voice over the intercom.

"Yes he is!" screamed the director.

"Okay, he's jerkin' my string. So what'll I do?"

"Is he sure?" I said to the stage manager. Mellow. Unfluttered. In control. "Please ask the soldier if he's one hundred percent sure the lady on stage is absolutely not his mother."

There was a pause.

"Yeah, he's absolutely one hundred percent sure," snapped the stage manager, angry, not bothering now to whisper or cup the intercom mike with his hand, sounding hurt, getting the feeling the director thought this mess was all his fault. "The soldier says he fucking knows what his own fucking mother looks like. Those are his exact words. So what the hell should I do?"

Meanwhile, our celebrity host was visibly anxious. He had been stalling for two full minutes, with no end in sight. And stalling wasn't his strong suit.

"You say you'd be surprised if your son was here in Camp Pendleton and not in 'Nam?" said the superstar master of ceremonies looking left and right, hoping to see a soldier on one side of the stage or the other ready to make an entrance. "You say you'd die if he walked out here on this stage to give you a little birthday hug and kiss? You're sure you'd die? You're not fooling us, are you."

"No, I'm not fooling you. But I hope I don't."

"Don't what?"

"Die. I want to see him," giggled Mrs. Dropp.

"Well, get ready to die," said our distraught host, out of ad-libs, giving up whether we were ready or not, "because your son is here! Ladies and gentlemen, let's meet this wonderful lady's lucky son whose trip back from 'Nam was arranged by us just so he could be with his mother on the little lady's birthday. Hold onto your hats 'cause here we go. Mrs. Beatrice Dropp, say hello to your son just back from Vietnam, Private First Class Raymond C. Dropp!"

"What'll I do?" pleaded the stage manager.

"What'll we do?" moaned my director pathetically.

"Send the soldier out," I said without hesitation. "Tell him to fake it or he goes back to Vietnam on the next plane."

And so to the cheers of thousands of servicemen in our audience, and to teary eyes everywhere I looked on stage, Mrs. Beatrice Dropp held out her arms to the wrong Private First Class Raymond C. Dropp who was walking, his arms outstretched, too, toward a fat little woman he never saw before in his life. As the unfamiliar marine came closer, Mrs. Dropp's expression changed. She seemed bewildered. Soon a strange young man was hugging her. She didn't know what to do.

"This is not my son," she kept mouthing to no one in particular. "This is not my son."

I don't think anyone figured out what Mrs. Dropp was saying. It could have been, I've got my son, or Ain't this fun. Anyway, I thought it was one of the best *Operation Entertainment* shows we ever did. And a few weeks later we got everything right. We united the real Ray Dropp with his mom, the wrong Ray Dropp had a great ten days in Hollywood before returning to Vietnam, and everybody lived happily ever after.

Not long after the *Operation Entertainment* show where Honey Dropp hugged a perfect stranger, we heard some timely news.

Lyn Bolin was no longer with NBC.

CHAPTER TWENTY-THREE

Our friend, Madeline David, replaced Bolin just as we expected she would.

And just as we hoped, bought the *Gong Show*.

I called a meeting of the company, poured the obligatory can of beer over my head, cheered and danced for a few minutes, then got down to the job of getting a new program ready for air. The first thing I needed was a master of ceremonies. It was a love/hate chore for me, one of a growing number of love/hate chores I was required to do when mounting a new game show. I loved the satisfaction of discovering exciting talent for the program, but hated looking for it.

I had always made it a practice to avoid using one of the always smiling, big-toothed saccharine slickos who adorned every game show on television. They were all members of a closed fraternity of entertainers who automatically rotated from a recently canceled program to one that was about to debut. So far I had been successful in going away from television for my hosts: A radio station in San Francisco for the *Dating Game*'s Jim Lange, a Los Angeles radio station for the *Newlywed Game*'s Bob Eubanks; off the beaten path for the rest of them. It wasn't easy to find someone fresh and talented who had never hosted a game show before, but I felt it was well worth the effort. A new face added another dimension to a new show.

Of course there was always the problem of breaking in the inexperienced master of ceremonies, making sure he knew the nuances of game shows in general and the one he was going to do in particular. I had to help overcome their festering insecurities, give them confidence, impart the tricks I had learned over the years. I would also have to address myself to the idiosyncrasies he was sure to have. In the beginning, the happy-go-lucky Jim Lange, host of the *Dating*

Game, was terribly vulnerable to public criticism. Jim was devastated when an early review of the Dating Game published in a Chicago newspaper said: Daytime TV Hits All-Time Low! Lange almost returned to San Francisco. I convinced Jim the bad review was the best thing that could have happened to us. I explained to him that newspaper television critics were originally from movies and the theater. "Free TV is beneath them," I said. "They still haven't learned they're not reviewing a major work of art, just something to get a housewife's mind off the kids for a half hour. A TV critic just can't admit he or she might enjoy a game show. In my opinion, a good game show review is the kiss of death. If for some strange reason the critic liked it, the public won't. A really bad review means the show will be on for years."

Jim stayed.

Bob Eubanks, host of the *Newlywed Game,* had the worst stage timing of any male performer I ever met. During the first two weeks we were on the air I was forced to stand next to his camera and hand signal Bob through the show, telling him when to stop, how long to stay, when to move on. "If the clod doesn't get the gist of this by the end of next week, he's outta here," I whispered to an associate as I rolled my fists one over the other ordering Eubanks to stop questioning wife Number Two and move the hell over to wife Number Three. The next afternoon Bob caught on. For some inexplicable reason it all fell into place for the cowboy. His timing has been impeccable ever since.

Now it was time to find yet another master of ceremonies, one for the new *Gong Show.*

That night, after driving around Hollywood on my motorcycle making my rounds of tapings and contestant auditions, I was heading for home happy in the warm night air, thinking of a thousand different things when a drunken bum appeared in my headlight beam. I swerved to avoid hitting him and fell off the motorcycle. Later, in the emergency ward of Hollywood General Hospital, I watched a farsighted intern sew six stitches into my leg.

"Motorcycle, huh?" he asked, his thick glasses inches away from the needle. "Car pull out in front of you?"

"It was a bum," I explained. "Standing there in my headlight beam."

Which made me think of another bum.

And a crazy idea.

"He could be the one!" I blurted out to no one.

"Who could be what?" asked the intern, his nose practically touching my wound.

The bum, I thought to myself. The one who slept in front of my office building every morning. He could be the new host of the *Gong Show*.

I was usually the first to arrive at our offices, generally between seven and seven-thirty in the morning and there was always this same bum lying on the grass by the building's entrance. He would be sleeping or staring at nothing. Every single morning, without exception, the bum was there.

He was your standard bum; wild unruly hair, torn clothes, scabs and cuts, filthy fingernails, soiled pants, soleless shoes, the ever-present wrinkled paper sack with the empty wine bottle inside. The only difference between this bum and all the others was this one could be a game show host. He certainly had all the requirements. He was well over six feet tall, well built, young—in his middle twenties I would guess—and quite possibly handsome. At least he might be if he was ever cleaned up.

The only problem was, there was something about the bum that scared me. He and I never said a word to each other. We just shot glances back and forth as I walked by. The one feature I always noticed about the bum was his eyes. They were piercing. I was never sure if his glare was one of interest or hostility. I hoped it wasn't the latter.

My secretary, Loretta Strickland, came for me at Hollywood General and took me home. On the way I told her about my bum idea. She looked worried. I think Ret thought I had suffered a head injury that had gone unnoticed at the hospital.

That night I didn't sleep. I just thought about the bum, considered the pluses and minuses of making a derelict the host of a new network game show, went over my plan to rehabilitate him. I would take him to Palm Springs tomorrow. Put him in the Betty Ford Clinic. De-tox the vagrant. De-everything him. Afterward get him a good suntan, a new wardrobe, a haircut. Teach him. Work with him. He couldn't be worse than Eubanks when he started, and look at Bob now. One of the best. The same fate could be in store for the bum. I could hardly wait to see his face when I told him I was going to make him a star. Talk about a rags to riches Hollywood story. What a publicity release this was going to make. I could see the *Variety* headline now: Bum Boffo! Idler Now Idol Of The Housewife Set!

I was in my car at dawn, racing along the Hollywood Freeway toward Sunset and Vine, and my office. And my bum. I wondered what his name was and whether or not I would have to change it. And if I did, to what? Biff? Biff Barker. Todd? Tim? Derk? Derk Todd? I drove into my parking space, locked my car, and ran to the front of the building. As I rounded the corner I saw something I absolutely refused to believe.

The bum wasn't there.

And he was never there again.

I had thought about the bum one day too late.

Madeline David loved the *Gong Show* but didn't like the host I eventually selected, a feeb named John Barbour.

I didn't like him, either. I never understood why I chose the man for the job in the first place. Punch drunk, I guess.

From the very start Barbour had this notion the *Gong Show* was a legitimate talent hunt, a stairway-to-the-stars sort of thing, and he was Major Bowes reincarnated. Each time I tried to explain the show's slapstick tongue-in-cheek attitude to him, he always appeared to understand. And then as soon as he returned to the stage, he would make the same mistakes. During one of our final rehearsals, Jaye P. Morgan—one of the three celebrity judges—smashed the gong with her mallet, ending a woman's torturous rendition of the song "Friendship." Though she plainly couldn't sing, I must say the woman's act was different. She sang to a hidden pet orangutan, which she exposed from time to time by opening her baggy overcoat.

"Why did you do that, Jaye?" asked our horrendous host. "Why did you gong Mrs. Klebenoff?"

"Because Mrs. Klebenoff showed her little monkey once too often," she replied.

"What kind of a reason is that, Jaye?" sniffed Barbour. "You should be ashamed of yourself for being so flip with someone's career."

I couldn't believe my ears. I was stunned by Barbour's rejoinder to Jaye. As soon as the rehearsal was over, I confronted John. I told the dense host that Jaye was playing the show exactly right. "Instead of Jaye saying the woman exposed her monkey once to often, would you rather Jaye had said she gonged Mrs. Klebenoff because she was the worst singer Jaye ever heard in her entire life?"

I then proceeded to spend one hour relecturing the man on the machinations of the program: How the *Gong Show* was a parody, a takeoff, an attempt to poke fun at the old amateur-hour programs. *The Gong Show* was for laughs, not careers. When I finished, Barbour looked at me with furrowed brow and clouded eyes, and said, "But Jaye didn't have to insult the woman the way she did."

"Right," I told the dunce, walked to the first telephone I could find, called Madeline David, and said, "Barbour's got to go."

"Fine. He's history. So who will host the show?"

"I'll find somebody."

"You know who should host the show?"

"Who?"

"You should."

"Me!"

"You. I watched you try to teach Barbour. I've seen you run the auditions. You know the *Gong Show* better than anyone else. Either you do it or I don't put the program on the air."

PART II

CHAPTER TWENTY-FOUR

A week before we began taping the *Gong Show* I started to cough. I thought I had a cold. Then one night while driving my car down Sunset Boulevard—hacking and wheezing, and gasping for air—I realized I had asthma. I knew it was because of my decision to host the *Gong Show*. I was convinced I was on the verge of making a public fool of myself.

Doctors gave me inhalers and pills, and injections every week to help defend myself against asthma-producing allergies. The attacks would come at any hour and any place, severe assaults that left me weak and exhausted. The only time I was sure I wasn't going to suffer a seizure was during the actual taping of a show. It never happened while I was performing. And I knew, as well as I knew my name, the day I stopped being on television would be the last day I'd ever have asthma again.

The doctors scoffed.

"Asthma is not a psychosomatic ailment as most people think it is," they said. "It's a serious disease."

They were wrong, at least as far as I was concerned. The day the *Gong Show* ended the asthma stopped. But that wouldn't be for many years because the *Gong Show* was a huge success.

I became famous.

Which was good and bad. Good for getting excellent restaurant tables, and parking lot spaces. Good for having airline public relations people meet you at airports to get you through all the petty rigmarole and keep you protected from the loons, the star fuckers, the hero worshipers and general all-around oddballs. Good for never having to stand in line again, any kind of line: movies, US Customs, concerts, ice-cream parlors, theaters, you name it.

Bad because I lost my privacy.

Everywhere I went I was recognized as the host of the *Gong Show*. Everyone would yell, "Chuckie, baby! Chuckie, baby!" wanting an autograph or an audition. No matter what time of day it was, total strangers would walk up to me and perform in my face. I couldn't eat breakfast at the counter of a coffee shop anymore or read my morning paper in peace without somebody doing Ed Sullivan introductions or whistling a few bird calls. I was unable to mingle with the rest of the folks at pizza parlors or hot dog stands because if I did, some bozo would tap dance or ask me to pick a card, any card. On an airplane, traveling from New York to Los Angeles, a dignified businessman knelt down by my aisle seat and did his lizard imitation, licking my cheek with his tongue.

Fame was also bad for sporting events, particularly baseball's seventh-inning stretch. That's when the fans were drunk enough to really become obnoxious. Once at a Dodger game a man followed me all the way back to my row from the men's room strumming a toilet seat strung like a guitar. The guitarist's beery friend played "Dixie" by thwacking his armpit. In New York, between the second and third period of a Ranger Hockey game, a woman slithered down my aisle and sang "Hello Dolly" standing on her hands. At a basketball game a belly dancer humped my knee. Once, during the halftime festivities at the Penn-Yale football classic in New Haven I had to be rescued from a mob of beer-drinking auditioners by the police.

Being famous also meant being vulnerable to any jerk, crackpot, or idiot's indignities. A woman once yelled to her husband across a crowded bookstore, "Hey, look, Morris, the moron can read!" While waiting for a red light to change to green, two pretty young girls in the car beside mine signaled me to roll down my window. When I did, the girl sitting closest to me said, "My girlfriend and I just want you to know we can't stand you." They both threw their heads back and laughed. Or the night the attractive and elegantly dressed lady sitting at the restaurant bar beckoned me to come over. When I arrived she smiled and said, "My husband owns a chain of television stations in the Midwest."

"Is that right," I replied, feeling good, acting humble.

"You know, my dear," she continued, still smiling, "you and your program are a disgrace to the industry."

These insults, and my inability to protect myself against them, were scary and humiliating, and always a surprise. Didn't the studio audience applaud riotously every night when I made my entrance? Wasn't I always told by my staff and crew how much everybody liked me?

I was confused. But then, instantaneous stardom is a new phenomena. Bigtime television is less than fifty years old. None of us really know a whole lot about how unanticipated notoriety affects the psyche. We all react in a different manner when suddenly the entire world recognizes us. My friend Dick Clark smiles happily each time he's asked for his autograph. He goes so far as suggesting fans can even take a picture with him if they desire. I'm amazed at his congeniality. I behaved exactly the opposite. I never fully understood why I acted the way I did. Perhaps the wild and wooly *Gong Show* I had begot was recreating its creator.

And the *Gong Show* was wild.

Gabriel singing from inside a garbage pail. Big Nose dancing a fandango in his silk bathrobe and high-heeled platform shoes. An entire half hour where eight different acts sang the same song: "Feelings." Paul Reubens playing different characters until he settled on Pee Wee Herman. The Unknown Comic wearing his paper bag with the two eyeholes over his head, his sleazy brown-and-white checkered sport jacket held together by a large safety pin and his scuffed black-and-white shoes, rattling off his foul-mouthed humor:

Unknown Comic: Is my fly open?
Chuck: No it isn't.
Unknown Comic: Well, it should be. I'm peein'.

Unknown Comic: Chuckie baby. Chuckie baby.
Chuck: Yes. What now?
Unknown Comic: What do you call a Mexican with a vasectomy?
Chuck: What?
Unknown Comic: A dry Martinez!

Maybe it was our incorrigible behavior that attracted the lunatic fringe to the *Gong Show*. The ex-Vietnam war veteran, a demolition expert, who made weird facial expressions by pressing his nose and mouth against a slab of plate glass. This obviously disturbed man, recently released from a federal mental institution, threatened to blow me up because he was gonged. (I needed a bodyguard for two weeks.) And the black woman who left her two newborn twins in my office reception room claiming I was the father and if I didn't take care of the infants she'd kill me. (I needed the bodyguard for another two weeks.) And the mysterious young girl who followed my car everywhere I went; the eerie sensation of looking into my rearview mirror and always seeing her face driving behind me. Or the time a tough female rock singer got gonged and I said, "Your time's up," and she said, "Time's up, my ass," and punched me in the stomach, dropping me to my knees. Or the rash of death threats I received after John Lennon was assassinated that forced me to take a different way home every night for almost a year.

Obviously not all of our *Gong Show* acts were menacing psychopaths. Nor were they household names. Just strange. Praying Mantis, The Yukettes, Blanche Labord: The Queen of Long Beach, Tiny Brooks, Halivah, Little Fitty, Nate Arm and the Armpits, Geriatric Mouse, Quasimoto Bel Aire, YourAnus, The Dumps, Mr. Toe Jam, and Dr. Flamo. And the things said on the show were a far cry from the *Dating Game* days.

Clifton Davis to singer Linda Kirby: "You may have a song in your heart, but you've got a frog in your throat."

Jaye P. Morgan to Louise Muerello who performed with magic doves: "On her shoulder may be a bird, but under her skirt there's a beaver."

Dick Savage to Pearl Burnett who sang "Tie A Yellow Ribbon 'Round The Old Oak Tree": "She should tie a ribbon around her neck."

Steve Garvey to singer Anitol: "You sound like a manure salesman with a mouthful of samples."

"What'd he say?" asked Anitol as I walked him off the stage.
"He said you have a splendid voice. It just needs a little work."
The *Gong Show's* idiocy never seemed to end. The day I read a letter on the air from the Elhart Reform School explaining how they forced their kids to view the *Gong Show* as punishment. The time I

cleaned up a duck's doo-doo while his handler held him, and then when I stood up, the duck bit my cheek. The girl with the enormous breasts who sang "Memories," only she said "mammaries," and the two seventy-year-old twin sisters who played a violin duet so badly I was forced to bring the entire UCLA Marching Band on stage—one hundred and ten pieces strong—to drown them out. And the Reverend Vert who sang "Amazing Grace" with his fly open. *And* the eighty-five-year-old Jewish granny who gave a peppy rendition of "Hava Nagila," received a standing ovation, went backstage, and died. And her thrilled husband who said, "If she had to pick a way to go, that was it!"

As crazy as they were, most of the acts never bothered me. There was, however, one type of act that did, and that was dog acts. The dogs were always barking, disrupting rehearsals, getting on my nerves. And they all did basically the same thing—jumped through hoops or slid down slides. Since we had a lot of dog acts on the show I needed something to bolster my spirits when they were about to appear. I devised a way of doing that. I would touch a few dabs of Alpo dog food to the crotch of my jeans or tuxedo pants, and watch with great anticipation what happened next. The dog act would be introduced, the curtain would go up, and the dog and his trainer would walk to center stage. Immediately the dog would start to sniff. Then turn. Then race for my crotch, hitting my fly with his nose so hard I generally jumped several feet into the air. The dog's trainer, holding the hoop or ball, would inevitably stand thunderstruck at his mutt's curious disobedience.

One day during a *Gong Show* rehearsal, I noticed Gene Patton—one of our stagehands—sweeping up backstage. Gene always swept our stage, but this time he was doing it differently. He was dancing as he swept. There was Gene—a huge man, sweet as sugar, perpetually smiling, forever happy—shaking his big black ass to the rhythm of Count Basie's "One O'Clock Jump." Not moving his feet, just wriggling his booty while holding his broom. I put Gene and his broom on the show. He danced to "One O'Clock Jump." Overnight Gene Patton became Gene Gene The Dancing Machine and a national celebrity. Another stagehand, Ed Holland—a tough Irishman who massacred the King's English—became Father Ed, a wise man of the cloth. While an act was setting up, Ed Holland—dressed as a priest—pontificated various religious thoughts.

Father Ed: When a man asketh you for five thousand dollars, giveth him five hundred. He wilst not bother you anymore and you wilst be forty-five hundred dollars ahead.
Chuck: Interesting, Father Ed. Where did you discover that pithy religious proverb?
Father Ed: I'm not sure. At the track, I think.

Makeup artist Peter Mims as Rhett Butler and wardrobe man Jefferson Becker as Scarlett O'Hara dressed up in *Gone With the Wind* costumes, reciting outlandish repartee, most of which was invariably bleeped out of the show.

Rhett: I've created a love sonnet for you, Scarlett.
Scarlett: Oh how wonderful, Rhett honey.
Rhett: I'm going to read it to you. Are you ready, Scarlett?
Scarlett: Yes I am, Rhett dear.
Rhett: Okay here goes. Hickery, dickery, dock. The mouse ran up the clock. The clock struck one. The mouse shit.
Scarlett (shocked): Oh, Rhett, you can't say things like that on television.

Bookkeeper Diane Saborine playing her musical adding machine. Lighting man Danny Lies accompanying his singing by strumming a side of beef. And then one day the networks insisted I stop using their employees on my show.

"Why?" I asked their battery of lawyers.

"Because you've now forced them to join two unions. The stagehands' union and the actors' union. It's against our corporate policy to allow employees to join more than one union."

"Why?" I asked again.

"We now become vulnerable to strikes from not just one union, but two. We want you to cease and desist using network employees as actors right now."

I refused. The networks changed their policies.

Chuck: Hello, Father Ed. What words of religious wisdom have you brought us today?
Father Ed: An uplifting Latin quotation I found in a medieval version of the Scriptures.

Chuck: Interesting. Can we hear it?
Father Ed: Certainly. It goes as follows: Quertus Varicum Parkus Plurius Scun.
Chuck: I'm sure the quotation is filled with deep religious connotations.
Father Ed: Yes it is.
Chuck: Could you translate that for us, Father Ed.
Father Ed: When the photographer giggles, the camera wiggles.

As the years rolled by, the *Gong Show* continued to elbow itself into television history propelled by its own internal fury.

When I think of all the time I spent teaching my hosts to keep their performances steady and routine, never succumbing to the fear of being boring, then I as a host go out there and immediately succumb. The hours I invested in making sure the hosts knew that if they felt their performances were repetitious and uninteresting, the audiences didn't. Programs that are on five days a week, I warned over and over again, will appear wearisome to the show's staff and cast but not to the public. The public enjoys habit, predictability. They like you the way you are, I explain to Lange and Eubanks and Race and Edwards, and all the others. They don't want you to change. The TV stars that never wore out their welcome, who went on forever, were for the most part low key: Perry Como, Ed Sullivan, Andy Williams, Walter Cronkite. Then I go ahead and perform about as low key as a whirling dervish, busting every one of my rules. There I was panicked that I was becoming a bore, upping my energy quotient a notch every month until, by the fourth year, I was running myself, and every one else, into the ground.

We filmed five daytime and two nighttime *Gong Shows* a week. I auditioned a hundred acts in the studio a weekend; fifty on Saturday and fifty on Sunday. We started at nine in the morning and quit between nine and ten at night, with just an hour break for lunch and another hour for dinner. We all tried to get along with each other. Tempers and tantrums were not acceptable. One of the more pleasant rewards of working with unknown performers was our leeway to throw them out of the building if they turned prima donna on us. Unfortunately we weren't allowed the same luxury when it came to the network censors.

The networks' censors—employees of the company's strict and

squeaky clean Standards and Practices Department—were ever diligent and watchful, always on the lookout for what they considered
tasteless acts; someone they could expel from the stage and so justify
their jobs. If there wasn't an act to banish, they would banish one
anyway. This arbitrary aspect of the censors angered me. It also hurt
our program. In order to protect the show, I began bringing conspicuously gross acts down to the studio each Saturday and Sunday
specifically for the censors to eject. All of us on the *Gong Show* staff
knew these acts were our offerings to the Gods of Good Taste: the
program's sacrificial goat. We tossed sly smiles back and forth when
the decoy was told to leave and never come back by the holier-than-
thou censors.

That was how the Popsicle Twins got on the air.

The Popsicle Twins were originally a throwaway. I was certain
when the censors got one look at those two sexy teenage cutie pies
licking up a storm they would do what they always did: come running down the aisle screaming, "You can't do that on television!"
Only this time they didn't come running or screaming. What were
they doing, grabbing a cigarette in the hall? Off to the men's room?
Dozing? Or did I simply overreact? Maybe it was okay to give great
fellatio to a couple of orange creamsicles on national television. (Unfortunately I had it right the first time.)

Yet no matter what the censors cut and the critics condemned, the
country forgave. It seemed America couldn't get enough of the *Gong
Show*. There were *Gong Show* toys, games, playing cards, and magazines. Baskin-Robbins had Gong Show ice cream as one of their
flavors. Gong Shows were being performed in bars and churches all
over the United States, and rebroadcast around the world. There I
was in Tokyo, waving my arms and clapping my hands, speaking
dubbed Japanese.

And so we spiraled on and on until the night Gene Gene The
Dancing Machine and I played basketball while Jaye P. Morgan
bared her tits, and the unicyclist exploded through the gasoline-
soaked hoop.

CHAPTER TWENTY-FIVE

The unicyclist wanted to use his own assistant and his own fire extinguisher. I said no. Too expensive. I couldn't afford to pay the unicyclist and his assistant. Besides, I could do what his assistant did, whatever that might be. The unicyclist didn't agree. But before going on, perhaps I should explain the unicyclist's act.

The unicyclist pedaled around the stage on his unicycle, going over little hurdles, up and down teeter-totters, things like that. After just so much of that junky warm-up nonsense, the unicyclist got down to business. This consisted of his assistant lighting a large gasoline-soaked hoop with a flaming torch. When the hoop was on fire, the band held a sustained C note, the drummer rolled his drums, the unicyclist rode around in a circle a few times, then dashed up a teeter-totter and cycled through the flaming hoop. The unicyclist's assistant—hopefully unnoticed to the audience—quickly touched the back of his jacket with his torch as the unicyclist went by. This caused the jacket—also lightly doused with gasoline—to burst into moderate flames. To the audience it appeared as though the unicyclist caught on fire as he went through the flaming hoop. As he went down the other side of the teeter-totter, his assistant ran to him with a small hand-held fire extinguisher and squirted white fuzz all over the unicyclist's back smothering the slightly burned jacket. The audience would breathe a gigantic sigh of relief, everyone would cheer, the band would play the finale, the unicyclist and his assistant would bow, and the curtain would close.

I told the unicyclist we didn't need his assistant. I could ignite the hoop with a torch, touch his jacket as he went by, grab the small hand-held fire extinguisher, and put out the fire on the back of his jacket. Nothing to it. A piece of cake. The unicyclist didn't like it but had little choice. Not if he wanted to do the show. So he agreed.

As I recall, the night began with a rebellious vibe in the air. I felt more mischievous than usual, the celebrity judges appeared to be somewhat unmanageable, the band extra impish, the acts a tad incorrigible. The first performer was an Elvis Presley lookalike who loved to bow. When his act was over I let him bow longer than we usually allowed for a curtain call, which the impersonator accepted ungraciously as his due. This bothered me. So did his get-up. He looked like one huge powder-blue rhinestone. I told the band to keep playing farewell music and the impersonator kept bowing. He bowed when we stopped taping to take a ten-minute break, and thinking we were still on the air, bowed while the rest of us (with the exception of the band) grabbed a cup of coffee, freshened our makeup, and made some telephone calls. The fool was still bowing when the break was over and we came back on the air. All told, the impersonator bowed for thirteen minutes straight, collapsing from exhaustion as soon as he left the stage.

I did my usual Alpo trick on a Great Dane whose talent was his ability to say the word "Mama." What I failed to consider was how big those Danes are. When the huge animal smelled the dog food on my crotch, it went berserk. The Dane's charge flattened my testicles and knocked me down. While I writhed in pain in the wings trying to catch my breath, I sent the revived Elvis Presley impersonator back on stage to take a few more bows.

If our celebrity judges that night—Charlie Brill, David Letterman, and Jaye P. Morgan—were down and dirty when that show began, they grew worse as it went on. Jaye in particular. When asked by one of the Swinging Seminarians why she gonged them, Jaye said, "I'm sorry, Father, I thought you were a Mother." When Charlie Brill gonged a comic, the comic told Brill he wished Charlie would drop dead. Brill told the comic he hoped a diseased yak would sit on his face. And Jaye explained to me that she gonged Fifi La Mass, a fat ballet dancer wearing an ill-fitting tutu, "because I think she has a little dump in her pants."

Then it was the unicyclist's turn.

The unicyclist did all his preliminary tricks, the dinky stuff, riding back and forth on his one wheel with his arms straight out from his sides, pretending to almost fall, making it look harder than it was. I was backstage gathering up the torch and looking for the small hand-held fire extinguisher, which I couldn't seem to find.

"Where's the small extinguisher?" I asked the prop man.

"Don't know," he answered. "It was here a minute ago."

"I need an extinguisher for this act, and I'm going to need it in about one minute."

"You'll have it," said the prop man. "If I can't find that one, I'll get you another."

I thanked the prop man, slipped into my circus top hat and tails, grabbed the torch, and ran on stage just in time to catch an angry where-have-you-been glare from the unicyclist. He had been vamping, ready to make his move through the flaming hoop, which I had yet to set aflame. I lighted my torch, ran to the hoop, and touched the torch to the gasoline-soaked ring. It burst into flames with a woosh that startled me. While I was collecting myself, the unicyclist went by. I forgot to touch his back with my torch. When he appeared on the other side of the hoop, he wasn't on fire. I knew being on fire was a major part of his act, so I chased him around the stage trying to ignite him. The unicyclist was saying something to me, but I couldn't quite hear what it was. I finally caught up with the unicyclist and torched his jacket. That's when I heard what he was saying. He was saying, "Never mind. Never mind."

It was too late. The unicyclist's jacket was on fire. Now I needed the small hand-held extinguisher. I dashed backstage. Two prop men were dragging something toward me. It was a huge fire extinguisher the prop men had wrestled off the wall. "Couldn't find the little guy," one prop man said to me cheerfully. "You'll have to use this."

"I can't lift that."

"We'll help you," said the prop men in unison.

The band was still holding their C. The drummer was drumming a constant roll. The unicyclist was pedaling his ass off, trying to swat out the flaming jacket with the backs of his hands. "Let's go," I told the prop men. The three of us positioned the huge fire extinguisher on the stage and waited for the unicyclist's next pass. When he came by, the first prop man tilted the monster extinguisher forward, I aimed the hose at the unicyclist's back, and told the second prop man to let her rip! A spray came out that was so powerful, I was thrown back onto the seat of my pants. When I looked up, the unicyclist was airborne.

The expression on the unicyclist's face as he went into orbit was a sight to behold, a countenance so rigid with surprise I shall never forget it. Eyes bulging, mouth locked open in horror, body still in a sitting position, legs straight ahead as if there was a sled under him. The spray from the enormous fire extinguisher catapulted the performer into the first row of the audience. The unicyclist, covered from head to toe in white foam, landed on the laps of a newlywed couple from Bloomington, Indiana.

At last the band could stop playing C and strike up the finale—at least with those musicians who weren't rolling on the floor laughing —and the crowd, once they regained their composure, cheered wildly. The celebrity judges rewarded the unicyclist with a standing ovation. Jaye P. Morgan went so far as to unbutton her blouse and bare her tits. Gene Gene The Dancing Machine and I threw a basketball back and forth, happy no one was hurt. Confetti dropped from the ceiling and everyone—me, the acts, the stagehands, the celebrity judges— all danced on stage as though someone had announced the end of the world was at midnight. It was during my frenzied dancing—my maniacal, out-of-control twisting and writhing —that I realized I was having my midlife crisis on national television.

It was during that show's final commercial break, while the makeup lady patted my perspiring face with handfuls of Kleenex, that I began to wonder why I was hosting the *Gong Show* and acting the way I did.

Today when I think back, I'm more confused than ever, frustrated and sad. I still don't know why, back then, I insisted on being such a profound ham so that now, years later, the mere thought of some of those antics of mine can make me moan aloud with embarrassment. One night, during an ice hockey game at the Philadelphia Spectrum, the electronic scoreboard that hung over center ice flashed this message: *Welcome the Gong Show's Chuck Barris,* and sixteen thousand seven hundred fans booed. My wife said they were booing a bad call by a referee, but I've never been sure.

Why, I muse over and over again, did I pursue such violent theatrics on camera when I was so shy and self-conscious off camera? If I would never dance with a bowl on my head in front of my family, why did I dance that way before millions of strangers; perform in such a demented manner that I was never able to watch myself on television then or now. Did I self-destruct because I loathed the possibility of having the same job for the rest of my working life? Or was I merely unequipped to handle success? And who could I blame for my on-screen personality? Was it my parents' fault? My teachers'? My DNA? Could it have been the result of smoking cigarettes at an early age?

Who knows?

CHAPTER TWENTY-SIX

There's a *New Yorker* magazine cartoon I'm particularly fond of. It shows a middle-aged Eskimo couple fishing by a hole in the ice. Other than snow, there is nothing on the entire landscape but another Eskimo couple leaving on their dog sled. The husband by the fishing hole says to his wife, "There go the summer people, thank God."

The summer's over. The tourists have departed. It isn't crowded on the roads anymore, or on the streets, or in the restaurants and parking lots. I'm thrilled. Now the town looks like the Saint-Tropez I discovered in November of 1953.

I was twenty-two.

I had just finished college and was driving through France as a graduation present to myself. I drove into the seaport late one evening because that's where the road ended. My first impression of Saint-Tropez was far from favorable. It was cold and damp, and very windy. The streets were deserted, the buildings gray and foreboding. Pale-yellow puddles of light from ancient lampposts outlined dark boats creaking in their moorings. The remains of my badly battered spirits dropped into my socks. I smacked the rented Citroën's steering wheel, furious at the fates for bringing me to this eerie dead end.

I parked the car, pulled my raincoat over my head, and made a dash for the entrance to a small nondescript hotel. I had a lonely meal in an empty dining room and later tried sleeping on a sagging mattress in a drafty, sparsely furnished room. I pondered the misconception that bumming around Europe was a profitable bridge between college and real life. I finally drifted off to sleep resigned to return to New York on the first plane out of Nice.

The next morning I awoke and checked the time. Though the room was pitch black, my wristwatch with the luminous dial swore it was nine o'clock. Still hung over with gloom and despair, I stumbled to the window, pulled open the curtains, threw apart the shutters, and looked out onto the port of Saint-Tropez. It was a sight to behold. The sun was shining brightly. Everything was crystal clear. One could savor how fresh the air was. The brilliant colors. The sailboats rocking back and forth at anchor. It was love at second sight and I guess it's been that way ever since.

Five minutes later I ran down the hotel stairs and out into the sunshine. I walked along the port until I found the Gorille Bar-Restaurant. I sat in one of its chairs with the green canvas back and stared at the astonishing yachts berthed in front of me. A waiter came for my order. I asked for a café creme. The waiter, typically French, didn't smile or make small talk. He just slid the previous customer's tip off the table with one hand into the palm of the other, and left. A small boy was sitting on top of the bar inside the Gorille near the cash register, bouncing the heels of his shoes off the side of the bar. The boy never took his eyes off me. He was about six years old.

He could have been my friend Henri Bruni.

It is early Sunday morning almost forty years later.

I'm walking from our little house near the sea to the Gorille for coffee. As usual I pass under the window of the mean old widow.

I wave. Speaking with exaggerated mirth and pep, I say, "It's almost October. Winter's almost here."

The widow glares at me. If her eyes were daggers, they would be embedded in my chest. Why does she dislike me so? Because I'm an American who will bring disgrace to the neighborhood and a decline in real-estate values? Does she think it's only a matter of time before I have a TV dish on my roof, a mambo band in my courtyard, and a Rolls-Royce parked in front of my door?

Down at the port two ancient Tropeziens are standing on a corner arguing about the growing traffic congestion. These two old relics have been quarreling about the same thing on the same corner at the same time for the last thirteen years. The two crusty Tropeziens give me a morning nod. Janot the retired mailman passes by on his bicycle and waves. He's on his way to feed the stray cats living in the rocks at the end of the port. Loulou the electrician is the only one in the Gorille besides Henri. I have a quick cup of coffee with Loulou and then head for the Place des Lices. It's still early. No one will be there. I'll be able to practice *boule* in peace.

The church bells toll the half hour. It's seven-thirty.

This morning I'm working on a particularly difficult section of the Place des Lices ground; a sloping knoll that seems excessively cruel. No matter what I do, or how often I do it, I am unable to make my *boule* ball remain anywhere near the *cochonnet* I have placed at the top of the knoll. The *boule* ball does stop near the little wooden *cochonnet* as planned, but then always rolls down the knoll ending up an embarrassing distance from where it should be.

And then this little old man appears. He's walking across the park on his way home, I suppose, with bread under his arm. He comes to where I'm crouched in my throwing position and watches one or two of my futile tosses. Without saying a word, the little old man walks a few steps away from me, bends down, and makes an X on the ground with his finger. He's telling me that's the spot, the X is what to aim for. So that's what I do. I throw my *boule* ball through the air, it lands on the X, rolls up the knoll, stops inches from the *cochonnet,* and stays there.

The little old man smiles and continues on his way.

"It's fall in the States, my favorite time of year." I'm talking to Henri Bruni the next morning at the Gorille. "I miss the World Series, the new football season, stuff like that."

"I miss the horses," says Henri dejectedly.

Henri loves to bet horses and knows he shouldn't. He has a wife and three children to support. He's in no position to squander his cash on the nags. Unfortunately he does, and has been spending the last month attempting to recoup from a disastrous weekend at a racetrack in Cannes. I feel terrible about Henri's financial problem. I'd lend Henri money, but I know he won't take it. Henri has principles. "I got myself into this mess, I'll get myself out," he tells me.

This morning the two of us are standing at the bar. Henri's on a break, watching his spoon stir his coffee.

"Henri, why do you stir your coffee? You drink it black."

"It's part of the tradition."

"Henri, I hate to tell you this, but I got a hot tip from America on a horse. I swear, it's a sure thing. It's from a friend in California who owns horses and knows a hot tip when he sees one. I'm going to telephone my friend this afternoon and ask him to put ten dollars on the nag's nose for me. Do you want to bet ten dollars, too?" Of course all this stuff about a friend in California who owns horses and knows a hot tip when he sees one is my imagination talking. I just made it up. It's part of a plan I developed earlier that morning to help Henri recoup a few bucks without him knowing it.

Henri says he wants to bet, but not ten dollars. That's too much. He decides on two dollars, goes behind the counter, finds his change purse and gives me ten francs.

A few days later I come in for my morning coffee and tell Henri our (mythical) race horse went off at 20–1 and won going away. I hand him two hundred francs—forty dollars—and he goes berserk with joy. He begs me to thank my friend for the tip. I'm pleased with my little scam.

A week passes. I announce to Henri the same friend telephoned again from California with another hot tip on a horse. "My friend said this filly is a sure thing. He swears she'll win going away. I'm going to call him back this afternoon and bet ten dollars. Do you want to bet, too?"

Henri says he does, goes behind the bar to find his change purse, and returns with two dollars.

Four days go by. I come to the Gorille and tell Henri the horse won just like my friend said she would and give him thirty dollars. Henri kisses me on both cheeks, hugs me, and calls me Papa Noël. He says my friend in California is Papa Noël, too.

All is going well with my plan. I've managed to slip Henri small amounts of money on several occasions without embarrassing him. And then one day I come in with the same story. My friend called from California, a sure thing, etc., etc. As usual I ask Henri if he wants to make a bet. He says he does and goes behind the bar to fetch his purse. When he returns he gives me two thousand two hundred and fifty French francs.

"Here," he says. "Four hundred and fifty American dollars!"

I gasp. "Four hundred and fifty dollars!"

"It's my savings."

"All of it?"

"All of it."

"You can't do this, Henri. You can't bet your entire savings on a goddamn horse."

"It's my savings and I can do anything I want with it."

I take his money, leave the Gorille, and suffer a minor nervous crisis. What am I going to do? What can I do? Even if I tell Henri the horse was a big favorite and went off at even money, I'm still going to have to pay him his original four hundred and fifty dollars plus the four hundred and fifty dollars he hypothetically won! What was the alternative? There wasn't any. Two days pass. I go to the Gorille and give Henri nine hundred dollars. He kisses the top of my scruffy head. He treats the bar to coffee. Everyone congratulates him.

A week later I tell Henri, "You know my friend, the guy in California who gave us all those wonderful tips."

"Yes?" says Henri.

"He died."

CHAPTER TWENTY-SEVEN

The problem with *Three's a Crowd* was . . .

Was what? I muse, sitting on a bench in the Place des Lices, pondering the show that was our first major disaster.

. . . the problem was, the contestants had a miserable time. It's the only show I ever created, I tell myself, where the contestants didn't enjoy themselves.

How could you? everyone would always ask me.

How could I what?

How could you put those contestants through such torture and misery?

Torture and misery?

Yes. You humiliate them so—poor souls—playing with their emotions like you do. Making them say such revealing things. You embarrass your contestants way beyond the point of good taste.

I heard that continuously: from radio and TV talk show hosts, newspaper interviewers, friends and acquaintances, prime time news stars.

"It's been said," said Mike Wallace on *60 Minutes,* "that you revel in your ability to degrade and make fools of the contestants on your game shows."

"I don't think that's true at all, Mike," I replied.

And it wasn't. Not at all.

The contestants on all of our programs had a wonderful time. They enjoyed being there. They wanted to be there. They came off the streets and into our offices with nothing, and went away with something: a gift, cash, a memory they'd never ever forget, a few minutes of glory . . . and if none of those, than just a break from their mostly drab and fruitless lives. I always believed if you asked our contestants, they would all agree with me, admitting they enjoyed themselves thoroughly.

Except the contestants on *Three's a Crowd*.

Three's a Crowd was an entirely different experience. True, it was a game show just like my other programs, spontaneous, highly identifiable, and meant to be funny. Its potential to draw a big audience was there like the others, and it did. Even after it turned mean and vicious.

Three's a Crowd brought to life the most dramatic triangle of the twentieth century and asked one of the most visceral questions of the times: Who knows the husband better—his wife or his secretary?

First the four husband/bosses were ushered on stage. The men were all asked the same four questions; questions like: How many times did you and your secretary go to Palm Springs on a "business trip?"

"I never went on a business trip alone with my secretary," answered the first husband.

After all the husbands' answers to the four questions were written down on cards, we would go to commercial.

Then the four secretaries would come on stage.

The secretaries would sit to the right of their bosses. This was an interesting tableaux; more often than not the whimpish boss had a sexy secretary while the manly boss sat beside a matronly one. The same questions were asked the secretary. How many times did you and your boss go on a "business trip" to Palm Springs?

"Never," said the first secretary.

Her boss would then hold up a card with his answer. Never.

"Correct!" shouted the host, and the secretaries received a point.

"Twice," answered the second secretary.

Her boss held up his card. Never.

"Never!" snapped the secretary, angry to not to have scored a point for her team when she was absolutely right. "What about the time we met your brother at Rancho Mirage? Or the meeting with the sales managers at the Hilton? They don't count?"

Her boss sat stuttering and chagrined.

The last two secretaries each scored a point so their team was leading 3–0.

Then the four wives came on stage.

Red and Chuck Barris.

Jean Aponte

The villa in the hills, from the front and from the rear.

The house in the port. It is the one in the center, behind the trees.

Bam Bam: Chuck driving, Patrick, Red waving, and Teetee next to her.

Chuck and Loretta Strickland, his secretary.

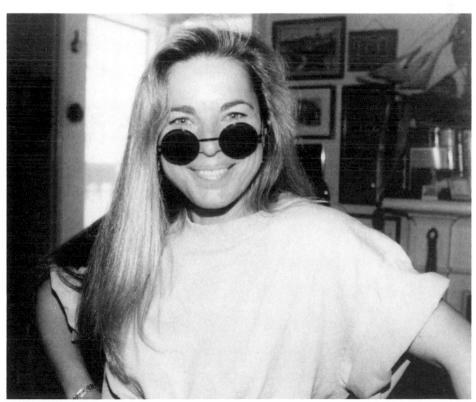

Tita Teetee Mercurio.

Marquis Chimps play the *Dating Game*.

Danny Cahill.

The wives sat on the other sides of their husbands and the tableaux was complete. Pretty wife, ugly secretary (and vice versa), and the increasingly ill-at-ease man in the middle.

"How many times did your husband say he took his secretary to Palm Springs?" asked the host.

"Alone?" said Wife Number One.

"Yes, alone."

"Never," said the wife emphatically.

The husband held up his card saying—Never.

"You're absolutely right," bellowed the host. "That's a point for the wives. And Wife Number Two, Mary Matson, how many times did your husband say he went to Palm Springs with his secretary Annie Franke sitting there on the other side of your husband?"

"Well, he better have said never."

Wife Number Two's husband held up his card that said—Never.

"You're right! Another point for the wives!" hollered the host while the husband and wife kissed. "However, you might be interested to know, Mary, your husband's secretary, Annie Franke, said she and your husband have been to Palm Springs together twice."

"What!" gasped Mrs. Matson, whipping her head around and bending forward to see the secretary on the other side of her husband better. "Twice? Alone?"

"Yes siree," cooed Annie Franke, loving every minute of this confrontation. "Once when Paul's brother was . . ."

"I don't believe this," hissed Wife Number Two at her husband.

And if that was embarrassing, the wives' reaction to the anniversary present question was *humiliating*.

"All right, Wife Number One," said the host, "how many times has your husband's secretary purchased your wedding anniversary present for him?"

"Purchased my anniversary present? You've got to be kidding. My husband would never stoop that low."

"So what's your answer?"

"Never."

The husband held up his card that said—Never—but the expression on his face was one of deep anxiety.

"Correct!" shouted the host, and the happy wife reacted accordingly.

But we all knew. We knew what the husband knew; that he had

allowed his secretary—the thin, blond-haired, cat-eyed shrew sitting on his right—to buy a revealing nightie. "For my boss's old lady," as the secretary put it. And we all knew the show's host was going to tell the wife. It was his job. He was required to do that so we could all moan and groan, and relish the stricken wife's misfortune. So we all held our collective breaths as the host said to the pitiful husband: "Your card says—Never—but as you know, your secretary said something else."

"What did she say?" asked the wife, at first confused and then quickly alarmed, repeating herself. "What did she say?"

"She said she bought you a filmy nightie for your last anniversary. She said your husband was too busy with the new—"

When the show was over, the couples left the studio humped-back and devastated. Except the secretaries. They seemed to love playing *Three's a Crowd*, especially if they won. Which they usually did.

When I first thought of *Three's a Crowd*, I explained the program idea to my old friend Ed Vane, the ABC-TV vice president.

He not only rejected the show, he threw me out of his office.

For the life of me, I couldn't think of the reason for Ed's violent reaction.

"He's obviously having an affair with his secretary," explained my secretary Loretta Strickland, as we walked to the elevator, Ret carrying the cardboard model of the game show's set.

I retraced my steps to get a better look at Mr. Vane's secretary. No great shakes, I thought. How could Ed be having an affair with that? He wasn't. He was merely incensed by my stupidity. Ed Vane knew *Three's a Crowd* would provoke a disastrous reaction throughout the country, a response that would come back and haunt me. And it did. Ladies picketed the local stations that carried *Three's a Crowd* in what may have been the initial call to arms of the Women's Rights movement. Another first for my company, though a dubious one.

The show continued on the air for a few more stormy months. Nothing got better. Things actually got worse. Wives reached across husbands to claw at secretaries. Husbands sat stupefied, attempting to calculate how much of their marriages were salvageable, and if not, what was it going to cost them.

"You asked us questions I never thought you would ask," said a wounded husband, a practicing psychiatrist. "You forced me to lie."

"I didn't force you to do anything. You chose to say what you said."

"The lights," he mumbled.

"What about the lights?"

"The lights—and cameras—put pressure on us, on me." The doctor's voice trailed off.

"That's silly," I said, knowing it wasn't.

"I never thought you would ask us those kind of questions," repeated the doctor and walked away.

"The man's right," said Ruthie Goldberg. "The questions are vile. They create reactions between the wives and secretaries that are absolutely virulent."

"But if we didn't ask those kinds of questions, Ruthie, the show would be bland. It would be pablum."

"Happy pablum will never get us into trouble?"

"What kind of trouble can *Three's a Crowd* get us into, Ruthie?"

The public backlash from *Three's a Crowd* not only caused the program to be canceled, but it took three other TV shows of mine with it. I went to my house in Malibu and stayed there for a year.

CHAPTER TWENTY-EIGHT

It's October.

Laborers from France, Spain, and Germany descend on Saint-Tropez and help the farmers harvest their wine crop. So do migrants from eastern Europe and gypsies from everywhere. Anyone can work harvesting French grapes. The workers fan out in the vine-yards. For two weeks they slowly move across the land taking its color away. Gone are the purple clusters of grapes and the bushes' green leaves. Small tractor wagons roll into town with masses of grapes heaped in the back. The grapes are heading for the crusher. Cars line up behind the tractor wagons as they drive into town waiting patiently for them to pull over so they can pass.

I invest in a satellite TV dish for our house in the vineyard. I want to see the World Series. When the satellite is installed, everyone in our house celebrates: our weird guardians, our crazy housekeepers, the Ultimate Cooking Machine, Buddy The Wonder Dog, the gang. We all clink wineglasses with the satellite man.

"I have opened the gates to hours and hours of exciting entertain-ment for you wonderful people," he announces dramatically, his arms open wide, letting in the wonders of the world for our family to enjoy.

Unfortunately I enjoy very little.

In the days and evenings that follow I cannot get the World Se-ries. What I can get is innumerable talk shows from Finland, Esto-nia, Bulgaria, Switzerland, Spain, Latvia, and Italy. I don't under-stand anything anyone is saying. By the looks of the various programs' hosts and guests, I'm not missing a thing. There are, how-ever, a great many steamy pornographic movies in the evening, particularly from pristine Switzerland, ostensibly the most conservative country in the world.

It's around the time of the World Series I'm unable to view that Red and I meet Just Plain Bill.

"His name is"—Simone Binfado puts on her reading glasses and checks the notebook on her desk—"Vice Admiral William A. Owens."

I'm sitting in Simone Binfado's office at the port. Simone is Saint-Tropez's harbormaster. She's also head of the Chamber of Commerce and runs the language center.

"Admiral Owens is"—Simone checks her notebook again—"Commander In Chief of your entire Sixth Fleet. I am told every United States soldier, sailor, and marine in this part of the world reports to this Vice Admiral William A. Owens. The admiral's flagship, the USS *Belknap*, is coming to the port of Saint-Tropez on a mission of goodwill." Simone Binfado looks up from her notebook and takes off her reading glasses. "I was just wondering if"—Simone puts her glasses back on and looks down again to the notebook—"Admiral Owens, his wife Monika, his second in command Captain Joe Mobley, and Captain Mobley's wife Mary can stay at your house for a long weekend." Simone removes her glasses. "It's so much better than putting the admiral and his wife in a hotel room."

"Why me?" I ask.

"Because I know your house in the vineyards and it's charming, and you and your wife are charming, and American." Simone smiles.

Something tells me to be wary of Simone's flattering sales pitch. I ask, "How long is a long weekend?"

"Five nights."

"Five nights! Isn't there a saying, Simone, that house guests are like fish. After three days they stink. Make it three nights."

"Okay. Three nights in your house and two nights in a hotel is far better than five nights in a hotel." Simone thanks me profusely.

I go home and tell Red a three-star admiral, the Commander in Chief of the entire Sixth Fleet, his wife, and another couple—the admiral's second in command—are going to stay with us for three nights.

"Are you crazy or something?" she barks. "A house full of strangers for three nights!"

"I was asked if they could stay five nights. I cut it down to three."

"You should have aced it altogether," growls my wife. "Just remember, you're no great shakes with friends, let alone strangers. Besides, they're Navy. That means they tell boring sea stories, have tattoos and get falling-down drunk."

Red's right. I never thought about that. Sailors do tell boring sea stories and sport revolting tattoos. Snakes wrapped around anchors that say "Mother." Stuff like that. And they drink like fish and throw up all over your living-room rug. And you can never get the smell out.

"But I made a commitment to Simone," I say. "I can't go back on my word."

"When are they coming?" asks my wife, resigned and dejected.

"In two weeks."

A few days later I inform Red that I'm going to build a flagpole in honor of the admiral.

"Why?"

"So we can fly an American flag when he arrives."

"Did you ask the contractors if they're going to make a huge mess like they always do?"

"The contractors said a flagpole's a piece of cake."

"There is no such thing as a piece of cake when it comes to building anything in France."

"I'm going to call it the Admiral William A. Owens Flagpole."

"The whole thing's revolting," says my wife.

"What's revolting?"

"This red, white, and blue side of you I never knew. The patriot has come out of the closet. The next thing you'll want all of us to do is sing 'The Star Spangled Banner' when the admiral arrives."

"That's not a bad idea."

Red makes a nasty remark I can't hear and walks away. My wife walks like Charlie Chaplin. It's a very cute walk. I always get a pang of love when I see her waddle off like that.

Anyway, I have the flagpole installed, and Red's right again. There's no such thing as a simple construction job in France. Everything's a major production. Massive tractors, earth movers, and cement trucks invade our property. They dig for days. There are gigantic piles of earth all over the place.

The day after the flagpole is finished and the lawn is restored, a naval officer telephones to say the admiral's plane has landed. I relay this news to the Redhead.

"Big deal," she mutters.

"The admiral should be arriving at your home at approximately 13:50 hours," says the naval officer crisply.

Red hrrumphs at the exactness of the message. "Living with the admiral must be about as much fun as hanging out with an Amtrak Metroliner."

Being discreet is not my wife's strongest suit.

She is, however, more than a little surprised when at exactly 13:50 our front gates swing open and Vice Admiral William A. Owens and party roll up our driveway. Seconds later, aides step out of the two limousines followed by the admiral and his wife. All of the officers are in uniform: gold braid wrapped around their shoulders, rows of ribbons on their chests. The admiral's wife is smiling. She has a great smile. She walks directly to Red and introduces herself as if the Redhead is an ambassador. The two shake hands warmly. Red likes her right away. I can tell.

The Barris Bunch—our caretakers Mad Janot and Crazy Solema from Portugal, the legendary UCM who was born in Algeria, our dog Buddy who hails from New York, our housekeepers Sweet Doris from Munich and feisty Barisa who is a Tropezienne, my valley girl wife from California, and me from Philadelphia—we're all impressed with our first look at the Admiral's entourage. The setting helps. A light breeze makes my huge American flag flap back and forth on top of the Admiral William A. Owens Flagpole. The young naval officers stand about smiling. It's a pretty day. All in all, a rather patriotic tableau, the kind that gives you goose bumps. At least it gives *me* goose bumps. Like watching the corps of cadets during a dress parade on Saturday morning at West Point.

And then the admiral steps forward. He reminds me of the great-looking prince the ugly frog always turns into. Admiral Owens is a young fifty, tall and handsome. The admiral shakes my hand, then walks up to Red, introduces himself, and tells her how happy and honored he, his wife, and the others are to be spending the next three nights in her home.

"Five nights," says Red quickly.

"I'm sorry, five nights."

"What do I call you?" asks Red. "Admiral Owens . . . Mr. Owens?"

"Try just plain Bill," says the admiral.

"Just plain Bill," sighs Red.

She's smitten.

I can tell.

And then Red turns to our motley group, to Mad Janot and Crazy Solema and the rest, and says, "I think we should all sing 'The Star Spangled Banner.' "

"We should do what?" I hiss out of the side of my mouth. "Nobody knows the goddamn words."

"We'll fake it," Red hisses back, and then starts it off. " 'Oh say can you see . . .' "

You had to see it to believe it. Solema, Janot, Teetee, Doris, Barisa, Buddy The Wonder Dog, the Redhead, the admiral, his Chief of Staff, their wives, the other officers all standing at attention facing the Admiral William A. Owens Flagpole; the officers saluting, everyone else with their hands over their hearts, all singing "The Star Spangled Banner" on this little patch of land in France.

True, some of my French employees don't know the words to our national anthem, but they fake it like Red said they should, including Mad Janot, whose eyes are filled with tears.

I turn to him and say, "What the hell are you crying about, Janot? You're French."

My handyman puts his arm around my shoulders, looks me right in the eyes and says, *"Va te faire enculer."*

What I think Janot says is literally, "I am proud to make with you my uncle," a cliché translated into everyday English meaning, "I am proud to work for you, my boss." I smile and playfully sock him on his chin.

What he really said was, "Go fuck yourself."

CHAPTER TWENTY-NINE

I was thinking of Saint-Tropez, wishing I was there. Wishing I was anywhere but the city I was in. Cleveland. It was 1971 and I was on a forty-city promotion tour for a book I had written called: *You And Me, Babe.*

I had just returned from the south of France where I had been visiting my friends Nadia and Larry Collins, and Dominique Lapierre. This time when I left Saint-Tropez I was more in love with the place than ever. It was so clean there, and tranquil, and crime free. And now here I was in grimy, polluted Cleveland (with three locks on my hotel-room door), standing in a dark TV station hallway sucking a cup of black coffee in a Styrofoam cup. I was waiting to be interviewed by two local morning television personalities with major attitude problems. Soon one or the other would ask me bland questions about my book they never read or cared to read, eager to be through with me so they could move on to the really good guest, the short lady sex therapist with the big mouth who loved saying clit and penis. The woman—a doctor of something, specializing in orgasms —was apparently on the identical forty-city tour as I was. Consequently we found ourselves on most of the same radio and television shows. During that part of each program when the telephone lines were open, she received all the calls.

Book tours—touring for anything—are a serious drag. It's also a grind; bouncing from city to city, struggling to wake up for the A.M. TV program, trying to be alert for all the local newspaper, radio, and television interviews throughout the day, fielding questions you don't want to answer, never being asked questions you do want to answer, straining to stay awake for the Night Show. Then, after the last show is over, dashing to the airport in a hair-raising attempt to make the last flight to the next city.

That morning in Cleveland, while a technician pinned a small microphone on my shirt, I was introduced to the program's co-host and hostess. They were both white, supercilious, and resentful about being local personalities who had never made it to the big time. The third member of the team was a beautiful black girl who was charming, well informed, and had read my book. Naturally she didn't interview me. The white girl did. When we shook hands, she forced a rigid smile that showed a lot of upper gum and small square teeth. Her head was long and narrow with close-set eyes under rimless eyeglasses. She wore a tight pony tail that hung down to her ass. While I waited to go on the air, I couldn't help noticing the gorgeous black girl looking at me. When I returned her glance, she didn't look away, but smiled and lowered her eyes.

The interview was a mess. All the hostess wanted to know was why I insisted on humiliating the contestants on my game shows and all I wanted to talk about was my book and its bittersweet love story.

"Aren't I here to discuss my book?"

"Quite so, still I'm sure our audience . . ."

We seemed to be fighting with each other for my entire seven minutes of airtime, she insisting I go in one direction, me stubbornly pushing her in another. Before she could hold up my book and mention that it was published by Harpers, I was sitting next to the sex therapist listening to her say clit and penis.

A month later I was back in Hollywood putting together a new game show called *Cop Out*.

A panel of ten celebrities, sitting behind a long dais, were asked personal questions. After the celebrity answered his or her question —whether they had just told the truth or were "copping out," i.e., *lying*—they would press one of two buttons under the arms of their seats sending their answer to our giant scoreboard. The rest of the panel of stars would then debate the veracity of the celebrity's answer. When all the other stars had given their opinions, the contestant made a choice. Yes, the celebrity was telling the truth or no, the celebrity was copping out. Everyone would then turn and look at the floor-to-ceiling scoreboard where it would flash: Truth or Cop Out. If the contestant guessed correctly he or she would win a prize.

The sample show of *Cop Out* had a high-tech set whose center-piece was a magnificent scoreboard filled with blinking chaser lights, bells, and whistles, and the ability to flash Truth or Cop Out in letters twelve feet high. The scoreboard was very impressive. The only problem was, it never worked. We prayed it would by the time we filmed the show. The network engineers labored day and night on the scoreboard promising it would be fine by airtime. I hoped they were right. Without the scoreboard we didn't have a show.

It was during this tryout period that I received my first letter from the beautiful black news reporter on the Cleveland television station.

I so much wanted to talk about your book. I've always been a big admirer of yours. I'm sorry if I seemed uncomfortable. I was so much in awe of you.

I wrote her back immediately.

I wanted to talk to you, to spend time with you, to ask you out for dinner, but I couldn't because I'm shy.

And so began a torrid correspondence that lasted for months. The two of us were unattached at the time, both having just ended long involved relationships. If we were rebounding, so much the better. Our letters always included an attempt to rendezvous somewhere, in a city midway between Los Angeles and Cleveland, and then any city, but our work schedules intervened. Once there was a chance we would be in San Francisco at the same time but at the last minute she had to cancel. She wrote:

I save all your letters. You must write often. And I must also. Then after we die someone in one of our families can publish our letters much like Jean-Paul Sartre and Simone De Beauvoir's and make a lot of money. I miss you terribly. If we can't arrange to see each other soon I'll fly to Los Angeles and to hell with the repercussions. So people will see us together. So what?

In the meantime the day had arrived to film the *Cop Out* pilot.

The studio had a standing-room-only audience. The roped-off VIP row was filled with network VIP's. The celebrities were seated behind the dais and the engineers, pleased with themselves, reported to me that the scoreboard was working perfectly.

The show started nicely. The host projected himself well, seemingly secure in his new job, the stars were talkative and chipper, and the lady contestant cute and perky. But things went awry quickly. The first question was: "Burt Reynolds, are you gentle or harsh when you break off a love affair?"

"Gentle," replied Burt. "I tell the unfortunate female the bad news over dinner at a fabulous restaurant. The next day I send flowers and champagne."

When it was time to hear the other celebrity's opinions as to whether Burt was being truthful or copping out, Theresa Graves leapt to her feet and yelled, "Who the hell is he kidding? He's the worst. Know what he does? He dumps you right on your ass, that's what he does. Flowers and candy? Ha! His way of ending an affair is never showing up again."

"Do you know that for a fact?" asked the anxious host.

"You're goddamn right I do. I was a dumpee."

Burt asked Theresa, "Are you sitting there with a straight face and claiming we had an affair?"

"Are you insinuating we didn't?"

This diatribe was interrupted by our perky, peppy lady contestant who, for some reason, announced: "This is a stupid show." Just the kind of comment you want your best contestant—the one you hand-picked yourself—to make in front of an audience filled with network buyers.

Our new host, to his credit, jumped in quickly and said, "Okay, Burt Reynolds has told us how he ends his affairs. Was Burt telling the truth or was he copping out? Let's find out what answer Burt gave our giant scoreboard." Everyone looked at the giant scoreboard.

The giant scoreboard didn't work.

And that was that. The lights came up, the show was over, the audience and the network buyers went home. I was so angry I went over to the giant scoreboard and kicked it so hard I broke a toe. And then it suddenly worked. The chaser lights blinked on and off, bells and whistles tooted, and in letters twelve feet high it flashed Burt Reynolds's answer.

Cop Out.

The beautiful black news reporter and I were finally going to meet. In New York.

I had asked her if she would stay with me in my Plaza Hotel suite. She said she would. My secretary, the ever-efficient Loretta Strickland, thought she'd better check the Plaza Hotel to make absolutely sure they allowed blacks to stay as guests.

"Are you kidding," I said angrily. "This is the seventies. Of course blacks can stay at the Plaza."

But Loretta checked anyway.

We were to meet at the Palm Court at five o'clock. At four-thirty I was seated in my best suit and tie at a table for two. I wanted to make certain I wouldn't miss her. I played with a cup of tea while checking my notebook, making sure everything had been taken care of: flowers in the room, champagne in the fridge, theater tickets, after-theater dinner reservations. While I was busy doing that a girl's voice said, "Hello again."

I looked up from my notebook. It was some stranger, a hippie dressed in a shawl and an embarrassingly long, formless shmata that ended at her dirty, sandaled feet. "You don't recognize me, do you, dressed like I love to dress, not the way you saw me in those serious duds I have to wear on the program."

No, I thought, I couldn't have.

"It's me," she said.

And it was. The long narrow face and the rimless eyeglasses. Only her hair was different. She made a full turn for me. I didn't know why until she said, "My long braid's gone," and I saw that it was.

I was stunned. I had been corresponding all these months with the wrong girl. I had been conducting a love affair by mail with the mean and obnoxious white news personality from Cleveland and not the beautiful black one.

"You look surprised," she said, smiling her thin smile, showing me lots of upper pink gum and little white teeth. "Have I changed that much?

CHAPTER THIRTY

I have an appointment to see the mayor of Saint-Tropez. His name is Spada. He's a thin, wiry man with a bush of black curly hair on top of a narrow and very serious face. He is never without a coat and tie and he always walks with short quick steps. Spada is a very determined man, a man on the move.

The reason for my visit is to ask the mayor about the big trees in the Place des Lices. The trees are old and diseased and will die if something isn't done to save them. If they die there won't be any shade, and if there's no shade, no one will be able to play *boule*. I can't imagine how the town can survive without *boule*. It isn't that the locals don't care. They just don't know what to do about it. The mayor, on the other hand, says he knows what to do about everything. If that's true, then he'll know what to do about the sick trees on the Place des Lices.

I've brought along my friend Larry Collins. Larry speaks French fluently. Since the mayor doesn't understand a word of English, Larry has agreed to assist my pig-French. Or just act as my translator.

Although the mayor is not sure why we've come, he's pleased to see us. The mayor presumes all Americans are rich. Men on the move like Mayor Spada tend to be more hospitable to rich people than poor ones. The mayor shakes Larry's hand vigorously, then my hand vigorously. He ushers the two of us into his office with a serious whisk of his right arm. It's a spacious, airy office with large bay windows that overlook the sea. It's been said that Mayor Spada, with the help of a pair of binoculars, checks on passing offshore racers to see if they're obeying the posted speed limits. If the mayor thinks a boat is going too fast, he copies its number down and sends the owner a summons.

Larry and the mayor go through the opening formalities which require them to chat about nothing for a prescribed amount of time. It appears to me this is going on forever. I'm so bored I can't see straight.

"Yo, Lar," I say in English, "get to the point."

Collins finally alerts the mayor that he's about to tell him the purpose of our visit. The mayor adjusts his face accordingly, making it attentive and solicitous. Larry proceeds to translate my concerns regarding the diseased trees. When Larry and I finish, the mayor counters with a rather lengthy diatribe about the obvious: the importance of the trees, the need for shade, the inherent danger a shadeless park would pose to the continuation of *boule* as we know it, the community's indifference to the slow death of the trees, the lack of financial support from the individual citizens of Saint-Tropez that would help combat the disease and get to the root of the problem (so to speak), especially among the *boule* players themselves.

"Perhaps the *boule* players can't afford to help financially," I suggest in French.

"What?" says the mayor to Larry.

Larry tells the mayor what I have just said.

"Perhaps," says Mayor Spada to Larry, "but what about the celebrities who live here? Brigitte Bardot? Eddie Barclay? Johnny Halliday? What about them?"

Larry translates what the mayor has just said for me.

"Perhaps the celebrities don't play *boule*," I say to the mayor.

"What?" says the mayor to Larry.

I stop talking to the mayor and just tell Larry what I want to say, and Larry translates.

"Mr. Barclay plays *boule*," says the mayor to Larry. "I've seen him playing in the park. Many times."

The mayor's right. I don't know what to say.

Larry and the mayor chat some more; laughing and tsking, hrumphing and oooh la-la-ing, doing all those idiotic things the French do when they talk seriously. I'm impressed by my friend Larry's performance. He gives great Frog. And then, right out of the blue, Larry turns to me and says, "How much?"

"How much what?"

"Money. How much money do you want to give the mayor to help save the trees?"

"Twenty thousand," I say.

Larry tells the mayor what I've just said.

The mayor is stunned.

I'm stunned, too. It's especially surprising to me since the thought of donating money never entered my mind. I just wanted to bring the matter of the sick trees to Mayor Spada's attention. And why the wide eyes on Spada? Is the mayor insulted by my meager donation? What goddamn reason does he have for being insulted? He's not donating twenty thousand francs for a couple dozen dumb trees.

"Twenty thousand?" Larry says to me, double checking.

I nod yes to both Collins and the mayor. If that's not good enough for the mayor, then fuck him and the horse he rode in on.

The mayor rises, comes around his desk, and shakes my hand. He doesn't seem as startled now as he was a few moments ago. Just hyper. And extremely happy. Perhaps Spada is a man of many moods. Larry and the mayor shake hands, then I shake hands with Spada again. Larry and the mayor shake hands again, Larry and I shake hands, which is a bit bizarre, and then Larry and the mayor shake hands for the third time. I think the mayor wants to shake my hand once more before I leave, but I've had enough.

As Collins and I walk down the hallway toward the steps, Larry says, "You did say twenty thousand, didn't you?"

"Jesus, Larry, how many times are you going to ask me? Yes, twenty thousand francs."

"Francs?" says Collins, stopping dead in his tracks.

"Of course francs. What did you think I meant? Dollars?"

"I told the mayor dollars."

"Dollars!" I roar. "Are you crazy? Twenty thousand dollars for a bunch of goddamn dying trees! No wonder the mayor was stunned!"

I drive Larry to his house, cursing all the way. Little do I know that in the future this horrific screw-up in communications between Larry and myself would make me a local hero.

CHAPTER THIRTY-ONE

It's early Saturday morning. Henri Bruni and I are once again on *Bam Bam,* fishing. It seems extra quiet this morning. The only sounds are the squawking of passing sea gulls and the lapping of waves against our boat. A light, balmy breeze is blowing off the land out to sea. The breeze ripples Henri's hair into his eyes.

"Your hair's getting gray," I tell him.

"Yours *is* gray," he grumps back.

Henri baits his hook and tosses it into the water. After the hook sinks, he wiggles into a comfortable position at the rear of the boat and turns on our little portable radio.

"That's 'California Dreaming,' " I tell Henri.

"What is?"

"The song they're playing on the radio. It's one of the rock classics of the sixties, 'California Dreaming' by the Mamas and Papas."

"Yes, I remember. Did you know them, the Mamas and the Papas?"

"I only knew one of them well."

"Which one?"

"Cass Elliot. Mama Cass."

"You did?"

"Yes. I knew her very well. In fact, I think I loved her." Remembering Cass makes me sigh.

"But she was very fat."

"So what?"

"You said you were lovers."

"I said I loved her. I didn't say we were lovers. And so what if she was fat?"

"Were you?"

"Were we what? Lovers? No."

"I liked Mama Cass."

"Yeah," I say, and we both fiddle with our fishing lines.

"What was she like?" asks Henri.

The Mama Cass Television Program was my first prime-time network television "special;" a one-hour program that would be on television once, maybe repeated a second time if we were lucky.

As it turned out, the entire Cass Elliot project was a royal pain in the ass. When it was over I vowed never to do another TV special. Too many bosses. First there was the ABC network vice president in charge of specials who was kept informed by his assistant, the director of specials, who was kept informed by the two outside producers, the ABC network vice president of special programs hired to keep their eyes on me. Then there was Mama Cass's agent, Bobby Roberts, who had the reputation to uphold of being difficult to deal with most of the time and obnoxious all the time. There were also all the guest stars' agents who considered the talent he or she represented the real star of the show and were constantly whining about this or demanding that so they could feel important and justify their jobs.

Everything about the undertaking was debilitating. I lost ten years of my life just booking the guest stars. It took incredible diplomacy to find big-name talent acceptable to all the goddamn bosses. And that was just one of a dozen arduous chores we were required to overcome before we had to film the show. A nightmare is what *The Mama Cass Television Program* turned out to be. But if you dug deep enough into all that miserable glop you'd find Cass, and she made it all worthwhile.

Mama Cass was most definitely fat. And dank. She sweated like a race horse, all the time, whether she was exerting herself or not. So when you hugged her, your arms went around a lot of damp girth and your cheek came away from her cheek uncomfortably moist. (You had to watch not to wipe your face with your hand for fear of embarrassing Cass.) If she was large and clammy, she was also warm and funny and alive. Very much alive; loving life, loving to be alive. And when we had trouble on the show, she was always there, right by my side, backing me to the hilt. Fortunately I didn't need her often. If I remember correctly we got through the special with only two calamities. Neither required Cass's help, but both of them were memorable.

The first calamity was Cass Elliot's chocolate cake.

We had to work on the show through Christmas and New Year's. Though that didn't bother any of us on the production team, Cass felt bad about it. On the day of New Year's Eve, Cass brought a homemade chocolate cake to my office. When she arrived, we were in the middle of a production meeting. Mama Cass put the cake on my desk and said it was to buck up our spirits. We all thought it was a sweet thing to do. I took a big slice with a glass of cold milk. Not long after I finished eating the cake, my office spun around. I became very concerned. I thought I might be suffering from exhaustion, or I had a brain tumor. I excused myself from the meeting and went to the men's room. I locked the door and splashed cold water on my face. With both hands gripping the sink, I looked at myself in the mirror. While I looked, the bathroom spun around. I walked out into the hallway and asked the first person who came along—one of my producers named Larry Gottlieb—to drive me home.

Larry saw me to the front door of my apartment, and left. I went inside and sat down on the living-room floor. I remained sitting on the floor staring at the opposite wall for hours. Sometime during the afternoon it dawned on me that Cass probably spiked the chocolate cake. (She did, with hashish.) Cass was always doing something like that, hoping to make everyone happy, never intending any harm. Anyway, since I had never fooled around with drugs, I didn't know what to expect. Rather than relax and enjoy Cass's foolish way of expressing her appreciation, I panicked and fought it. I lay on the floor frightened. I developed this intense desire to jump off my balcony. I thought perhaps I might fly back to my office and surprise my staff. I decided to telephone Larry Gottlieb first and explain to him what I was about to do. He might consider returning to my apartment as quickly as he could and stop me. I crawled to the phone but found to my horror I barely could read the letters and numbers. I was convinced that if I couldn't make the call before the numbers disappeared for good, I was a dead duck. They'd find me on the first day of the New Year twenty floors down, squashed among the tulips. I dialed Larry eleven times before I got it right. He returned and sat with me for the entire night. The next morning I drove out to Santa Monica, parked my car, and went to the beach.

I lay down on the sand, arms and legs flung out spread-eagle fashion, and slept for twelve straight hours without moving.

Then there was the Mary Travers—of Peter, Paul, and Mary—calamity.

All Cass's friends on the special—Joni Mitchell, John Sebastian, and Mary Travers—were told they could sing two songs. But there was no guarantee both songs would be used on the show that would eventually air. If we ran short of time we would have the right to cut one song from the singer, or singers, of our choice. It was a monumental task getting everyone to agree, but eventually they did. The day before we filmed the special in Hollywood, Ruth Goldberg received a telephone call from Mary Travers in New York. The call was very upsetting to Ruthie.

"Mary says she's at Kennedy Airport and about to get on her plane, but she won't come unless we promise to use both her songs."

"She said what? That's goddamned blackmail!" I yelled, slapping the desk with the flat of my hand, seething with outrage and confusion.

Ruthie appeared shocked by my quick burst of anger, as if I thought she was to blame for Mary's treachery.

"What should we do, Ruthie?" I asked mournfully, reaching for her hand.

"What *can* we do?" she said, sitting down. "If you say no, she won't come. And if she doesn't come there will be a gaping hole in the show that'll be impossible to fill at this late hour. We'll never find a replacement by tomorrow morning who can possibly meet everyone's approval. And if we don't find a really great replacement, all the network bosses will have major shit fits."

"But goddamn it, Ruthie, if I say yes, then all the other guests are going to want to be guaranteed their two songs make the final edit. And then what happens if we run long? Where are we going to cut?"

Ruthie and I stared at each other, dazed and worried.

A few minutes later I made my decision.

"Tell Mary her two songs will air. But between you and me, Ruthie, I'll still cut one in the editing room if I have to."

"I can't tell Mary that!" snapped Ruthie Goldberg. "In all the time I've known you, you've never gone back on your word. You and I have made deals with talent strictly on your word alone, no contracts, nothing. Everybody in the business knows your word's as good as a signed contract. I'm not going to help damage that reputation. If you promise Mary Travers both her songs will air, then both her songs will air. Don't make me promise her something you know isn't true."

I made Ruthie do it.

I met Mary Travers that night, after she arrived in Los Angeles. We had a bite to eat in her hotel room. She read me some poetry that I thought was quite nice. I told her stories that made her laugh. I think we liked each other. At least that night we did.

Mary's second song never made it to the final edit, and Mary and I never spoke to each other again. Years later I stood right behind her in a movie line. The two of us moved along as if we were perfect strangers. The funny thing is, I never regretted doing what I did to Mary Travers. I always figured she tried sticking it to me first, and in a really cheap way.

But Ruthie never forgave me.

Cass and I promised to continue seeing each other after the special.

I wanted to, but lots of things were happening then and I ended up canceling most of our dates. One night, fed up, Mama Cass got a bucket of paint, a paintbrush, and a ladder, and painted *Do You Think Chuck Barris Is Ever Going To Show Up?* in big red letters across the living-room wall over her fireplace. The sad thing is, I always enjoyed the nights we did go out together.

At some point in our friendship, Cass had to go to England for a week. The night before she left, we had dinner at the Steak Pit restaurant on Melrose. We sat in a booth by ourselves. I held her sweaty hand while Cass tried to talk me into going with her. I told her I couldn't, I had too much work to do. She was disappointed. To soften her dashed hopes she suggested that after dinner we go back to her place and make love. When I said no, she became upset. "Why don't you want to screw me? Because I'm too fat? Do I gross you out? Do I disgust you?"

I begged her not to say things like that.

"Then what's the problem?"

I told Cass we were friends,

"Friends fuck."

I shrugged.

"I'll give you a blow job. I give the best head in the whole entire world. I have to give good head to get guys to fuck me. You'll see. I'll give you head and you'll be so happy and so surprised, you'll want to fuck me immediately. Real bad. But I won't let you. I'll make you suffer. What do you say? A little head at my place after dinner?"

I begged off saying I was beat.

"You're some fucking piece of work," she said, depressed.

"We'll make love when you come back. I'll meet you at the airport and we'll go right to bed."

"You promise?"

I said, "I promise," and crossed my heart. "As soon as you come back."

But Cass never came back. She choked to death on something she ate a few nights later in her London hotel room.

"What was she like?" repeats Henri Bruni, turning around in the back of *Bam Bam* to face the sun. "Tell me about Mama Cass."

"No, Henri," I say, pulling up my fishing line; no fish on the hook, not even the worm, "there's nothing to tell."

CHAPTER THIRTY-TWO

Gigi's a retired fisherman; a little guy, less than five feet tall, but stocky. Gigi's in his late fifties. Since giving up fishing, Gigi spends his time smoking and drinking, reading the newspapers, kibitzing with the other fishermen. A cigarette's always in his mouth, a glass of beer or wine always in his hand, a baseball cap always on his head. In the forty years I've been coming to Saint-Tropez, I've only seen Gigi without his baseball cap once. It was then I realized that Gigi's bald, and ashamed of it. Though Gigi drinks a lot, I've never seen him drunk. But since he drinks and drives a motor scooter, he's constantly bandaged or discolored by mercurochrome from the falls he takes. I like Gigi. The reason I'm so fond of him is because whenever we see each other, he grins and gives me a big hug. We can be apart for years or hours, I still get the grin and the hug. So this morning I'm not surprised when I walk into the Gorille for my coffee, see Gigi, and receive his infectiously happy greeting. I hug the little guy back and ask him how he is.

"*Bien!*" he says with gusto. I am well.

We hug again and Gigi leaves. He walks out the door of the Gorille, lurches forward, crashes through two chairs, knocks over a table and falls on his face on the filthy, wet ground. Gigi's head's resting on his left cheek. His forehead is scraped and bleeding. His baseball cap is nearby upside down, his bald head exposed. His right eye is open wide.

I stand in a small semicircle of people looking down at Gigi, waiting for the SOS medical car to arrive. I stare at Gigi's open right eye. I'm suddenly reminded of the lady on *Treasure Hunt*. What a bizarre memory to dredge up at a time like this.

* * *

Treasure Hunt was one of my game shows that was on day and night in over a hundred and fifty cities for two years.

On the program, a lady contestant won the right to select a large gift box from twenty-five that were on stage. Inside one of those boxes was a check for twenty-five thousand dollars. In the other boxes were prizes that ranged from a new car or sailboat down to a pair of wind-up chattering false teeth.

Before the lady was allowed to open the box to see what was inside, she was given a choice. The program's quasi-sadistic host, Geoff Edwards, would say, "Do you want this five thousand dollars that came with the box you selected"—at which point he would count out fifty one-hundred dollar bills and place the bills in the woman's hand—"or give me the money back and take your chances on whatever may be in that box?"

While the audience howled, "Take the money!" or "Take the box!" the woman stood there holding five thousand dollars cash in her sweaty palm agonizing over what to do. If the lady took the money and not the box, our host would open the box and show her what she missed, which might have been the twenty-five thousand dollars. If she chose the box and not the money, our host would open the box and show her what she actually won—but not before the lady was subjected to a series of misleading teases and stunts that left her completely bonkers. This was the heart of the show: the emotional roller-coaster ride the program's writers inflicted on these women. In the end the ladies were always left drained and exhausted, but happy. What the hell, even a pair of wind-up false teeth and some complimentary gifts were more than the woman had when she arrived; plus—and perhaps most important—her moment on coast-to-coast television, her fifteen minutes of stardom. Believe me, contestants never regretted their day on *Treasure Hunt*. At least I didn't think they did.

A perfect example was Mrs. Ivy Flotsam.

The irony of it all was that Mrs. Flotsam never intended to be a contestant on *Treasure Hunt*. She drove by the ABC television studios at Prospect and Talmadge avenues in Hollywood by mistake. She didn't intend to take that route home, but a road construction detour sent Mrs. Flotsam past the studio's gates just in time for her to see the line of prospective *Treasure Hunt* contestants forming. On a spur-of-the-moment whim, Ivy Flotsam parked her car and joined the line.

"What the hell have I got better to do?" she asked an ABC guide.

The ABC guide said nothing. He didn't feel an answer was required.

No one was more surprised than Mrs. Ivy Flotsam when she found herself shouting as loud, or maybe even louder, than most of the other two hundred women waiting in line, hoping to attract the attention of the program's beady-eyed producers. The producers were walking back and forth checking the women out, searching for animation, hypertension, groveling wide-eyed screamers; the characteristics of the perfect *Treasure Hunt* contestant. And who do you suppose had those qualities and therefore was one of the lucky six ladies chosen to appear on the program that day? Ivy Flotsam, of course.

All of a sudden there she was, the good Mrs. Flotsam—wearing her little yellow blouse with the dirty bra strap hanging down her right arm, her flowered Bermuda shorts tucked neatly into her ass— standing right next to the show's master of ceremonies, Geoff Edwards. Mrs. Flotsam's little palms were pressed together in front of her nose praying she'd be a *Treasure Hunt* winner. While watching her pray, I wondered about the state of Mrs. Flotsam's health. I couldn't help but notice her blotchy red face and odd body movements. I began to wonder if our lady contestants should have physicals before being selected to go on the program. Were we being lax about something that could come back and haunt us?

Add to all of this the sadistic nature of our host Geoff Edwards. True, I had instructed Edwards to milk all the suspense he could when revealing the contents—good or bad—contained in the gift boxes. I not only demanded he do this, I trained him, filling Edwards with all of the tricks I had learned over the years on how to drive a contestant nuts. I must admit Mr. Edwards improved on my teaching to the point where the student surpassed the master. The longer the show was on the air, the more fiendish Edwards became. I had created a sick character. Unfortunately it was too late that afternoon to do anything about contestant physicals and a zealous host. And while my mind was ruminating about all of this, guess who managed to slither through the program's obstacles and emerge a winner? Mrs. Ivy Flotsam, of course.

Mrs. Flotsam couldn't believe her good fortune. She jumped up and down with joy, clapping her hands, kissing the cruel Edwards, crying, laughing, the works. Eventually she settled down to a reasonable anxiety level just in time to watch our host lift the gift box lid and shout, with eardrum-blasting intensity, "Guess what, Mrs. Flotsam?"

"What?" whispered Mrs. Flotsam.

"You have just won . . . twenty . . . five . . . thousand . . ."

Mrs. Ivy Flotsam went weak in the knees. I was convinced she was going to pass out. Or worse, suffer a fatal heart attack. Right on our stage. In front of twenty million viewers across the United States.

". . . *coffee beans!*" shouted our demented host.

"Coffee beans?" mouthed the wobbly and confused woman.

"That's right, Mrs. Flotsam," continued yelling host Edwards, "you've won twenty-five thousand coffee beans! Aren't you thrilled? Here they are in these six packages. And that's not all, Mrs. Flotsam, no sireee, that's not all. You're going to put those coffee beans in something else. That's right, another gift. Can you guess what that something else might be?"

The good Mrs. Flotsam, in her yellow blouse, dirty bra strap, and Bermuda shorts, had no idea. All she could do was stand there and allow her blood pressure to soar, her movements to become more spastic. She stared at the floor, her lips silently repeating over and over again: What might that be? What might that be? What might that be?

My heart began beating faster too, a warning that danger was in the air. I tried willing my sadistic host to cool it. Couldn't he see we had a potential hospital case on our hands? It seemed obvious. But apparently not to Mr. Edwards. He just couldn't wait to say, "You've also won a brand new . . . automatic . . ." and then yell with unctuous joy, "*coffee grinder!*"

Mrs. Flotsam, who had been happily soaring through the stratosphere with joy and expectation, zigzagged back to earth like a punctured balloon. Her extreme sadness and disappointment were obvious. A coffee grinder? Not a new car, or a camper, or something expensive? And then our infamous host, looking once again into the box, said, "Wait a minute, Mrs. Flotsam! You've won something else!"

Once again the studio was electric with excitement, to say nothing of the distraught Mrs. Flotsam.

"Mrs. Ivy Flotsam," said Edwards, starting slowly then picking up steam, you've won . . . your very own . . ."—again the required heart-palpitating pause—*"picnic basket!"*

"A *what?*" said Mrs. Flotsam, more annoyed than inquisitive.

"That's right," boomed Edwards, "a picnic basket to put the coffee and coffee grinder in!"

Big deal, was the now somewhat hardened Mrs. Flotsam's attitude. She stood silently gazing at nothing discernible, wishing she could get the hell off the stage. She was obviously the butt of this never-ending joke which she could certainly do without, thank you very much.

Our host put the bags of coffee beans and coffee grinder into the picnic basket, and the picnic basket into Mrs. Ivy Flotsam's arms. He congratulated her for being a winner and waved good-bye. It was a mauled and beaten Mrs. Flotsam who headed back to her seat in the audience.

She hadn't gone far when Edwards hollered yet again, "Mrs. Flotsam! Mrs. Flotsam!"

Mrs. Flotsam slowly stopped walking, slowly turned to face Edwards, slowly lifted her chin, slowly squared her shoulders.

"Yes," she said.

Poor Mrs. Flotsam, damp and exasperated, her yellow blouse, bra strap, and flowered Bermuda shorts hanging wet and wrinkled on her bent and worn-out body, grimacing as she struggled to hold the heavy picnic basket filled with twenty-five thousand coffee beans. The last thing Mrs. Flotsam needed now was the embarrassment of dropping the heavy picnic basket and spilling twenty-five thousand coffee beans on the studio floor.

"Mrs. Flotsam," said our malevolent host, "why don't you put that picnic basket down somewhere? You don't know where to put it? Well, why don't you try putting it down . . . in the back of your . . . *1960 classic Rolls-Royce!*"

That's when Ivy Flotsam went down for the count.

CHAPTER THIRTY-THREE

First her eyes rolled to the back of her head. Then her chin dropped into her chest. Then she pitched forward without bending an arm or a leg, like a tree chopped down at its base, landing stiff as a board, facedown on the floor. Dust puffed up on both sides of her after the crash, and then settled. Ivy Flotsam's head rested on its left side. One eye was open, staring, not blinking.

"Oh my God," wailed my director. "We've pushed it too far." And then he shouted, "Cameras break for the audience! Cameras break for the audience! Find me happiness!"

Off went the cameramen—jerking the television cameras backward, turning them, then pushing them forward—scurrying around, looking for something cheerful—a smiling face, a joyful kid, a young couple in love. My director was quick to discover that mirth and gaiety seldom pal around with sudden death. Everywhere the cameramen focused they found shock and wonder: gaping mouths, wide eyes, fingers and palms pressed against cheeks, hands hiding faces distorted in confusion and disbelief. The director finally settled for people's shoes.

Me? Well, I had a million questions. Was a death on the show good for the ratings, or bad? Would it be a first, or had it been done before? Would this macabre event secure a renewal for the show or send us packing? While all of these scenarios were running through my head, Mrs. Ivy Flotsam's unblinking right eye was staring at me from the wall monitor of camera #2.

And then—just like that—Mrs. Flotsam jumped sprightly to her feet.

She obviously hadn't died. She had only fainted. Taken respite on our stage floor. Now refreshed, Ivy Flotsam was ready to hear about her classic Rolls-Royce.

"It's been said," said Mike Wallace many months later, when he interviewed me on *60 Minutes,* "that you revel in your ability to degrade and make fools of the contestants on your game shows."

"I don't think that's true at all, Mike."

"No? You can sit there and tell me with a perfectly straight face that you do not purposely humiliate your contestants? Or go out of your way to demean them?"

"Absolutely not. If these people knew they were going to be humiliated or made fun of, why would they be contestants in the first place?"

"I don't know. You tell me why."

"Because they want to. Nobody has a gun to their heads telling them they must come. The contestants on our shows come because they have a good time. If we intended to embarrass them, they'd know it and never show up for auditions. I don't think anybody wants to knowingly be embarrassed. I believe game show contestants want to be seen on television. They want their families to cheer for them, and everyone at the office or at the factory to say, 'Hey I saw you last night on TV.' It's their chance to break away, if only for a moment or two, from their ordinary lives. These people don't take participating on a game show as seriously as you think they do, Mike. It's not a big sociological thing. They just want to have some fun."

"Hmmmm" went Mr. Wallace.

His hmmmm bothered me. I didn't know what it meant.

"I understand," said Wallace, "that you and your staff put a woman through such an emotional wringer that she collapsed on stage. Is that true?"

"Collapse sounds harsh, Mike. I'd say she fainted."

"Collapse, fainted. Neither sounds like a lot of fun to me."

"Well, first of all," I said, shifting in my chair to make myself more comfortable and sorry I did, worrying that my nervous wriggling was making me appear guilty, "the lady you're talking about. . . ."

"Flotsam. Mrs. Ivy Flotsam."

"Right, Ivy Flotsam . . . a good example, Mike. If I remember correctly, the lady won an automobile. A Rolls-Royce. As a matter of fact, that's what made her faint, hearing she had won a Rolls-Royce."

"I saw the tape of that show. I got the feeling she was an emotional basket case from all the torture you put her through before she heard about the Rolls."

"I wouldn't call that torture . . ."

"Then what would you call it?"

I wriggled in my seat.

Wallace said, "In your heart of hearts did you think Mrs. Flotsam was having a good time before she fainted?"

"Absolutely," I answered confidently. "If you went out to that lady's house and asked her if she had fun on our show, I guarantee you she'd say yes. I'll bet you anything you want, Mike, Mrs. Flotsam would say she had the time of her life that night."

Six months later I saw Mike Wallace again, this time on television talking to me.

I caught the program in a Boston hotel room. I was touring the country for something, a book, a record, a TV show, I can't remember which. I was all alone in this big depressing suite, sitting in an armchair facing the TV set nervously playing with a salad that room service had just brought me on a rolling table. There I was on the tube saying: "I'll bet you anything you want, Mike, Mrs. Flotsam would say she had the time of her life that night."

And Mike saying to the television camera, "So we took our *60 Minutes* crew and went out to visit Mrs. Ivy Flotsam in her tidy little row house in Pasadena, California."

I dropped my fork.

There was Mrs. Ivy Flotsam, sitting on her ratty old couch, wearing (I swear to God) the same yellow blouse with the same dirty bra strap hanging down her right arm, and the same flowered Bermuda shorts. Ivy smiling at Mike, concentrating very hard on what he was saying.

"I saw the tape of that show," said Wallace to Mrs. Flotsam, "and when you fainted you went down like a felled tree."

"I sure did," giggled Mrs. Flotsam, embarrassed.

"You were on the floor quite a while."

"Yes I was."

"Well, Mrs. Flotsam, how exactly did you feel about your experience on *Treasure Hunt?* Was it a happy experience or were you sorry you ever saw the inside of that television studio?"

I held my breath, my heart beating like a drum.

"Are you kidding, Mike?" said the perky little woman. "I had the time of my life that night. I'll never forget it as long as I live."

The next day I sent Ivy Flotsam a magnum of champagne and two dozen long-stemmed roses. There was a card attached that simply said: From a fan.

Gigi's dead before the SOS ambulance arrives at the Gorille.

A week later Henri tells me no one has gone to the morgue to claim Gigi's body. I go. I make arrangements to have Gigi cremated. I'm given three choices of burial jars: expensive, not so expensive, cheap. I pick not so expensive. The next day I fetch Gigi's ashes from the mortuary and take him to *Bam Bam.* I drive *Bam Bam* out to sea in the direction of Corsica. An hour from Saint-Tropez I stop and pour Gigi into the Mediterranean. Then I drop the burial jar over the side. It sinks immediately. It has disappeared from earth never to be seen again, just like Gigi.

I sit in *Bam Bam* for an hour and think about all of this, about the meaning of a life like mine, and Gigi's—a guy who, on eternity's ledger, was an invisible person, a zero. The one thing I never wanted to be was invisible. I worked hard not to be a zero, to be somebody. I did what I wanted to do, I did it my way, with integrity, and never over someone else's dead body. Now I'm reaping the rewards. So why not sit back and savor the success I achieved instead of berating myself for not being more than I already am? Gigi wouldn't have castigated himself? Maybe that's what fascinated me about the man, his philosophy—the Tropezien philosophy: Happy to have been given the blessing of life, thankful to have more good days a week than bad, thoroughly enjoying the rewards that come your way, hoping to be around for as long as possible, knowing in the scheme of things you're probably a zero yet never feeling contrite about it. And why should they feel contrite? In the last analysis isn't it all a big so what? A case of who cares? Colin Dexter wrote: "Nothing matters very much and in the end nothing really matters at all."

* * *

The sun is up now.

It is going to be a beautiful day. I am reminded of a Russian saying: The morning is wiser than the evening. I fire up *Bam Bam*'s engines and go back to Saint-Tropez.

CHAPTER THIRTY-FOUR

We own two houses in Saint-Tropez.

Decadent, to say the least, more so in that they're ten minutes apart. Do you really need two houses in one small town? No, not really. Then why not sell one? Hard to explain.

We became involved with the first house the summer we arrived in Saint-Tropez. We rented it to see what the expatriate life would be like. The owner of the house was a nasty mean-spirited millionaire builder named Giancarlo Verdi. He's still nasty, a bigot with pockmarked cheeks, a bent nose, and a long face; a cross between Manuel Noriega and Sea Biscuit. The repulsive man loves money so much he stutters when he talks about it.

Giancarlo Verdi had constructed his home in the vineyards for himself and his wife. The two planned to live in the house for the rest of their days. Consequently Verdi selected a superb location and built the house using the best materials available. It's a beautiful big rambling home made of stone and wood. It has a comfortable master bedroom and bath, two snug guest rooms, large spacious living and dining rooms, and a cozy kitchen. There's a vineyard on one side and a forest on the other with views of the Mediterranean to the east and the ancient hill town of Ramatuelle to the west. Verdi and his wife decided to return to Italy for a few years. They planned to rent the house while they were gone. Red and I were the only couple, other than Giancarlo and his wife, to live in it.

We loved the house but detested the abominable Verdi, his mongrel dog—a big black cur that had a humped back and sores and loved to bite little children—and his dense and evil caretakers Joseph and Josette Lupere. The couple reminded me of two famous literary characters: Lenny (*of Mice and Men*) and Mrs. Danvers (of

Rebecca). Joseph and Josette lived in the guardian's cottage on the property. Joseph was a huge lout of forty some years, strangely good-looking, with the mind of a pea. I can safely say Joseph was perhaps the most rancid-smelling person on the Côte d'Azure. When holding a conversation with the oaf you had to stand at least five feet away. Josette, his sinister wife, was roughly her husband's age with a thin face, a pointy nose, rat eyes, and a malicious smile.

Also aggravating to me was the house's name. In Ramatuelle, the wine country above Saint-Tropez where the home is located, there are no addresses such as 123 Oak Street. Your address is the name of your house: Le Bastide Blanch, Les Biche Niche, Les Arbors, La Bignole, Tailla. That's what the mailman goes by when he delivers his mail. Some of the names I can handle. Others make me gag, like the one Verdi chose for his house.

Holy Mother of the Vines.

The name was burned into a large wooden sign. The sign was embedded in the earth on the road near the entrance to our drive-way. I despised the name Holy Mother of the Vines almost as much as Verdi, the child-molesting dog, and the dull-witted guardians. Every time I turned into my driveway I felt as if I was entering a monastery. I asked Verdi if I could replace his guardians, get rid of the dog, and change the name of the house, albeit temporarily.

He said, "Absolutely not."

Two years later, Verdi came by to announce that he and his wife were filing for divorce, that he was moving to a smaller home near his favorite golf course not far away in St. Maxime, and that his wife was going to remain in Rome. Since neither he nor his wife had any intentions of living in the big house alone, Verdi had decided to sell it. He offered us the first opportunity to buy Holy Mother of the Vines. Red and I were excited. We had grown accustomed to being in the hills, had always considered it "our house." (We lived in it longer than Verdi had.) And so the negotiations began.

Actually it wasn't a negotiation, it was a war. The battle pitted a tough, squat bully from the rough slums of Milan against a tough, squat hustler from the mean streets of south Philadelphia. The war raged for almost a year and a half. During that time my rent doubled and my gas and electric bills soared, while Verdi's wooden Holy Mother of the Vines sign and his mongrel mysteriously disappeared.

Rumor had it that the sign and the dog were last seen in the sea floating toward Corsica.

Now I must digress.

One morning—in the middle of all this—while having my coffee at the Gorille, I looked out the door and noticed my friend Moineau Mercurio trying to get my attention. Moineau was sitting on his motorcycle wearing a surplus World War II US Army jacket and a Baltimore Oriole baseball cap with a snakeskin brim. Moineau was motioning to me to join him on the rear of his bike. The word around town is: If Moineau Mercurio beckons, you'd better go because there's always a good reason why Moineau's beckoning. So I finished my coffee toot sweet, climbed aboard Moineau's motorcycle, and we took off.

We rode up and down the narrow streets of the village, turning right and then left and then right again, coming to a stop in a part of town called the Old Port. We were idling by a small house that faced the sea. Moineau Mercurio patted the house's side. "It's for sale," he said.

Houses are rarely for sale in the Old Port. They're simply handed down from generation to generation. You have to know a local to hear about a house on the market in this section of Saint-Tropez. Everything here is a landmark. No facades can ever be changed. Its inhabitants—sailors, fishermen, artisans, artists, and writers—are an introverted collection of isolationists. They protect their old-world neighborhood against foreign encroachers with fierce expressions and frigid shoulders.

"I'll buy it," I told Moineau.

"Are you crazy?" said Red when I explained to her what I had done. "What are we going to do with two houses?"

"What if the negotiations on the big house in the vineyards fall through?" I asked. "And they very well might. That bastard Verdi is tough. If the negotiations do collapse at least we won't be shut out of Saint-Tropez. We'll still be able to live in the little house I just bought. And if we do end up getting the big house, we can always sell the little one in the port. Houses in the Old Port are hard to come by. I'm sure we'll be able to get our money back. Besides, when you see the little house, you'll love it."

When Red saw the little house, she hated it.

I couldn't blame her. It was truly horrible inside. My new acquisition was three hundred years old and looked it. It had fifteen very small rooms on three small floors, and a total of two tiny windows. Electric wires, broken pipes, and hunks of molding hung from the ceilings. Anything dependent on hinges had either fallen from them, or were about to. Paint was peeling off all the walls and stray cats stared down at us from filthy nooks and crannies. Red cried.

The French architect who accompanied us, a little guy named Roger Herrera, ignored my sobbing wife and continued his exploration of the ancient dump. When he finished, he turned to Red and said, "With your help, I can make this into an incredible love nest."

That's all Red had to hear. Roger had said two magic words. Love and nest. She stopped crying.

A month later we gutted the place. All that was left of the structure were its four thick stone walls. The Redhead, with the help of the architect, slowly put the house back together again—only this time her way. Instead of fifteen little ratty holes, there was going to be one master bedroom and bath on the third floor, one office-studio and bath for me on the second floor, one living room, one dining room, and a state-of-the-art kitchen on the first floor, a bunch of fireplaces and lots of windows. Red's desire to make our small home cozy went from dedication to passion, from passion to a manic fixation. She thought about the house twenty-four hours a day. She left home and traveled far and wide throughout France and England seeking unusual furnishings and antiques. When my wife found what she was looking for, she returned to Saint-Tropez puffed up with the thrill of discovery as though she were Thomas Edison.

"Isn't it wonderful," said Red when the jail door she exhumed in Marseilles was installed in our downstairs bathroom. My wife looked through the door's latched peephole the guards employed to check the prisoner inside and said, "We can always open this to see if the toilet's available."

I agreed the peephole was wonderful. I also wondered how a guest would feel if she noticed someone's eyeball watching her while she peed.

And the wonderful stone baptism basin we use as a sink that my wife rescued from a condemned church in Lyon. And the shutters from Dijon, the miniature pillars from Chartres, the wood ceiling beams from Orléans, the cozy couches and armchairs from all sorts of flea markets, warm drapes and curtains from Paris, hat racks and andirons from London, the oak shelves filled with books, the thick rugs, the stereo systems spewing Mozart and Van Morrison, the five fireplaces, and the large shuttered windows that overlook Place Henry Pearson and the sea. The little house is a gem. It's our love nest. How could we sell it to anyone else?

Meanwhile, the deadly negotiations over the big house were coming to an end. Giancarlo Verdi and I had inflicted upon each other everything but public death threats. Now, tired and spent, we devised an uneasy peace. We had an agreement and it was time to sign. All the responsible parties and their seconds gathered at a notary's office. Verdi was there first. I came last.

I walked into the room and said, "The deal's off."

Verdi went deathly pale. He actually staggered backward one or two steps.

Then I quickly added, "April fool!" even though it was mid-January.

No one laughed. They were too busy watching Giancarlo Verdi. It appeared he might be on the crest of a massive heart attack. Giving Verdi a coronary wasn't the point of my jest. (Technically the deal would have fallen through if Verdi had died.) I just wanted to leave the contemptible sod with one last jolt to remember me by. As it turned out, all that Verdi suffered was a painful stab of anxiety.

An hour after the house was legally ours I fired Verdi's revolting guardians, Lenny and Mrs. Danvers, and changed the name of the place from Holy Mother of the Vines to Maison Très Cher, which means Very Expensive House. I'm glad that war's behind us and I'm glad we won. Red and I would have hated to lose our home in the hills.

So do we really need two houses in one place ten minutes apart? Not really. Then why don't we sell one?

Which one?

I tell my right-hand man, Michael (pronounced Mee-SHELL) Allard, I want to improve the grounds around Très Cher.

Allard sets up a meeting for us with a lawn specialist. Red explains to the lawn specialist what we would like to see happen: a few more trees here, a bush or two there, some wildflowers in the front, some roses and tulips in the back . . . don't go crazy, just spruce it up a little. The lawn specialist nods his head knowingly and says he'll take care of everything. We go to Paris for two days and return home to find our entire sprinkler system—all these long muddy rubber tubes —stacked up one atop the other in our driveway. I can't believe my eyes.

"Why?" I ask the lawn specialist.

"Because it is an old system."

The lawn specialist is wearing the customary light-blue jumpsuit most working men wear in France. He's big and bald. The little hair that remains has been cut close to the sides of his head by an electric shaver. To make up for his shiny dome, he sports a ridiculously large mustache with waxed, circular tips like Salvador Dali. There's a prominent wart between his eyebrows. I wonder why the lawn specialist hasn't had it removed.

"Couldn't you have asked us whether we wanted our old sprinkler system torn out of the earth before you tore it out of the earth?"

"We had to see for ourselves."

"See what?"

"Whether it was an old system."

"Well, put it back."

"I cannot."

"Why not?"

"That's someone else's job," says the lawn specialist, the smoke from his dangling cigarette closing his left eye.

"What do you mean, someone else's job?"

"We don't install old sprinkler systems," he replies, smiling. "Just new ones." The lawn specialist thinks he has just said something funny.

I consider kneeing the man in his balls, and, when he bends over in agony, breaking his forehead with the iron *boule* ball I hold in my hand.

"And how much will a new sprinkler system cost to install?"

"One hundred and fifty thousand francs."

"Thirty thousand dollars! Are you out of your mind?"

The lawn specialist shrugs.

I turn once again to my right-hand man Michael Allard. Allard is the young bilingual Frenchman I employ to secure my best interests in all matters—personal or business—that take place in Saint-Tropez. I ask Michael Allard in English what he thinks about this bozo ripping out my sprinkler system and then charging me to put it back.

Allard shrugs his shoulders and says, "It's the way the French do business."

Unfortunately it's difficult for Michael Allard to maintain total loyalty. Michael is going to receive a kickback from the lawn specialist for suggesting him to me. That, too, is the way the French do business.

Not long after work ends on the sprinklers, we need something else. We need a new pipe connected to the city sewer system. Our pipe is apparently old, carotid, and ineffectual; brown water is backing up into our sinks and showers. This means I must deal with another contractor: a pipe specialist.

"How much for the new pipe?" I ask the pipe specialist. He's a thin and nervous little man, and wears rimless spectacles. The pipe specialist could very well be a serial killer.

"Forty thousand francs."

"How much?"

"Forty thousand francs."

"Forty thousand francs!"

"Yes, forty thousand francs."

"Eight thousand dollars for a new pipe! Isn't that a lot of money for one pipe?"

The pipe specialist shrugs his shoulders.

The French love to shrug their shoulders. If they're not shrugging their shoulders they're saying Oooh-la-la, or making that tsk tsk tsk sound with their tongues while waving their forefingers in your face as though you were a three-year-old. The French have perfected the art of tsking. They do the loudest tsks of any nationality in the world. A French sports announcer on television never describes the action. He just tsks. If a player makes a great shot, the announcer tsks in awe. If a player is injured, he tsks grievously. If the player does something stupid, the announcer makes his tsks sound like a reprimand. Occasionally if someone does something incredible, good or bad, the announcer may do serious tsking and then switch to a singsong Oooh la la. Otherwise it's dead air.

I ask the pipe specialist how long it will take to put in a new pipe.

"One week."

"Is it a big job?"

"No."

"Okay, do it," I say and walk away, knowing doom is just around the corner.

Two days later the front of our property resembles the construction site of Saint-Tropez's future municipal airport. Excavation machines and earth movers abound. The ground is in turmoil. Workers lie everywhere, eating and sleeping, burying their garbage under the flowers, eyeing the house in an effort to determine the best way to break and enter when we leave town.

"I thought you said this wasn't going to be a big job," I tell the pipe specialist.

"It isn't. You should see a big job." He smiles showing me his yellow teeth.

Three days later the pipe specialist informs me his work will cost sixty thousand francs, not forty thousand, and take a week longer than he first anticipated.

"Why?" I ask, my resistance ebbing, sweat beading on my forehead.

"Because we find new problems."

"How come you discover these problems now and not when you first made your estimate?"

He doesn't answer. He just shrugs.

"What happens if I don't agree to this extra money?"

"We leave."

"And my torn-up ground?"

He shrugs again.

I want to hit the pipe specialist so hard, the blow will kill three members of his family.

"I don't believe this," I say to my right-hand man, Michael Allard, who will receive five percent of the pipe specialist's fee. Michael and I have walked off to the side so we can talk in private. "Can you explain, Michael, why this creep with the yellow teeth estimated it would cost forty thousand francs before he did the work and then, when everything's all torn up, tells me it's going to cost sixty thousand francs and take a week longer?"

"It's the way the French do business," replies Allard. "You don't have to do it if you don't want to."

"But I do have to do it. If I don't, I'll bathe in mud and my grounds will look like a war zone. Is there another pipe specialist?"

"No. He is the only pipe specialist in Saint-Tropez."

"Where do I have to go to find another pipe specialist?"

"Paris."

Although there's nothing to think about, I tell the pipe specialist I will think about it.

The pipe specialist smiles and leaves. He goes into my garage where he plugs a small electric stove into a wall socket. He takes various condiments and utensils from his sack, and proceeds to cook himself a veal chop and lima beans on a small frying pan. The way he cooks, the smells that filter out of my garage from his grilling veal chop and sizzling lima beans makes me ravenous. When everything's ready, the pipe specialist takes his meal to the front lawn. He sits in the shade of one of my trees and eats with delicate movements. The pipe specialist drinks an entire bottle of red wine and wipes his plate clean with his last piece of fresh bread. He sleeps for twenty minutes, then comes to me and says, "Well?"

I tell the pipe specialist, "Put in the new pipe," but my mind is elsewhere. I am planning his murder. Killing him is the easy part. Getting rid of the body is something else entirely. That will be difficult.

It always is.

CHAPTER THIRTY-FIVE

"Hello. Paul Corrigan," says Paul Corrigan on the other end of the telephone. "I'm with *Variety*." *Variety* is the show business trade paper. "I'm here in Cannes. At the film festival. Just wondered if it was possible to come to Saint-Tropez and have a few words with you?"

"About what?" I ask.

"About what? About what you've been doing with yourself since you retired."

I hate the word *retired*. It connotes senior citizenry, walkers, park benches, leaky orifices, Florida, old age, death. "I'm not retired."

"Oh," says Paul Corrigan, the word filled with wonder.

"I've been writing."

"Writing what? Never mind. We can talk about that when we see each other."

"I don't think so, I have . . ."

"Promise I won't take up too much of your time. Just want to find out how and why the man with the golden touch . . ."

"Golden touch?"

"Why, of course. Didn't everything you create turn to gold?"

"No."

"No? Name one game show you thought up that didn't." *People Poker* was the first show I ever created. Even before the *Dating Game.*

The reason I never mention it is because I wasn't out on my own. I was still working for the American Broadcasting Company. I developed the program not long after I arrived in Hollywood to become the Duke of Daytime. I had asked permission from the network Powers That Be to allow me to produce a television game show "in house," meaning within the company. That way we would save all those royalties and production fees we paid outside game show creators. I never knew why they hadn't done that before, and said so. The Powers That Be agreed and I went to work on my first creation.

People Poker was a simple idea. I put sixteen people on the stage: five female hookers, five female surgeons, and five policewomen. The sixteenth person was a "Joker." Her vocation would be on the odd side. One would never be able to guess what the Joker did for a living. But if you chose the Joker you could use her as one of your hookers, surgeons, or policewomen. The contestants were allowed one question before making their choice. If one was searching for a doctor, the contestant might ask: How many pints of blood in the human body? (Clearly a doctor would know the answer.) The object of the game was to select a better poker hand from the bunch than your opponent. Three surgeons and two policewomen were better than two hookers and two surgeons.

I filmed the game show at the ABC-TV affiliate in San Francisco. The local contestant procurer, associate producer, set designer, and director had never done anything for the network before. It was a wonderful opportunity for them, and for me. We could all come out heroes on this one. Maybe a move to Hollywood for them, a promotion for me. As it turned out it was lucky none of us were fired.

The show was a catastrophe.

From that cataclysm came three important lessons that would stand me well in the future. One lesson was never to rely on your staff. Rely on yourself. Make sure you check and recheck all the details—large and small—satisfied in the end that everything is to your liking and no one else's. Lesson number two was to memorize the following sentence: It's all in the preproduction. Every one of your problems must be thought out and solved *before* you enter the studio to film the show. Any difficulties that haven't been resolved by then will wreak havoc. And finally, allow yourself plenty of time in the studio to fix things.

On *People Poker* I took my contestant booker's word that the hookers, surgeons, and policewomen would never be a problem. I assumed the set designer and the director knew what they were talking about when they placed the contestants as far away from the cameras as they did. I accepted as gospel my associate producer's

estimates regarding the time we would have in the studio to re-
hearse and tape the sample program as being sufficient. So it
shouldn't have come as a surprise when I went into the control room
to see how everything looked on the monitors and became stricken
with a thick nausea.

The people were so far away from the cameras you could hardly
see their faces, let alone guess their occupation. "Move in closer!" I
shouted to the inexperienced director. His immediate reaction was
to go rigid. My tone of voice coupled with the changing situation
was too much for the frightened man. He was reduced to mumbling,
"Move where?" into the palms of his hands over and over again.
"Move where? Move where?"

And then the fight broke out.

Between the hookers and the policewomen.

The lady cops just realized some of the other women on stage had
warrants out for their arrest.

"I thought you said we wouldn't have any problems with the
policewomen and the hookers," I said to the contestant getter.

"We won't," the woman replied as a hooker hit a policewomen in
the face with her purse, knocking the cop off the platform and onto
the floor.

"Tighten up on that policewoman on the floor," I yelled to my
director.

"Tighten?" he asked his palms. "Tighten where? Tighten where?"

I turned to my associate producer. "We've got to stop," I said.
"We've got to start again."

"We don't have enough time to do that," he replied brightly,
proud to have an immediate answer to any questions I might ask.

I left the studio in midshow, and then the television station. I
walked across the street to a bar and ordered a scotch and soda with
a lot of ice. I drank seven of them and spent the night sleeping at the
airport, waiting for the first plane to Los Angeles. I had to resign
from the American Broadcasting company before I would ever be
able to sell them another game show.

"People Poker?" said Paul Corrigan, on the telephone from Cannes.
"Never heard of it."

"I hope not."

"Listen, we have a little thing we do at *Variety*, a where-are-they-now column? There's a lot of interest in people wanting to know what's become of you."

"Is that right?"

"Yeah. A lot of people think you're dead."

CHAPTER THIRTY-SIX

My wife develops a pain in her back, down near her right kidney. I secretly think it might be a scary problem. Red's had trouble before with a damaged fallopian tube. The symptoms are similar. I'm sure my wife is thinking the same thing. After a few days the pain disappears. We write it off to a pulled back muscle. I'm relieved to know my private fears were unfounded.

And then one evening the pain returns, this time more intense. Red lies awake the entire night suffering. In the morning the pain has become unbearable. Teetee and I drive Red to the hospital. She's taken into a room where a doctor examines her. As I've said before, I can't speak decent French, especially under pressure. The French doctor cannot speak English. Teetee is our translator. She tells me the doctor says Red is suffering from appendicitis.

The doctor's full of shit.

I tell Teetee to tell the doctor he's wrong. "Tell him my wife and I have been through this before. Tell him she's had fallopian tube problems in the past with this exact kind of pain. Tell him it's either a tubular pregnancy or one of her tubes has torqued. Just tell him that."

Teetee tells him that. They talk back and forth for an eternity. Meanwhile, Red is lying on a spare hospital bed in the fetal position, writhing in agony. Teetee and the doctor are still talking. They're taking forever. Red is moaning. It's like a rolling nightmare. I feel as though I'm trying to run down the train tracks ahead of an oncoming locomotive and suddenly I can't move my legs.

"Tita, will you please tell me what the fuck the doctor's saying?"

"He says he's sure it appendicitis," answers Teetee frightened by my outburst.

"Ask him," I say, fighting my anger, trying to be calm, "if Red can see a gynecologist."

Teetee and the doctor discuss this. The doctor's young, long, and narrow. He's dressed in green hospital scrubs. His green skullcap covers his forehead. His green mask, half tied around his neck, lies on his chest. He reminds me of a grasshopper. The doctor never smiles. Teetee and the doctor are still talking.

"Jesus Christ, what's he saying?"

Teetee is tense and worried. My yelling has shocked her. She wants to help me but feels certain from the sound of my voice and the expression on my face that she's letting me down miserably. And now she's afraid to tell me what the doctor said. She's sure I'm going to be upset with her.

"Tita, what the hell is he saying?"

"The doctor says there is no gynecologist in the hospital. He says he has had training as a gynecologist and just examined Red as well as any gynecologist could have done. He says it is appendicitis and that he is going to operate right away before things get worse."

Two orderlies wheel my Red away. There's nothing I can do about it. Besides, she can't go on suffering such excruciating pain.

The appendicitis operation is supposed to take no more than an hour. Teetee and I sit on a bench near the swinging doors that lead to the operating room. I'm sorry I was so angry with Teetee. She's as worried as I am. She did the best she could. I hug her and apologize.

She says, "Fink nothing of it."

Two hours later we're still sitting there and no one has come out of the operating room to tell us anything. I'm certain the doctor is now aware the problem was not Red's appendix. But what *is* the problem?

Three hours pass, and then four.

The doctor finally pushes his way through the swinging doors. He tells Teetee Red's appendix wasn't the problem. But he took her appendix out anyway.

I ask Teetee, "Do you think the doctor would be kind enough to tell me what the problem is?"

Teetee asks the doctor what the problem is. She listens to his answer and says, "It was her left tube. It had twisted into a knot. The doctor says he removed the tube."

I'm scared to death to pose the next question. The butcher's already sliced out a perfectly healthy appendix and a torqued fallopian tube. What else has he removed? Please, God, I pray, not her ovaries, too. Holding my breath, and with the fear of God rushing through my bones, I say, "Tita, ask the doctor if he took anything else out?"

Teetee asks the doctor. They talk for what seems like forever. I try desperately to control myself. Finally Teetee turns to me and speaks.

"No," she says, "nothing else."

I could cry with joy, but I don't. Instead I growl, "Where is she?"

For the next two days and nights, Red lies in her hospital bed attached to intravenous jars and a urine bag.

Teetee cooks all her meals at Très Cher and brings the food to the hospital. But Red hardly eats. She's pale. Her hair is damp with sweat. I wipe her forehead with a cold washcloth. When I'm not doing that I sit in a chair and watch her sleep.

The doctor comes to see my wife once a day. At ten in the morning. He arrives with an entourage of resident interns and nurses. They circle Red's bed and discuss her situation as if she were on exhibit. At some point they always laugh. I wonder what's so funny. They ignore me. I might as well be in Pago Pago. On the second morning, as the entourage prepares to leave, I block their way. The entourage is perplexed. I ask if anyone speaks English. One of the interns says he does. The intern is a flippant young man, smug, impressed with himself for being bilingual. The intern wears a white jacket with a stethoscope around his neck and eyeglasses framed in thick tortoise shell. There are several ballpoint pens in his jacket pocket and a name tag over the pens that says: H. Fochet.

"I'm the patient's husband," I snarl at H. Fochet. "Do you think someone in this goddamn crowd of yours can tell me how the fuck my wife is?"

H. Fochet looks at me for a long moment. I'm not sure if he's furious or alarmed. He speaks to the surgeon. The surgeon speaks to H. Fochet. H. Fochet speaks to me. He says, "Your wife is getting better."

The entourage leaves.

The next afternoon a nurse removes the intravenous needles and the urine bag. In the early evening Red develops a terrible headache that will not go away. It hurts so much she can't sleep. At two o'clock the following morning, Red asks the head nurse if she can have a pain pill for her headache. My wife knows her French is less than adequate so she mimes her dialogue by pounding the sides of her temples with her fists.

"I do not understand what you are saying. If you want help, learn to speak better French," the nurse says angrily, and leaves. No one answers Red's buzzer or comes to her room for the rest of the night. Four and a half hours later, at six-thirty in the morning, I arrive with coffee and a fresh roll in a white paper bag. Red tells me about the early-morning incident with the nurse.

I explode.

At ten o'clock the doctor and his entourage appear. To his visible surprise, the doctor finds his patient sitting on her bed wearing her street clothes. He sees Teetee and me standing next to her. He sees a packed overnight bag by the door.

The doctor speaks to Teetee.

Teetee says to me, "The doctor wants to know what is going on?"

"Tell the doctor we're leaving now. Tell him he can, or cannot, do the decent thing and give us prescriptions for whatever drugs Red should take during the next few weeks. That's up to him. But tell him if he doesn't give me the prescriptions I'm going to sue his ass black and blue for removing my wife's perfectly healthy appendix. Tell the doctor he has two minutes to decide."

The doctor writes out several prescriptions and hands them to me.

We leave.

Buddy, our neurotic labrador, was happy to see us all come home.

But that was yesterday. Today he's pissed. I'm about to go to town without him. Buddy doesn't like being told he can't come and he's letting me know it. He's sitting in the back of my car pouting, and he won't come out. Sometimes Buddy can be a big pain in the ass.

Buddy Barris The Wonder Dog.

For a long time Buddy didn't know he was a water dog. Every time we tried putting him into the swimming pool, the pup would howl pathetically. This was a labrador howling! We were convinced we had a defective dog on our hands. Actually we never realized how lucky we were. The day Buddy came to his senses, when he finally figured out that unlike other dogs, his toes were webbed, we hardly saw him dry again. From that moment on he was always in the water. Now he jumps off *Bam Bam* whether we want him to or not. He jumped into the sea once when we were going sixty miles an hour.

The French have a saying. *Quand le chat est parti, les souris dansent.* When the cat's away, the mice will play. When the Redhead isn't around, when she's off antiquing somewhere or in Paris for an exhibition, Buddy and I have a ball. I eat chocolate candy and salted peanuts, never shave or change my clothes. Buddy lies on all the furniture my wife has proclaimed off-limits to him, and sleeps at night on Red's side of the bed, his head in her pillows. If she knew, she'd die.

Sometimes Buddy suffers these heavy love pangs. When he does, he'll run over to where I'm sitting, put his paws around my waist, and lay his head on my chest. He's giving me a hug as best he can. Or he'll put his paws on my shoulders and lick me with his big wet tongue from the bottom of my neck to the top of my forehead. Quite often Buddy and I remind me of a couple of homosexuals; I'm the old fag and Buddy's the young stud. "It's perfectly fine to have that kind of relationship with your dog," a friend once told me. "Just make sure you're using the proper protection."

Anyway, today Buddy's pissed at me.

He's pissed because I don't want to take him to the Place des Lices to watch me play *boule.* He wants to go this afternoon in the worst way. When I walk into the garage he's in my car. I tell him to get out. What Buddy doesn't understand is that the whole hospital thing with Red was stressful and tiring and I just want to go to the Place des Lices by myself and relax. I don't want to be responsible for Buddy's craziness. I have to pull the dog out of my car by his collar. He's not happy. When I back out of the garage, I notice Buddy sitting nearby, scowling. I stop and think twice about bringing him with me. But I don't. As I start down the driveway I see Buddy trotting off in the opposite direction through the vineyards.

I go to the Place des Lice. I play *boule* and have a Perrier-menthe with some of the boys. Later, on the way to my automobile, I see Henri Bruni coming toward me on his motorbike. He looks grim. Henri waves me down. I know something terrible has happened. I wonder where Red and Teetee are. Were they driving anywhere? Henri stops his motorbike and turns off the key. He puts his hand on my shoulder and says, "Buddy's been killed."

First I'm relieved. It is not Red or Teetee. And then I'm sad.

"On the Route du Plage," says Henri. "He was hit by a motorcycle."

Buddy was only fifteen months old.

It's a dark, moonless night.

Red and I are sleeping. Red soundly, the effects of a sleeping pill. The last two nights since Buddy died she's been taking a sleeping pill before going to bed. I'm tossing and turning thinking about Buddy. Sometime after midnight I hear a strange whining outside. I think it's a couple of hostile cats. And then I realize it might be oinking. Lots of oinking. But how could it be pigs? It's cats, I decide, not pigs. By now I'm annoyed at what I think are two toms getting ready to fight. I know their screeching is going to become louder and louder. I get out of bed and lower the storm door. The storm door blocks out the sounds of the night. Almost completely.

When I wake up the next morning, I kiss Red on the top of her head, go over and raise the storm door. Something about the lawn catches my eye. It's different. I don't know why but it is. I walk outside barefooted wearing just a T shirt. My first thought is that we're in the process of replanting our lawns. The gardener has begun turning over our topsoil so he can spread fresh new grass seed. I didn't know we had decided to do this and wonder why I wasn't told. But that's not what happened. Something else has taken place. Something bad; worse than bad, a catastrophe. Wild boars have decimated our property.

It's been an extremely dry summer and fall in the wine country above Saint-Tropez. Because of the drought, the animals are dying of thirst. When wild boars are thirsty they become desperate and do what they least like to do: approach mankind. Mankind shoots wild boars on sight. That doesn't stop the animals from leaving the hills. The boars travel in packs down from the hills toward homes and farms rooting for water, destroying the land with their sharp tusks as they go.

I stand in my T-shirt stunned by what I see. The wild boars have destroyed everything that grows around our home. They've dug up all the lawns. They've grooved trenches into the ground with their tusks as though they were bulldozers plowing irrigation ditches. They've torn apart our sprinkler hoses and water pipes, ripped up our gardens, mowed down our pretty flower beds, laid waste to our bushes and small trees. There are no more cobblestone pathways. There's just devastation and destruction. I can't help thinking that if I had looked outside when I thought I heard oinking, I could have chased the wild boars away. But I didn't look outside, and now our once beautiful land is ravaged and ugly.

Red is getting out of bed. From inside the bedroom I hear her say, "Is anything wrong?"

Red is still grieving for our dead dog. She has taken Buddy's death much harder than I ever expected. Maybe that's because, after being so sick, her emotional reservoir ran dry. The Redhead's been crying for two days now. Nothing I say helps.

"Is there anything wrong?" she asks again, walking up to my side.

"Yes, there's something wrong."

Red sees the plundered grounds. Without hesitating, she says, "The animals are angry with us for letting Buddy die."

Red's losing it.

And I'm suddenly and hopelessly enraged. I lose it, too.

"I've had it," I yell at Red. "I'm sick and tired of wild boars and dogs getting killed and Michael Allard and lawn specialists and architects and contractors with their grimy hands in my pockets every five minutes trying to grab as much money as they can from the rich Americans. I'm sick of French doctors and nurses who won't help you unless you can describe what hurts in fluent French. You want to know the truth?"

My wife says nothing. She looks vacantly at the havoc in front of us.

"The truth is, I'm fed up with France and I'm fed up with the French. I've had it up to here with their holier-than-thou attitudes, their this-is-the-way-the-French-do-business bullshit. I'm sick of walking around town every day like goddamn Helen Keller because I can't speak their language and I'm sick and tired of trying to learn it."

My wife slides her arm around my waist and lays her head on my shoulder.

"No kidding, Red, I've had it. I hate when I can't go to the Gorille in the morning to get my coffee because lightning screwed up the electric gates and they won't open, or not being able to write because lightning screwed up my computer. I'm tired of having to unplug every appliance in the entire house whenever I hear thunder. This is the goddamn twentieth century. You'd think France would know how to handle lightning and thunder by now. Fucking third world country is what it is."

"Buddy would have chased the boars away," says my wife to herself.

Ignoring her, I rail on. "I want a cup of American coffee. In an American coffee shop. I want to read an American newspaper and hear an American radio station. I've had it up to here with the goddamn BBC and messing around with my radio every night trying to raise them like it was World War II. And then when I finally find the BBC, what do I hear? I hear what's happening in Angola and Sierra Leone. I don't give a rat's ass about Sierra Leone. I want to hear American football scores and I want to hear them the day of the game, not a week later."

"What are you trying to tell me?"

"What I'm trying to tell you is, I want to go home."

"But this is our home."

"Not anymore."

We stand there in the grass with nothing on but our T-shirts, arm in arm and brokenhearted.

PART III

In all of life the odds are six to five against.

—Ward Just

CHAPTER THIRTY-SEVEN

We arrive in Los Angeles a month later at one o'clock in the afternoon. Danny Cahill picks us up at the airport and drives us to Beverly Hills in a new limousine. The limo's black and long. Inside there's a bar, glasses, whiskey and champagne, a basket of hard candy, today's newspapers, assorted trendy magazines, all the show biz trade periodicals, bottles of Evian water, and a bucket of ice cubes. The darkly tinted windows make reading impossible. The air-conditioning makes opening them unwise. What interior illumination there is is provided by two rows of little yellow lights in the limo's ceiling. These lights give me a feeling that I'm attempting an airplane landing at night, upside down at a rural airport. There is, however, a small pin spotlight embedded in each rear corner. One can read a magazine and feel like a Vegas headliner at the same time. Things haven't always been so opulent for my driver Danny Cahill.

I've been using Danny to chauffeur me around Los Angeles for over thirty-five years. I was one of his first customers. He drove me in his first limousine. He had purchased the limo from a hustler. It was a used limo the slippery car dealer promised was "almost like new." An hour after the sale, Danny Cahill turned on the radio and watched the automatic antenna emerge from the front fender, rise a few feet, then fall over dead, like a broken twig. When I opened the ashtray lid, the lid fell to the floor.

In the early days of our business relationship (it was during those mind-expanding sixties) Danny Cahill would drive around town throbbing with delight and detachment from a few tokes of vintage ganga, talking to me through his rearview mirror, me usually slumped down in the backseat staring out the window thinking about some new show, watching the neon signs go by. In those days the meaning of life for the two of us was extremely simple: Every day above ground is a good day.

No one threw us a curve, nothing bent us out of shape, few things fazed us. Like the night we were cruising down Highland Avenue and this man up ahead of us stepped out of his automobile parked by the curb to check something in his trunk. Danny—laid back, eyes at half-mast, smiling as usual, talking quietly to himself—sliced off the guy's car door at the hinges. The door flew up in the air, came down on top of Danny's engine hood, rode with us for a couple of blocks, then slid lazily onto the street. Danny just kept going. We giggled about that for hours.

But times have changed. Now Danny Cahill's a big success. He owns several spiffy new "stretch" limousines; some black, some white. The limos are so long we can't talk to each other. I sit too far away. If I want to tell him something I have to use a gold telephone located in a wall bracket by my right ear. Some of Danny's customers are Jack Nicholson, Bob Hope, and Anjelica Huston. Today he's known as Danny Cahill: Chauffeur-To-The-Stars. I enjoy Danny's success. I know he enjoys it, too. I also know neither of us are likely to ever have as much fun again as we had the evening we sliced off that poor sucker's car door on Highland Avenue.

The afternoon sun is blasting the City of Angels. The buildings are a chalky white. So are the pavements and streets. It's November and it feels like I'm in the tropics. We roll through the glare and shimmering heat on our way to the Bistro Gardens restaurant in Beverly Hills. We stop at a red light. Bored, I push a button and roll my black-tinted window down. Hot air smacks me in the face. There's a battered dusty-green Chevy idling beside us. Its driver is very wide and very black. He barely fits in the front seat of his car. Several lightning Z's have been sculpted into his hair above his ears. The rest of his hair is shaved in a semicircle around the bottom of his head leaving a thick flat whiskbroom effect on top. His eyes, some of his forehead, and part of his upper nose are covered by a pair of extralarge aviator sunglasses. His movements, as he turns to look at me, are slow and torpid, his expression full of contempt. I get the feeling that if ever there's a revolution and this guy is one of its leaders, an early proclamation of his will be to have ostentatious me in the long stretch limousine, shot. I roll my window up ever so slowly hoping he doesn't think me rude.

The Bistro Gardens restaurant is on Cañon Drive in the heart of Beverly Hills. The restaurant is crowded with flashy men showing lots of gold and striking half-dressed girls. Everyone has everything unbuttoned down to the waist. Everybody can see the lines of everybody else's underpants beneath their slacks and shorts.

The restaurant is jolly and festive. It has freshly cut flowers everywhere in brightly painted flower boxes. The dining area is divided in two halves with inside and outside seating. A piano player works at a baby grand half inside and half outside. "A" people are placed inside in the evening and outside in the afternoon. It's vice versa for the "B" people.

"How good to see the two of you again," says the Bistro Gardens maître d'. He shows us to our table and helps Red with her chair. It's a nice table in the shade of a red-and-green-striped beach umbrella. Of much greater consequence is the fact that it's afternoon and the table is outside. I'm secretly thrilled. How quickly, I muse, the chameleon changes colors. It was only a few weeks ago in Saint-Tropez that I confessed to Henri Bruni at the Gorille how mangle-brained and phony I must have been back in the "old days" when the table I was given in a Hollywood restaurant could make or break my day.

A waiter in a sport shirt and slacks gives us menus, recites several specialties of the day, tells us his name is Ronnie and that he wants to help us in every possible way. He smiles and leaves. A hostile busboy places bread and butter on our table without looking up. We see someone waving. I recognize his face but can't remember his name. I'm horrified to see he's heading our way.

"Yo!" he yells, coming quickly, slithering between the other tables and chairs like a skier hip-swiveling through slalom poles. When he arrives he shakes my hand and kisses Red's. He flashes large, very white capped teeth. He wears a canary-yellow sport jacket, a yellow sport shirt, and green slacks. His smile is fixed and he speaks in question marks. "How's it going?" he asks cheerfully. "You two look great, been workin' out? Hey, come to think of it I haven't seen you two for a while, been away? Keepin' busy? Got anything in the works, Chuckie baby?"

I try to answer, but he won't let me.

"Me?" he continues as though I asked. "I've got so much on my plate I can't see straight. Paramount just optioned my latest script. Know when? Two days ago! You want to know who the leads are?

Can't tell you. Sworn to secrecy. Did I tell you about my syndicated TV pilot? Get this. A tits-and ass late night *cooking* show. Can you dig it? One of those why-didn't-I-think-of-that ideas, right? It's a go for guess when? September! Can you believe that? I'll know this coming week for sure. King World's distributing it. They do all the big ones. *Oprah, Wheel, Jeopardy.* Did I tell you about my book? Jesus, how could I? I haven't seen you, right?"

For a reason that escapes me, whoever he is throws his head back and laughs.

"It's going to be published by Random House," he says after pulling himself together. "Coming out just in time for Christmas. You know what the title is? Are you ready for this? *Marilyn and Me.* Did you know Marilyn and I were very close? Hello," he says to my wife. "Keep punchin'," he says to me. He gives my right cheek an affectionate though surprisingly hard slap, and slaloms off to another table.

Whoever he was leaves me more than a tad depressed. I perceive that I have returned voluntarily to a land where everyone is a renaissance man and everybody talks to each other in resumes.

"Guy's really on his toes," says Red, buttering a piece of bread. "Realizes he hasn't seen us for a while. We've only been away for two years."

I tell Red I remember who the man is we were just talking to. Not his name, only that about three or four years ago he had a string of flop television shows on the air; one bomb after the other.

"Doesn't seem to have hurt him," says my wife.

"That's true. But then failure isn't always detrimental to one's career out here. A good run of ineptitude can often be a stepping-stone to success. A perfect example is the modest geek we were just talking to."

The Redhead and I are slip-sliding away into hostile land.

Another man strolls up to our table. I know who he is. He's Willard Siegel, head of ComTex, a huge media conglomerate. Willard smokes a large cigar. He always smokes a large cigar. Willard tweaks my shoulder, nods to Red, and looking everywhere but at the two of us, says, "Hear about the Polish proctologist who uses two fingers because he wants a second opinion?" Siegel laughs at his own joke from behind a pair of dark-brown Ray-Bans. "Why doesn't Poland have a national hockey team? Because all the hockey players drown during spring training. How are you two?"

While I tell him, Siegel assesses the room. He locates where the influential people are sitting, rates their importance, plans who to talk to next and what to say. He hasn't heard a word I've said.

"I hear you have some good new TV game show ideas," he tells me, waving to someone sitting far away.

"Who'd you hear that from?" I ask.

"I heard. I heard. And how are you, you gorgeous creature?" Siegel is talking to my wife, but he isn't looking at her. He's looking instead at a group of power people sitting on the other side of the terrace, motioning to them that he'll be right there; two minutes, just two minutes. Still semaphoring this information to the other table, Siegel says to me, "So you couldn't stay away. Missed the action, right? I told you you'd be back. Let's face it, you're a workaholic and workaholics don't retire."

"I didn't retire," I tell Siegel rather petulantly. "I'm writing a book. Writing a book's hard work. I work eight hours a day, sometimes more." I'm vaguely embarrassed at how defensive I sound. "Funny thing is, Willard—"

"Sure, sure," interrupts Siegel, bending down and brushing cigar ash off his knee. "The Great American Novel, right? And if you get lucky and get it published, which is no easy trick these days, how many people will buy your book? Four people? Five people?"

I pop a forced laugh. "Four or five people. I'd like to think I'm a better writer than that. I mean, give me a break, Willard. Make it at least eleven or twelve."

I want to say more but don't. What I just said sounded stupid. Nothing is coming out right. It doesn't matter. Willard isn't listening. His mind has focused on the cigar-ash smudge on his light summer-weight beige pant leg. Rubbing it with his fingers has threatened to make the smudge permanent. Siegel is not thrilled. A waiter rushes over with an open bottle of club soda and a napkin. How did the waiter know? Does the Bistro Gardens employ a waiter just to keep his eye out for smudges and stains? Apparently such accidents are not to be taken lightly. Willard Siegel's cigar smudge has now assumed the importance of a brain tumor. Much to our relief, and to others close by, the waiter does a magnificent job of removing it.

Siegel is visibly pleased. He slips the waiter a fiver and the waiter leaves.

"Where were we?" he says, checking his gold Rolex.

"You said my new book would only sell four or five copies."

"Right," says Siegel, "and that's not your style, old buddy. An audience of five people—okay, I'm being facetious, make it five *thousand* people, that still ain't what you're about. You deal in audiences of millions. Tens of millions. Commercial TV is what you do, and you do it . . ." As he speaks, Willard is forming his forefinger and thumb into an imaginary gun. He aims his forefinger at a celebrity whose face I recognize and whose name I should know, but forget. The celebrity has just entered the outdoor terrace and is walking to his table. Willard clicks his thumb and silently shoots the celebrity dead. The celebrity smiles and winks at Willard. ". . . better than anyone. Creating TV shows is what God put you on this earth to do, not to write fucking books. Leave the book writing to the book writers. I'm giving you good advice. Trust me."

A waiter excuses himself profusely for interrupting. He has something of great import to tell Siegel. So classified is his news, the waiter has to whisper the information in Siegel's ear. I inadvertently overhear the waiter. You know what the waiter's highly confidential message is? It's that a chair has been added to the table in the far corner of the terrace—the table where all the powerful people are sitting—and it's there whenever Siegel's ready. Willard whispers something back to the waiter. This time I can't hear what's being said. If it's as important as the waiter's news, I'm not missing a thing. I use the break to push bread around in the bread basket. My wife takes my hand out of the bread basket and puts it back in my lap. Willard slips the waiter another fiver and the waiter leaves.

"Anyway," says Siegel, "I told you you were too smart to spend the rest of your life in Frogville. I told you you'd be bored to death there, that it was only a matter of time before the French would drive you crazy. Didn't I tell you that? Besides, you're too old to become a best-selling author."

"Too old?"

"Yeah, too old. After fifty, you are what you are and know what you know. Those oddball stories of late-in-life career changes that end up being hugely successful, those Grandma Moses things, are just that, oddball. For good or for bad, what you do when you're fifty you'll do the rest of your life. Thank God you do what you do well. Listen, there's no way you could've stayed away from Hollywood forever. Hey, like I said, it's where the action is, right? It's where every red-blooded American wants to be, right? You know why? I'll tell you why. It's where the money is, that's why. The money's not in the south of France, old buddy, the money's here in Hollywood. Am I right or am I right?"

"You're right, Willard," I reply, but I don't mean it. It's the first of a lot of things I'll say in the coming weeks I don't really mean.

Suddenly I'm aware of a thick knot balling up in the pit of my stomach. The palms of my hands turn clammy. My body is reacting to a fact. The fact: I'm definitely back. Back in The Orange. Back in La La Land. Back in Hollyweird. My dreams of living happily ever after in the south of France are officially over. My pontificating about the good life being the simple, unpretentious kind Red and I shared in the hills above Saint-Tropez appears to be nothing more than hypocritical hot air. If it was so good why did we come back? Evidently real life is not strolling arm and arm with my wife into the Mediterranean sunset like I thought. Real Life is having power lunches with the Willard Siegels of the world; the guys who never look at you when they talk. It's hard to believe I'd rather be lunching with Siegel at the Bistro Gardens than fishing with Henri off the back of *Bam Bam*. But I must, otherwise, like I said, why would I be here?

"Don't disappoint me," says Siegel while signaling one of the powerful people at the faraway table that he's coming right away.

I don't know what Willard means by not disappointing him, but then I don't care what Willard has to say, so what difference does it make? Before Willard leaves I want to ask him where exactly he heard that I had new good TV ideas.

I say, "Willard, where exactly did . . ."

"You better call me or I'll be heartbroken," he says, smiling at a pretty girl sitting nearby, "and that's the last thing you want to do? You don't want to break the heart of the best friend you have in this town, do you?"

He blows the pretty girl a kiss, mouths something to her with his lips, pinches my right cheek, says to Red, "I love this man," and flees.

My cheek smarts from all the slapping and pinching.

"Do you really have new good TV ideas like Willard says you have?" asks my wife.

"Not that I know of."

This evening we've been invited to dinner with friends.

It's our first night in Los Angeles in a long time and I presume everyone is dying to hear about our adventures abroad. We go to a new and extremely popular "in" restaurant called Laconda Veneta. The restaurant is on Third Avenue near La Cienega. Red and I step out of my car and someone in a red vest steps into it and drives off. I watch my souped-up Mercedes 190E disappear down Third Avenue. I have learned in Los Angeles to give my beloved automobile away without so much as a whimper to anyone who wears a red vest.

The restaurant is small, congested, and noisy. Everyone is sitting close to everyone else, listening to what the people at the next table are saying, looking at what others have ordered, and wondering if they should order the same thing. We are the last to arrive. The three other couples are already seated. We all hug and kiss. They're glad to see us, not because we've been away so long, but because they're famished and want to eat. As soon as we sit down they begin waving frantically for a waiter. He comes with a bouquet of menus. We listen closely as he recites the evening's specialties. This is followed by an intense question-and-answer period between my friends and the waiter.

"Is this dish very fatty?"

"No, not really."

"Has there been salt added?"

"None."

"Could you please tell the chef no salt?"

"It's not prepared with salt."

"Could you please tell him anyway?"

"Yes I will."

"Is the salmon broiled or grilled?"

"Broiled."

"In a Teflon pan or with butter?"

"In a Teflon pan if you prefer."

"Can the sauce be on the side?"

"Absolutely."

"Is it possible to have the cheese shavings omitted from the salad?"

"Sure."

"Could I get the pasta with garlic but absolutely no olive oil?"

"Yes."

"And no butter?"

"Yes."

"Please tell the chef no butter."

While collecting the menus, the waiter tells us his name is Ronnie. He's the second waiter named Ronnie my wife and I had today. When Ronnie leaves, the discussions begin. Our six friends talk about movie grosses, trade paper innuendo, what Hollywood studio mavens have lost their jobs or found new ones, the good news of friends in the biz who have failed and the bad news about those who have succeeded. They discuss terrible actors and actresses who are ridiculously overpaid. They nervously admit to projects hanging by threads because their patron saints at the studios are about to be fired. They exchange words of encouragement to each other they obviously don't mean.

Red and I haven't said a word. We're unable to. We're not up on the latest dish. We haven't anything substantial to bring to the table other than the less then thrilling news that we had two waiters named Ronnie in one day. Anyway, Red and I are too tired to talk. We're blitzed with jet lag, the scourge of the affluent.

So we just listen.

I realize nothing much has changed over the last few years. The grosses sound the same. The innuendo sounds the same. The same people have failed and succeeded. Only the names of the motion pictures are different. I'm bored and move the bread around in the bread basket. My wife takes my hand out of the bread basket and returns it to my lap. The check finally arrives. The waiter hands it to me. I don't mind paying the check, but I wonder what I did to deserve it.

Someone says, "Hey, this was supposed to be on us in honor of your homecoming."

The thought dies there. Everyone else is busy moving the table and chairs so that we can get up and leave. We go outside and stand in front of the restaurant shaking hands, hugging, and kissing cheeks. We make plans to see each other again. Men in red vests return our automobiles to us.

On our way home I say to Red, "Nobody asked us about France."

A week later I am having lunch with my friend Stanley Donen.

We're discussing Dominique Lapierre, and how his stationery has all the books he's written and published engraved at the top. Neither one of us has ever seen stationery with someone's credits listed like that. We laugh recalling a letter Stanley sent me mimicking Lapierre's. Stanley had listed some of the motion pictures he directed. There were so many titles he only had room to write, "Thinking of you," at the very bottom of the page.

As we eat, I can't help overhearing a discussion at a table behind me. The conversation is between five women; all Jewish, middle-aged, and loud. I listen to them debate the troubles of the world: Elizabeth Taylor's marriage to a stud twenty-five years her junior, Princess Diana's difficulties with Prince Charles, how Barbara Bush's white hair made her look so old. ("She should tint it a light orange.") They also discuss their own problems; their husbands' inability to get it up and keep it there, their teenage children's obnoxious behavior, their own amazing restraint in not mutilating their kids at least once a day. The mothers' solutions to these and other knotty situations makes them (and me) wheeze with laughter.

"That's my next television show," I say to Stanley.

"What is?"

"*Mothers.*"

CHAPTER THIRTY-EIGHT

My first thought is to have just Jewish mothers.

But then I think, why restrict myself? Italian mothers can be just as hilarious as Jewish mothers. So can African-American mothers. Maybe even WASP mothers. Maybe. So I tell my newly hired talent coordinator that I want to audition forty mothers and that I want them in all sizes, shapes, and colors. Their only prerequisite: They must have given birth to at least one kid.

My new talent coordinator is a blond-haired, blue-eyed, compact lady named Christina Ferra. She's thirty-three years old and legend has it she was a virgin until last year. Why Christina Ferra was a virgin until last year is a long but not boring story. Unfortunately it won't be told here. Anyway, Christina has a fantastic figure and sometimes wears micro-mini skirts so short you can see her panties when she reaches for anything two inches over her head. This is no reflection whatsoever on the girl's professionalism. Christina has one of the best creative minds in town. So I tell her to get me forty mothers.

She gets me sixty-five.

They jam the small rooms and hallways of the offices we've rented at the NBC studios in Burbank. We interview ten mothers every hour. We work for almost eight straight hours. I'm looking for five exceptional mothers: women who are funny, thoughtful, intuitive, and, most of all, characters. I intend to use these five mothers as my permanent panel. They will solve the problems of our celebrity and civilian guests, along with those who call or write us from our viewing audience. They'll even be able to handle the hypothetical personal disasters I'll create when everyone's gone and I'm all alone in my office. The mothers I'm looking for will be capable of doing all that, and doing it well.

In return, I'll make them stars.

I'm having lunch with my friends Willard Huyck and Gloria Katz at California Pizza in Brentwood.

Willard is a man of forty plus years with definite likes and dislikes. He likes flowered sport shirts and Omas fountain pens. He dislikes people. Willard's wife Gloria is well read, up to speed on current events, thinks she knows more than anyone else about everything, and shakes her legs while she eats. She's very intense.

Gloria says, "Something's bothering me about your new show idea."

"What's that?" I say, not paying much attention, concentrating on my vegetarian pizza.

She says, "I think you're going in the wrong direction with *Mothers.*"

"The wrong direction?" I'm paying attention now.

"Yes. Today's television viewers aren't interested in mothers."

"Oh?" I say, annoyed. I'm annoyed because Gloria thinks she knows more about television audiences than I do. The problem is, she might. She and her husband Willard created the motion picture screenplays of megahits such as *American Graffiti* and one of the Indiana Jones epics, among others. Grudgingly I say, "So, Gloria, what are today's television viewers interested in, pray tell?"

"Sex," says Gloria.

"Sex."

"Yes, sex. Lots of pretty young girls showing lots of tits and ass. If you had a show filled with pretty young girls you wouldn't call it *Mothers*, which is great because *Mothers* sounds like death warmed over."

"Death warmed over."

"Yes. If you do what I say, you could call the show something else."

"Like what?"

"*Bimbos.*"

Gloria could be right.

So I tell Christina to get me forty bimbos.

She gets me a hundred.

Pretty, sexy bimbos replace the mothers in our halls and offices. They're sitting and standing everywhere filling out forms. Strange, exotic perfumes thicken the air. One of my staff has an asthma attack. Great numbers of stagehands, carpenters, and mechanics arrive. They've come from near and far. They offer up lame excuses as to why it's absolutely necessary to be in my way; to fix this doohickey or that wall plug or vacuum some goddamn rug that hasn't been vacuumed in fifteen years. As they speak, their eyes follow the mass of pulchritude, the incredible breasts and behinds gliding through the clouds of perfume.

I go into the conference room where the auditions will take place. It's standing-room only. The first five bimbos arrive cooing and giggling. They make a big production out of crossing their legs. They have no idea they're here because they're bimbos, only that they might get jobs as models or hostesses on a new television program. They flap their eyelashes and smile seductively even when nobody is looking at them. I bring the meeting to order. I explain the basics to the girls. I tell them I'm going to ask for their opinions on various subjects. "Say anything that comes to your minds."

"Anything?" asks one girl coyly, recrossing her legs.

The room bursts into spasms of male hysteria. I'm always amazed at this power women have over men; how fast they can reduce a man to a boy. One word dropped from the moist lips of a sexy bimbo with crossed legs and a hiked-up skirt, and every man in the room is trying to laugh louder than the next guy.

I press on. "And if you can't answer a question, don't worry about it. You'll answer the next one."

The girls smile and recross their legs.

The first question is an easy one. I've made it easy on purpose. I want to make them as comfortable as quickly as I can. The question concerns the Russian leader, Mikhail Gorbachev. Gorbachev and his wife are being held captive in a dacha somewhere in the Russian republic of Georgia. That's all everyone in the world has been talking about for the last two days and nights.

I ask the girls, "If you were Mrs. Gorbachev, what advice would you be giving Mr. Gorbachev these days?"

"Who's he?" says Bimbo Number One.

I excuse myself and go home.

* * *

We've gone back to mothers.

The next weekend I interview sixty-seven of them bringing the total auditioned to one hundred and twenty-two. I now have more than five great mothers. I have at least fifteen. Some are hip, some homespun. All glib. All quick. All funny. All characters. They range in age from thirty-five to eighty-five. They're every height and weight, every color and nationality. I decide to try and sell *Mothers* on a Monday through Friday basis, nighttime or daytime, and rotate all fifteen mothers throughout the week. I'm convinced every one of them will discuss the show's problems with intelligence and humor. Now all I need are the problems.

"What kind of problems?" asks Christina.

"Every kind, with one big hook. Young people, people between the ages of eighteen and thirty-five, must be able to relate to these problems."

"How many problem people do you want?"

I suggest a few dozen.

Christina gets me sixty-five.

Now we can have a "problem" audition.

We listen to hardship, pain, and suffering for an entire day trying to decide if what we hear and see is usable, meaning how much of this is clean and interesting enough to air? Will these problems be identifiable to teenagers and young adults? Are they entertaining, or just morbid and depressing? How will the mothers handle honest-to-goodness real-life dilemmas? Like the one involving Raquel Vaccaro.

Raquel Vaccaro has a twelve-year-old daughter Kimberly. Twenty years ago Raquel was a *Playboy* centerfold. The presently divorced Raquel is proud she was a centerfold. The nude picture stands framed in all its glory on the coffee table in the Vaccaro living room. It's the first thing Mother Raquel's new boyfriends see. It's the first thing daughter Kimberly's new girlfriends see. The picture appalls and embarrasses young Kimberly. Every time one of her friends comes to visit and sees the picture of her naked mother on that awful zebra-striped rug, Kimberly wishes she could curl up and die. She hates the horrid picture and wants it removed and banished from their home forever.

"No such thing," says a defiant Raquel. "I'm proud of that picture.

Granted the ol' bod ain't what it used to be, but I see nothing wrong in letting my friends use their imagination."

The mothers tear into this one. They hoot and holler, agree and disagree. They're hilarious. Their heated discussion could have gone on for an hour. Their decision? Kimberly's right. The picture's an embarrassment. Get rid of the damn thing right away.

Then there's Charlie. He's a strapping, good-looking fourteen-year-old who wanted to know the facts of life. He asked his father and older sister but got short shift from them. He refused to ask his friends because he was supposed to be experienced in all those matters by now. In the old days a boy his age would have gone to a bordello, but old-fashioned whorehouses don't exist anymore, at least not in Charlie's neighborhood. So he asked his earthy, hot-blooded grandmother. Charlie really likes his grandmother. She's young as far as grandmothers go and spends most of her nights dancing at the local disco. Charlie's grandmother teaches Charlie everything he wanted to know.

Not long after his grandmother's lessons, Charlie's father asked him, more as a joke than anything else, if he ever learned the facts of life.

Charlie said he did.

"Who from?" asked his father, both curious and slightly alarmed.

When Charlie told his dad who from, the man's face turned white, then an angry shade of red.

"Pardon my French," says Charlie's father to our panel of mothers, "but Jesus Christ Almighty, my son here was fucking *my mother!*"

"So what, dad," replies Charlie. "You do the same thing to my mother every night."

I think this problem's going to throw our mothers. But it doesn't. Far from it. They take Charlie's father to task for paying scant attention to the boy's inquiries and scold the grandmother for being so anxious to teach. They agree it was a bizarre solution to Charlie's dilemma, but a solution it was nonetheless.

After watching and listening to the way the mothers handled Raquel and Charlie, I'm beginning to think my *Mothers* television idea could turn out to be a great one.

After the audition's over and everyone's left, Christina says, "Now what?"

"Now, Christina, it's time to sell it."

My first appointment is at the CBS-TV studios on Fairfax Boulevard in Hollywood.

I'm to see a man named Rod Perth. Perth is a vice president. He's in charge of late night programming. This means he's responsible for all the programs on the Columbia Broadcasting System's television network after eleven P.M. I think late night is good for *Mothers.* The ladies will be able to speak candidly without worrying about upsetting children and ministers. But I'm concerned about the man I'm going to see. I've never met him and I don't like his name.

I'm driving to CBS with Loretta Strickland, practicing my sales pitch on her as we go. Loretta was my first secretary. We were together for fifteen years. She went to work for me in 1965 when she was twenty years old. She sported an immense bouffant hairdo sprayed with liquid concrete to keep it in place. When I first met Loretta she was six feet eleven inches tall. The hairdo accounted for two of those feet. In those days Loretta was a hyper young lady, smart, incredibly efficient, with a lot of cleavage she was never ashamed to flaunt. Now, over twenty-five years later, she's a lot more mellow, still street smart and efficient and still flaunting her cleavage.

Loretta's agreed to come with me on my CBS sales call for old time's sake. On Loretta's lap is a small-scale model of our *Mothers* set made out of cardboard. Loretta holds it carefully so that nothing falls off; none of the tiny replicas of our scenery, logo, risers, stools, lectern, and banquette. As we drive toward the studio, Loretta and I recall the names of other television network executives we sold programs to in the past; me practicing my pitch as we drove. I mention Budd Grant and Ed Vane. She mentions Lyn Bolin and Madeline David.

We turn onto Beverly Boulevard. It's an overcast and humid day. The city is covered with the poisonous white haze they call smog. Everything we pass looks rundown. Every other store is closed or going out of business. Windows are boarded up. The ones that aren't have huge yellow-and-orange signs shaped to look like sunflowers pasted on them. The sunflowers are supposed to be cheerful, but they're not. They're depressing. The signs say: Free Pet Food, Used Cowboy Boots, 2 Eggs-Toast-Coffee-$1.99, Free Ammo With Every Gun.

Takeout joints are all over the place: Humphrey Yogurt, Winchell's Donuts, the Soup Plantation, Starbucks. Wire trash receptacles placed in front of their doors are packed with garbage. Bums sleep on the pavement. Beggars push shopping carts in the streets, the carts packed to overflowing with other people's waste. The rest of the world are in automobiles with their air-conditioning and hi-fi on full blast, their dark-tinted windows rolled up to hide the passing panorama of poverty and despair.

Hooray for Hollywood.

I hang a right at Fairfax Avenue, a left onto CBS Television Center, and drive to the gate. A guard steps out of his sentry box. He's Mexican. He has a very round face and a pencil-thin mustache. The guard wears an ornate uniform complete with Sam Brown belt. A large patch over his heart has the letters CBS Protection superimposed over a rippling American flag. I tell the guard who I am. He checks his list. I'm on it like I said I would be, so he smiles. He has lots of gold teeth.

The receptionist sitting in the main building smiles because our names are also on her list. The receptionist on Perth's floor smiles because we are on her list, too. Rod Perth's secretary smiles because we've arrived on time. She talks to me informally, very friendly, as though she, Mr. Perth, and I have known each other for years. She says, "Hi! I don't know where ol' Rod is, but I'm sure he'll show up in just a few minutes. Would either of you like coffee? Tea? Herb tea?"

Loretta and I decide to wait without coffee or tea.

We sit down on a leather couch and leaf through old trade papers. In the beginning Loretta and I are the only ones in the reception room. Soon the room's filled. All the others are carrying paraphernalia like Loretta and her cardboard *Mothers* set. Some carry scripts and drawings. If they have neither, they carry clipboards. Apparently one ought to carry something. Thank God we have ours. As each person is called away, he or she smiles smugly at those who are left behind. It seems the last to come and first to be called carry the most weight. Loretta and I were the first to come. The room is empty again and Loretta and I are still there. We have waited for almost an hour.

"Let's go," I say to Loretta.

Just then Perth's secretary returns. "I found him!" she exclaims, as if the executive had disappeared somewhere up the Amazon. "I swear this guy's goin' to be the death of me."

Who gives a rusty fuck? I think, not thrilled.

"Sorr-reee you two," continues Perth's secretary chock full of overblown gee-whiz joy. "Didn't mean to keep you waitin' so long but Mondays are always like this, you know, things pile up over the weekend, one crisis after the other. Anyway, Rod'll see you now."

Perth is tall and wears a blue shirt with a white collar, pink suspenders, and baggy tan slacks. Perth's office is small and crammed with Perth memorabilia: framed pictures of Perth with this celebrity and Perth with that celebrity, posters of Perth's favorite movies, his softball mitt, his favorite worn and rumpled baseball cap. Perth's assistant is a short man whose name I forget to memorize. The man has a roaring head cold. He stands around blowing his clogged nose into a Kleenex he holds with both hands. When he's finished blowing he tosses the soggy Kleenex into a wastebasket and offers me one of his germ-infested hands to shake. We all sit down on fuzzy couches and lean back against pillows covered with striped denim.

"Any time you're ready," says Perth.

I say, "The show is tentatively titled *Mothers.*"

"You got to be kidding!" says Perth, amazed.

This could mean any one of three things: From the sound of the title it's just the kind of show he's looking for. He already has a show called *Mothers.* The last thing in the world he wants is a show called *Mothers.*

He says, "The last thing in the world I want, for Christ sake, is a show called *Mothers.* I mean, Jesus Christ, the minute that title appears in *TV Guide* every octogenarian in America will turn it on, which is exactly the audience we don't want. They told me you were the king of the eighteen to thirty-five year olds. That's why you're here, man. If I thought you were going to bring me the Geritol set I'd of saved you the trip."

Snot Nose punctuates his boss's opening salvo by blowing into a new Kleenex extra hard.

I start again. "This program . . ."

"Since we've never met," says Perth, "let me tell you the way I work. Visualize my head compartmentalized into slots. The slots are to jam program submissions into. If your idea fits into one of these acceptable slots, say the Relationship-Game Show slot, or the Relationship-Talking Heads slot, or the Reality-Based slot, or the Beverly Hills Teen Sit-Com slot, or the Bare Your Soul late-night slot—to name a few—you're alive. If it doesn't, you're dead as a doornail and your idea is jammed into my Dead As A Doornail slot. Follow me?"

I start again. "Let me just back up and say . . ."

Perth says, "My most favorite slot of all is the eighteen to thirty-five-year-old slot. If an idea doesn't fit into that slot, if it doesn't skew young, then forget it. It's not worth shit. And hey, I don't think you've gotta be a genius to see that an idea called *Mothers* isn't a show that's going to appeal to eighteen to thirty-five-year-olds. Right?"

"Right," says Snot Nose, who wasn't asked.

"Sorry, but *Mothers* sounds old fartskies to me. Dull as cat shit and borrr-ring. I mean, call a show *Mothers,* and Christ, you'll be skewing sixty and seventy-five year olds before the program ever gets past the opening titles. Do we all agree?"

Perth's assistant, who's blowing his nose again, nods his head.

"Thanks for coming," says Rod Perth, standing now, stretching his long narrow body by clasping his hands above his head and tilting backward slightly, letting us know the meeting's over.

I say, "Before we go, can I pitch you three quick show ideas? Don't panic. They're just basically one-liners. I think now that you've explained to me what you like and don't like, these ideas might be right up your alley. If you like one let me know and I'll explain it in greater detail."

Perth frowns.

"One idea's called Stump The Shrink," I say without waiting for permission. "Three young eighteen to thirty-five-year-old certifiably neurotic contestants describe their chaos. The sicko that makes the guest psychiatrist speechless wins."

Perth sits down.

His assistant stops blowing his nose.

"Or how about America's Most Dysfunctional Family? There's three young yuppie families—all eighteen to thirty-five years old— and a panel of eighteen to thirty-five-year-old doctors. The family the panel thinks is the most mentally impaired, emotionally warped, and/or abnormally maladjusted wins a Winnebago. The winning family must partake in a group hug at the end of the show."

"Are you serious about these ideas?" asks Perth.

"The third one's tentatively titled *Greed*," I continue, ignoring the question. "We have four contestants. They're each given a thousand dollars. The premise of the show is: How low will you go to perform a certain task. By the way, you might consider calling the program: *How Low Will You Go*. Anyway, this is how the program works. We offer dilemmas for the contestants to wrestle with, such as bringing an eighty-year-old arthritic man on crutches on stage. The host asks the four contestants how little money they will take to kick the crutches out from under the old crippled man's arms. The contestants bid downward. See, that's the hook. They bid downward! No other game show has ever asked its contestants to do that. The contestants yell eight hundred dollars! Six hundred dollars! Five hundred and fifty! Three hundred! And so on. The contestant with the lowest bid must kick away the old guy's crutches before he gets to keep the money. After the poor man's dragged off the stage, we bring out a ten-year-old curly-headed, freckle-faced boy and his dog Spot."

"What do the contestants have to do with this one?" asks Snot Nose, moving to the edge of his chair.

"Shoot the dog," I reply.

"You've got to be kidding!" says Perth, barely able to hide his excitement.

I shrug.

In the elevator going down to the parking lot I say to Loretta, "I didn't tell him my favorite. Want to know what it is?"

"I'm afraid to ask," she answers, touching her hair.

CHAPTER THIRTY-NINE

Loretta and I, and our cardboard model of the *Mothers* set, go to Burbank to pitch the show to John Miller, the National Broadcasting Company's vice president in charge of daytime television.

Mr. Miller wears a suit and tie. He's tall and handsome, cordial and polite. His office is sparsely furnished. There aren't any papers on his desk, just a letter opener and a few ballpoint pens lined up in a neat row on the side. John listens attentively. He likes *Mothers*, particularly its unflinching patriotic red, white, and blue bunting that will hang from the rear flats, its homey apple pie spirit, its slogan: They Know Best. Mr. Miller does a bad news/good news job on us. He sadly relates that he doesn't have much money left in his development budget—Loretta's spirits sink along with mine—but says he'll scrape together enough for us to make a pilot show. Loretta and I yelp with joy. We shake Mr. Miller's hand many times and tell him thank you over and over. We skip down the NBC corridor, clapping and hooting, giving each other high-fives, delirious over having sold our first comeback pilot. Wait until Perth finds out about this!

But we never hear from Mr. Miller again.

Loretta has food poisoning, so I have to go see Michael King at King Brothers Company alone.

King Brothers distributes *Oprah Winfrey, Wheel of Fortune, Jeopardy,* and other smash-hit TV shows. The King brothers are very powerful. They have clout. Clout means you can make someone rich as Croesus by simply nodding your head. Clout is one of the most important possessions you can have in Hollywood. Some think clout is more important than good health. I once heard a best man raise his glass of champagne and toast the groom by saying, "You should have good health and clout for the rest of your life. Mostly clout." Apparently a little sickness was okay.

I sit in the King Brothers Company reception room. I have the cardboard model on my lap and my favorite Phillies baseball cap on my knee. My Phillies baseball cap has been with me through thick and thin, and lots of bumpy airplane flights. It brings me good luck. It's also been broken in just right. I'm very attached to the cap.

Michael King himself comes out to fetch me. He wears a green-and-white matching satin sweat suit, and sneakers. I follow in his wake down several halls to his office. My mind wanders. I think of being on *Bam Bam* and how I would follow some yacht's wake for miles and miles, riding happily on the flat sea the huge boat created.

"So," says Michael King after he's seated behind his desk, "how's it going? Just put that thing over there on the couch." He's referring to my cardboard *Mothers* set. I put it on the couch he points to, along with my favorite baseball hat and go to my seat in front of his desk.

Michael King clasps his hands behind his head, pushes back in his outlandishly large leather chair, puts his feet up on top of his desk so that his sneaker soles are in my face, and says, "You know what my goals in life were for a long long time? To beat your organization. To have more hit shows in TV syndication than you had. To make more money than you did."

"Well, I guess you did 'em all."

Michael King smiles. Then he frowns. "But I'm not sure I beat you. I mean, personally beat you. I probably have, but I'm not sure. How much did you walk away with? Hundred million? Two hundred million?"

I'm stunned by the conversation's direction. I'm shocked that this man would ask me these questions. I don't know how to answer him.

"You grabbed over four units, didn't you? I'll bet you did. So what? I'll have my fifth this year."

"Fifth what?"

"Unit."

"Unit?"

"Fifty million dollars," says Michael King. "A unit's fifty million dollars. Nowadays everything's measured in units. What's the matter, you been away so long you don't know the new lingo?" Michael

King laughs. "Listen, you're lucky you got out when you did. The business sucks. I mean, really sucks. It's cruel out there. Nobody's havin' any fun anymore. At least when you were around, the business was fun, you know what I mean? You wanna know something? You're my hero. My fucking number-one hero. You did what everybody dreams about doing but never does. You quit while you were ahead. Now you're livin' the good life while all of us greedy sons of bitches are out there still breaking our fucking humps. Every one of us is gonna drop dead from a fucking heart attack. We'll have all the money in the world, but what good will it do us? Do you know Thelma Orloff?"

"No."

"Thelma was the hottest real-estate saleslady in Beverly Hills, Brentwood, and Pacific Palisades. Sold all the celebrities and Iranians their homes. Always too busy to take a vacation. I must have told her a million times, Thelma, when are you gonna take a break? Go somewhere? Have a good time? In Italy every single year everybody takes a six-week vacation. It's mandatory. When are you gonna take one lousy week? Make a long story short, Thelma's on a dialysis machine now. Had pains in her kidneys. Too busy to go to a doctor. So she's on a dialysis machine now. Three times a week. Monday, Wednesday, and Friday. Uses all her money to pay shvartzas to do things for her; wheel her here, wheel her there, sit her up in her chair, wipe her ass, blow her nose, put her to bed. Doesn't take a hell of a lot of money to pay a shvartza to wipe your ass. So what's she gonna do with all the rest of her millions? Leave it to her fucking kids to piss away on dope? I saw Thelma yesterday. Looks like shit. She told me she'd give her right arm to be able to take a trip somewhere; take a sailboat ride, lie on a beach, climb a mountain. But the poor woman can't now. It's too late. Those days are over. Poor Thelma didn't get off the train in time. Remember when you told me that? I quote you all the time. Swear to God. Remember what you told me about getting off the train?"

"No."

"You once said to me, Michael, a smart guy is a guy who knows when it's time to get off the train. Thelma stayed on the train too long. I'm stayin' on the train too long. But you, you little fucker, you got off the train at just the right time. Now you sail around the Med in your fucking boat enjoying yourself, adding years to your life. I always said the one guy with brains in the business was you. So why are you here? What's that thing on the couch?"

Obviously I can't tell Michael King the truth. "I'm here," I say, "because we haven't talked to each other in a long time and I just wanted to see how you were holding up. That thing on the couch"— I turn and look at it, then turn back to Michael—"is something I found when I was cleaning out my office. I'm taking it home and getting it bronzed. I want it as a reminder never to be tempted to go back into the business again."

"See that!" says Michael King. "Another great idea. Bronzing that thing to remind you not to go back in the business. I always said you had the best ideas."

A few days later, at Tribune Entertainment's Channel 5, a seemingly nice man named George Paris listens attentively to my *Mothers* sales pitch.

I tell him about our wonderful mothers and what characters they are. I repeat some of the funny gems that came out of their mouths. I show him Polaroid pictures of the mothers' faces so he can see how great they look and how different one is from the other. I give him examples of the problems we'll deal with, explain why the eighteen to thirty-five-year-olds will love this show. I suggest that the timing is perfect for a television program that honors Mom and apple pie while still being acceptably titillating and full of sly innuendo. When I finish, I flop back in my chair, slightly winded. I am happy with my performance. I've finally shaken those early appointment jitters, that insecurity I experienced weeks ago in Rod Perth's office. I sneak a look at Loretta. She's sitting ramrod straight in her chair with the cardboard model on her lap. She sends me a clandestine smile back.

George Paris rearranges himself and clears his throat. Paris is in his forties, clean-shaven and jowly. He wears a bow tie and a cardigan sweater. His suit coat is draped around a silent butler behind him. He says, "May I address myself to the creative aspects of your show?"

We're in deep shit.

When some bozo lays a line like that on you—May I address myself to the creative aspects of your show?—you are going, going, gone. A dead fucking duck. This guy Paris could save Loretta and me a lot of time by simply telling us the program idea stinks, get lost.

Then the two of us can get up and go, and that's that. But no, he's got to spend the next what seems like a month babbling on and on about how (in his opinion, of course) it is drastically misleading to think that unfortunate souls can have their problems solved by laywomen. He thinks (in his opinion, of course) unfortunate souls with problems require the help of professionals: clinical and behavioral psychologists, psychiatrists, teachers, counselors, and the like.

I tune him out.

Loretta and I take the elevator to the ground floor. On the way Budd Grant steps into the elevator.

Budd Grant of *Parent Game* fame; the man who kissed my forehead and then canceled my pilot and never explained why. Eventually Budd left NBC to become head of all television programming for the Columbia Broadcasting System. A few years later he was fired from CBS, and that was the last I heard of Budd Grant. And now here he is, stepping into our elevator.

"Well, look who it isn't," he says to me. "Hi, Loretta."

"Hello, Mr. Grant," replies Loretta, smiling. I think Budd Grant had the hots for Loretta years ago when she was my secretary.

"You still walking around Hollywood carrying those goddamn models under your arm?" Budd says to me. "I thought you gave up selling TV shows."

"I guess I didn't," I answer.

"I thought you moved to France?" he says. "Just another lousy Hollywood rumor, huh? Too bad. When I heard you packed it all in and took off I said to myself, now that's a ballsy move. So you're not so ballsy after all. Just another shlepper like the rest of us."

On the drive home I say to Loretta, "Didn't Budd have the hots for you?"

"Yes he did. He would call me up late at night and ask if he could come over to my place and talk to me. He kept telling me I was the only one in Hollywood who understood him."

"Did you let him come over?"

"No."

"Did you two ever discuss why he spells his first name with two d's?"

"No, we never talked about that either," says Loretta, holding the cardboard model of the *Mothers* set tightly on her lap.

The next morning I fly to New York to see Willard Siegel.

Willard's the executive who runs the television domain of Com-Tex, the huge media conglomerate. He's also the one who's always smoking a large cigar, told me he heard I had great new TV show ideas, and is generally looking somewhere else when he talks to you.

Willard's office is enormous. It's the penthouse of a downtown skyscraper. The office has floor-to-ceiling windows that overlook all of Manhattan. You can see the Statue of Liberty out of one window and Central Park out of another. You hardly notice the exercycle and a treadmill stashed in a far corner of Siegel's vast and luxurious domain. A black female dressed as a French parlor maid appears, takes our beverage order, and disappears.

"Have a seat," says a beaming Siegel.

There are several places to sit. One is by his desk. Another is around a large coffee table. A third is at the bar. I'm confused. Willard, puffing a big you-know-what, points to a chair in front of his desk. His second in command, Mort Rosen, enters the massive room, shakes my hand, and sits down next to me.

"I've asked Mort to join us," says Willard.

Mort Rosen smiles at me. I smile back at Mort Rosen. I've met Mort before. Mort's a nice guy.

"Mort knows a good idea from a bad idea," says Siegel out of the corner of his mouth while relighting his cigar. He waves away the layers of smoke and says, "I'm a lawyer. What do I know about show business? Nothing is what I know. So what am I doing running this company? Good question. Speak."

I tell Willard and Mort the *Mothers* idea. When I finish, Willard asks Mort if it's a good idea or a bad idea.

"It's a bad idea."

"Well, I think it's a good idea," says Siegel to Rosen. "Why do you think it's a bad idea?"

"Because it'll skew old," answers Rosen.

"Well, I think it'll skew young," says Siegel to Rosen. "It's a talk show sideways with lay people instead of pompous know-it-all celebrities. I think if you keep the problems young, a young audience will eat the show up. *Mothers* are just what this country needs. They do know best. There's nothing like 'em." Turning to me, Siegel says, "What will a pilot cost?"

"Three hundred and fifty thousand dollars," I reply.

"You got it," says Willard.

I'm shocked and I show it. "Thank you."

"You're welcome. Didn't I tell you I was your best friend in this business?"

I fly back to Los Angeles amazed at life's strange twists and turns. Yesterday the *Mothers* idea was dead in the water. Today I'm about to begin producing my first new television game show in years. Just like that. And then a week later I'm shocked again.

I hear that Willard Siegel was fired.

CHAPTER FORTY

I'm sitting in my hole-in-the-wall office on Little Santa Monica, the same office I used when I first came to Hollywood. My good-luck office. My shrine. It's where I received the telephone call from Len Goldberg twenty-five years ago telling me he was putting the *Dating Game* on the air. I'm here because I need to think about things.

One of the things I'm thinking about is that I'm finished with the *Mothers* project. I haven't any drive or desire to continue selling that idea. I know this. But there are a lot of things I don't know. Like why, at this particular time in my life, I feel this compulsion to create and sell a new game show. Considering the fact that in seventeen short years I'll be eighty (God willing), and that I have enough money right now to live well for the rest of my life (thank God), why should I be wasting precious time scratching around trying to get back into the rat race? Doesn't make sense.

The other thing I'm thinking about—and this is a big surprise to me—is that I believe I'm homesick for Saint-Tropez. After all my blustering and growling about France and the French, it comes as somewhat of a surprise to me that I miss Henri and Loulou, and Janot le facteur, and Dede le boulanger, and all the other Janots and Dedes. I miss my café crème in the morning, my Perrier-menthe after the *boule* games in the Café des Arts with all the other guys. I even miss their rancid smells.

My reverie is interrupted by a ringing telephone.

It's a friend in The Biz. He says, "I heard a rumor the television chief over at MCA Entertainment wants to meet with you. The word is he'd love to do a late-night talk show with you as host, if—and it's a big if—if you can come up with an off-the-wall concept that would excite him."

"Him? Who's him?"

"Shelly Schwab. He runs MCA Television high atop the Black Tower in Universal City. Rumor has it they think you'd be a terrific late-night personality. Whacko, crazy, a sort of cross between Ernie Kovacs and Soupy Sales. So if you're interested, think of an off-the-wall concept, go to Universal City and sell it to Shelly."

I hang up the telephone and hoot with excitement. It's a knee-jerk reaction. The hell with France, I say to myself, although I'm not sure why. Maybe it's because I can smell the opportunity to sell another TV show. Maybe I get excited every time that possibility exists. Some kind of Pavlovian reaction. Maybe I just can't help myself. I open my office door, put my head out into the hall, and yell, "Put down those obituaries, folks, the fat lady hasn't sung yet! It's not over until it's over." Nobody sticks their head out an office to wish me well. I shut the door and realize I have a major problem. I have to think of an off-the-wall concept.

I'm lost. Nothing comes to mind. I pace and ponder, take a long walk, come back to the office, collapse on the day bed and stare at the far wall. On the wall is a huge framed enlargement—six feet by five feet—of one of my favorite photographs. Red took the picture when we were living in New York at the Wyndham Hotel. Why the two of us went from Los Angeles to New York for the weekend, checked into the Wyndham on West Fifty-eighth Street and stayed there for three and a half years is another story.

The Wyndham is a sort of Faulty Towers hiding behind the majestic and famous Plaza. Along with plain old-fashioned tourists, the Wyndham is a word-of-mouth hangout for show business people working on Broadway or making a film in Manhattan. The photograph that I'm staring at on my office wall was taken in the bedroom of our somewhat tacky Wyndham suite. The picture shows our queen-size bed, the night table, and wicker chair on either side of the bed, some dreary water colors suspended here and there, and a monotonously patterned wallpaper that you can see peeling in various places.

I'm in bed lying on my back on top of the covers in traction. I'm suffering from a herniated disc. A thick belt is strapped around my waist. Pulleys run from both sides of the belt over the end of my bed to a pair of large weights that hang a few feet from the floor. I'm dressed in a Phillies baseball hat, a T-shirt, sweat pants, and sweat socks. Lying on the bed beside me is John Cassavetes. Sitting in the wicker chair on my right is Ben Gazzara. Sitting in the other wicker chair on the left side of Cassavetes is Peter Falk. It's a Friday night in February some time after eleven in the evening. All of us, except Red, are eating deli food, drinking whiskey, and watching a professional basketball game on television. We've all wagered various quantities of money on the contest and are therefore wearing intense expressions. You can't see the television set. You can see a closet door and a bathroom door. I wonder why the blowup fascinates me.

And then I realize why.

It's the talk show idea Mr. Schwab at MCA covets.

The giant enlargement has given me the germ for a slightly demented and unquestionably different concept. I take the germ and mentally run with it. The show should take place in a bedroom, I decide, or a hospital room, or a hotel room; it doesn't matter as long as a bed is center stage. The room ought to be decorated to look like an overcrowded pawnshop, perhaps the same as my office was in the sixties, with everything from stuffed alligators to electric guitars hanging from the ceiling and all kinds of junk imaginable lying around everywhere else. I would be in bed in traction, or with my leg in a cast. One guest could be lying on the bed beside me like Cassavetes. Two other guests could be sitting in the armchairs on either side of the bed where Gazzara and Falk are. The guests will make their entrances and exits through the bathroom door. The closet will be for surprises. Who knows what we'll find when we open the closet door. Maybe we'll find Bruce Springsteen sitting in a rocking chair eating a pizza and waving. Maybe it'll be our midget weatherman. Maybe the UCLA marching band. Maybe D.B. Cooper.

I know I'm rushing things, but I'm excited. I telephone Mr. Schwab's office and make an appointment to see him at ten o'clock the next morning. Then I call my friend Robert "The Prince" Downey. Downey is the legendary film director of cult movies like *Putney Swope* and *Greasers Palace*. Downey's mind's a treat. His ideas are so weird, they're priceless.

He says, "What do you want me to do?"

"Go with me to MCA."

"Why?"

"For moral support."

The next morning, chauffeur-to-the-stars Danny Cahill drives Downey and me to the Black Tower in Universal City.

Danny Cahill suggests he come with us to the meeting. When I ask why, he says for good luck. I tell him I'll think about it. When we get to Universal City, Danny parks and hands me the immense framed blowup I had placed in the trunk of his limousine. He reminds me again about his wanting to come along. I decide against it. Three's a crowd. Danny's disappointed. He drives off searching for a cup of coffee.

Downey and I enter the Black Tower, find an elevator, and a few minutes later, Mr. Schwab's waiting room. A receptionist escorts us into the head of the television department's office. There are seven men and one woman, all dressed in black suits and ties, sitting on couches and chairs waiting for us. I'm somewhat startled by this impressive reception. I thought it was going to be just Shelly Schwab.

"I'm Shelly Schwab," says a nice, decent-looking man. Shelly Schwab is my size and kind of resembles me. I like him immediately. "I hope you don't mind the crowd," he says, "but we here at MCA Television have never had the honor of hearing one of your legendary sales pitches."

"No problem," I say, feeling a rush of sweat on my forehead. I haven't sweated like this since my meeting at Rod Perth's office. Why the sweat now, I wonder, and why isn't Loretta here? Because I'm not pitching *Mothers*, I tell myself, that's why. Am I nervous because Loretta's not here? Or because I'm pitching a show idea I'm suddenly not sure will work? Or because I'm overstimulated by the four cups of coffee I drank before arriving.

"Cup of coffee?" asks Shelly Schwab.

"Yes, please," I say.

"Why don't you sit there," he says, pointing to the cat-bird seat, the one facing all the others.

First I lean the framed blowup of Cassavetes, Gazzara, Falk, and myself against a wall, its back facing everyone in the room. When the time is right I plan to turn the framed picture around and surprise all the MCA executives. It's sure to be an attention grabber. I take my seat facing the crowd. Downey, in a long-sleeved shirt opened at the neck and jeans, is perched in the middle of a couch flanked by black suits. He looks out of place.

"A short preamble for the benefit of the younger members of our team," says Shelly Schwab to the multitude. "Chuck, as probably all of you know, is one of the most prolific and successful game show producers who's ever worked in television. At one time he had more programs on network TV than anyone, the big studios included. A couple of years ago Chuck retired and went off with his wife to live happily ever after in France."

I wince at the word "retired."

"The story goes," continues Shelly, "that Chuck swore he'd never do television again unless he had an idea that would make so much money he'd have no other choice but to return to Hollywood and do it. Well, as you can see, Chuck's back and we're the first distributor to get a crack at his hot new property."

Schwab flashes a smile to the black suits.

All the black suits smile back.

"With that in mind," says Shelly to me, "I'll turn the meeting over to you."

Right now all I want to do is find out who told Shelly Schwab all that bullshit about not doing television again unless the idea would make me so much money I couldn't refuse. Also I've become thoroughly insecure. I thought this MCA crowd was looking for me. But that's not true at all. Someone filled Schwab's head with a song and dance about me being television's Messiah doing a second coming with a blockbuster game show under my arm just for him. Who would tell Shelly that? Certainly not a friend.

"Yes," I say, "my idea was too good to let die in the south of France."

And then something remarkable takes place.

I can't speak.

It happened to me once before, not being able to speak in public. In Minnesota. I was chairman of the board and chief executive officer of my company. My associates and I had been traveling across the country doing a dog-and-pony show trying to complete a sixty-million-dollar stock offering. I was addressing a roomful of market analysts in Minneapolis at a breakfast meeting when all of a sudden I was unable to speak. I just stood there brain dead; my mind a total blank, my eyes glazed, my mouth a hole in the center of my face.

God only knows why. Exhausted perhaps? Unprepared? Insecure? Whatever the reason, I became mute. My audience didn't know whether I was a genius playing out some bizarre trick or a basket case with one foot in Minneapolis General.

I'm sure Shelly and his black suits are thinking the same thing. I can feel their discomfort, see Schwab and some of the others wriggling uneasily in their seats. I watch my friend Downey staring at the palms of his hands. Time passes by. My upper lip is covered with beads of sweat. I'm obviously going down for the count. I must talk. I must get on track. Any track.

"Okay," I say, the word cracking as it comes out, "let me start by saying I've been living in France for the past two years. During that time I thought of a lot of TV show ideas. But I made it a practice to sit on all of them. The last thing I wanted to do was come back here and do another game show. I did all that already." I pause. Do the MCA television executives really want to hear this crap? I take a sip of coffee. It's cold. I look up and smile. "By the way, have any of you ever been to the south of France? Nobody? Well, let me tell you, it's just incredible there. The sky and the water are bluer than anywhere else in the world. The air is so fresh, it's, I don't know, it's just indescribable. I write in a cozy little room that overlooks the sea with a view that's not to be believed. I usually start writing early in the morning when the fishermen are leaving, and finish in the afternoon when they're coming home. All day dozens of swallows swoop past my window and sea gulls stand on its ledge. And the colors are absolutely inspiring. You can see why all those master Impressionists lived in the south of France. The trees and houses, the sea and sky, even the laundry hanging out to dry is worth painting."

Downey's making faces at me trying to get my attention. His contorted, painful frown is trying to tell me something.

Ignoring Downey, I roll on. "And out where our big house is, out where the vineyards are, it's truly beautiful. There's wildflowers everywhere and wonderful weeping willow trees. They're really not weeping willow trees. I don't know what kind of trees they are or what they're called, but they're proud and majestic. And they're bent almost sideways by the mistrals that have been blowing there for centuries. Mistral is the name of those cold, magical winds that blow down from the Rhône River valley from the north. They say mistrals last for one, three, or six days. They're sexy, too, if you can believe winds can be sexy, and the—"

"I don't mean to interrupt," says Shelly Schwab irritably, not smiling now, checking his wristwatch, "but I think you'd better start talking about your idea."

"Right. Okay. Let me tell you the working title. I call the show *Late Night Something.*"

I wait for the laugh. There isn't any. Maybe that's because the title's not funny. I wonder to myself why I ever thought it was. The flop sweat begins to trickle down my chest. I say, "You know what I'm going to do now? I'm going to save all of us a lot of time. What I'm going to do is show you a picture that says it all. This picture describes my talk show idea better than anything I can think of. You know what they say about a picture being worth a thousand words? Well, this is one of those."

I get up, walk over to where the framed enlargement is leaning against the wall, and carry it to the center of the room. Everyone's eyes are riveted to the back of the picture. Everyone's anxious to see the front. You can feel the tension in the room. I'm pleased with this bit of show biz suspense. I came in a genius, dropped to mental case, and now maybe I'll be a genius again. I take a deep breath.

And then I flip the big blowup around.

CHAPTER FORTY-ONE

Downey, Danny Cahill, and I are sitting in a box at the Santa Anita Racetrack. It's a beautiful morning. We made it to the track in time for the first race. The horses are rounding the near turn, about to come down the stretch. Downey and Danny are shouting, "Come on! Come on!" rooting in a bet. I'm reviewing the meeting at MCA Television I walked out of an hour ago. The horses are rumbling down the stretch now right in front of us. Downey and Danny Cahill have bet Pick-Sixes, which means they have to pick six winners. If they do, they'll win millions of dollars. If five of the six come in, they'll still win plenty. Of course the chances of them choosing five winners, let alone six, are slim to none. Right now their first horse is out in front. I lift my eyelids up to see if the horse wins.

He does.

The boys only have five more winners to go. They leave to place a few side bets. I feel around my popcorn box for more popcorn. My fingers touch the bottom of the empty container. Disappointed, I drop my eyelids and slide back into my morning meeting, recalling once again the moment I turned the enlargement of the photograph around.

"So, there it is," I had said, pointing to the enlargement. "That's the show."

"What's the show?" snapped Shelly Schwab.

"That's the show," I replied irritably, never talking in that tone of voice to a prospective buyer before. My nerves were frayed. I was losing my bearings, falling apart at the seams.

Shelly Schwab sat unsmiling and said nothing.

"You see, Shelly," I continued, trying to sound as pleasant as I could, "I'm in this bedroom in traction, and my guests for the evening are all around me like Cassavetes there, and Gazzara and Falk. All the guests make their entrance through here, through this bathroom door." I pointed to the door. "That's the bathroom door. And that's the closet, over here. There's always a surprise in the closet. Inside the closet can be anything or anyone."

Silence.

"Like a midget weatherman?"

Here at the racetrack, Downey and Danny Cahill are in hog heaven.

I, too, am feeling better. The noon sun is baking the MCA debacle out of my body. I'm starting to decompress and enjoy myself. I'm even getting excited over the boys' three straight winners. What began as a cataclysmic morning has metamorphosed into a sort of happy afternoon. Downey and Danny Cahill are beginning to see sports cars and motor yachts in their lives and I'm reveling in unanticipated treats, things my wife would never let me eat in a million years: hot dogs, french fries, milk shakes, and Snickers bars.

Downey and Danny's horse wins the fourth race. They're now four for four. One more winner and they're assured of taking home between fifty and a hundred thousand dollars. Two more and they'll get millions. Downey leaves to telephone his wife Laura. Maybe she can run down to the corner and light a candle at the Church of the Good Shepherd, say a prayer, ask God to let the next two horses win. Other than Red and my sister, Laura's my favorite female. She's so pretty it's sickening.

Unfortunately the boys lose the fifth and sixth by a nose. They're out of the running for the Pick-Six but they're still way ahead of the track in winnings. They lose the seventh and eighth races and decide to go home.

I ask Downey, "What about the last race? The ninth race?"

"You gotta know when to quit."

"Is that like knowing when to get off the train."

"Yeah," he says, and the three of us leave.

CHAPTER FORTY-TWO

Red and I attend a fund-raiser. Clinton For President. It costs me
ten thousand dollars for this privilege. The fund-raiser is in the form
of a sit-down dinner at the Beverly Hills home of Lew Wasserman.
Wasserman's one of the most powerful men in the entertainment
industry. I've come to this fund-raiser because I have something
very important to ask Clinton.

Since I never have important questions to ask anyone in politics,
sports, or entertainment, I rarely go to fund-raisers or charity balls.
Most of these events are generally filled with affected Hollywood
types either talking glowingly about themselves or back-biting some
other Hollywood type to the bone. The food is generally awful and
you eat too much because you're bored and have nothing better to
do with your mouth. The next morning when you wake up you think
someone smaller than you has gone into your closet during the night
and hung all their clothes there.

On those infrequent occasions Red and I do go to an affair like
Clinton For President, I rationalize our being there by telling myself
I'm going to overhear interesting conversation that I can use in my
writing. Of course this never happens. Also, I don't know how to
mingle and make charming small talk with the other minglers and
charming small talkers. Invariably I end up standing in some corner
most of the evening, rigid and cold like a fudgsicle.

And finally the preparations for these bashes are both stressful and
dangerous to my marriage. Particularly when Red suggests what I
should wear. Tonight she lays out my severe black double-breasted
suit, a white shirt, a blue-and-black patterned tie, a black alligator
belt, and black loafers with tassels. The discussion that ensues is ill-
humored. Red keeps saying I must look "presidential." I whine. Red

glares. We compromise. I'll wear the loafers with the tassels, but we drive to the affair in my GMC Cyclone truck.

When we arrive at the Wasserman mansion, the parking attendants converge on Red who is about to climb down from the truck's front seat. They do this because she is the prettiest girl wearing the prettiest dress they've seen so far that evening. I am not adept at describing a dress, but I'll try. The dress is a sweet powder blue. It has a plunging neckline but you don't see an undue amount of bosom. It fits tightly around the waist and flounces out from her thighs showing sexy sections of the Redhead's great legs. I worry about Red getting out of the truck. I know the parking attendants and photographers are going to try and look up her dress.

We transfer to one of several small vans that will transport the evening's guests up the Wassermans' winding driveway to the mansion's front door. An elderly couple join us in the van. The two are a humorless pair, their faces reddened by sun or liquor, the latter I suspect. He's a large man, wears a Clinton button in his lapel, tucks his tie under his belt, and is the spitting image of Secretary of State James Baker. His wife looks exactly like Barbara Bush. It's hard to believe they're Democrats.

Inside the house, a photographer takes our picture and we shake hands with Mr. and Mrs. Wasserman. They appear to be friendly, nice people. Mr. Wasserman thanks my wife and me for coming and points the way to their patio. We step outside onto the formal rolling gardens. The gardens go on forever. A young waiter passes by and spills an entire glass of something on Red's beautiful powder-blue dress.

I'm stunned.

I want to kill the waiter. I look to heaven for guidance and compassion. I ask Him: why Red's dress? Why not any of the fifty other dresses on this goddamn patio? I turn to the young waiter, but he's so apologetic about the accident, I find myself feeling sorry for him. We discover it's only Perrier. Still, there's this massive dark stain. I'm sick. Red isn't. She says it's no big deal. "We'll chertle about this tomorrow." She means chortle. Red takes my hand and we mingle.

There are a great many people standing around eating and drinking and talking to each other, waiters and waitresses serving munchies on silver trays, Secret Service agents everywhere; on the roof, hiding in the hedges, standing conspicuously among the guests.

The Secret Service agents are easy to single out. There is a small plastic coil coming out of one ear. The coil is attached to a walkie-talkie hidden somewhere in their clothing.

"Why are we here?" I ask my wife.

"Don't start."

"But why *are* we?"

"I don't believe this," says the Redhead. She sighs. "Because you wanted to come. You had something important you wanted to ask Clinton."

"I paid ten thousand dollars to ask Clinton something?"

"That's what you said. You said you had something very important to ask him."

"You let me pay ten thousand dollars to ask the guy a question?"

"Please."

"What did I want to ask him, honey?"

"How the hell do I know, honey?"

"Ten thousand dollars to ask Clinton something and I can't remember what it is."

"Typical," says my wife, and waves to someone she knows.

It's apparent that everybody who is anybody is at the Clinton party tonight. All the motion picture chiefs are here. All of their lieutenants are here, too. So are major television and film celebrities. The party oozes clout. I see the famous movie producer, Jon Peters, with a famous model named Vendela. She's so famous she only needs one name, like Sting and Madonna. Vendela is wearing a white dress you can see through. It is very difficult not to stare at her very thin bra and bikini panties. I wonder if she should be wearing that dress. I tell Red, "She doesn't appear very presidential."

"She's not my responsibility," replies my wife.

I watch Vendela's escort, Mr. Peters, greet a very small but powerful Walt Disney Company executive named Jeffrey Katzenberg. I watch Peters wrap his arms around Katzenberg's waist, hug Katzenberg tightly to his chest and stomach, then lift Katzenberg completely off his feet. I watch Katzenberg's little legs kicking helplessly in the air. I watch Jon Peters hug and lift another famous producer, Peter Guber, off his feet. And do the same to someone named Sandy Gallin. I tell my wife, "It seems lifting people up in the air is Jon Peters's way of saying hello."

"He's only being playful."

"Well, I'll tell you this. If he lifts me up I'm going to punch him right in his fucking mouth."

"Right, honey, you do that."

Two baby-faced studio executives are talking to each other nearby. They wear silk sport coats with wide lapels, white dress shirts buttoned at the neck, no ties, baggy slacks tucked into unlaced high-top sneakers. One has wild, curly blond hair. The other's hair is black, wet, slicked down, and parted in the middle. Both are holding their drinks in one hand, feeding each other their munchies with their other hand. The one closest to me is saying, "We shouldn't be looking for fulfillment in our work. Not at our age. We should simply focus on getting rich. We'll do fulfillment later, when we're old."

David Geffen walks by. David's an old friend. He's become a billionaire since I saw him last. He looks good. His face is charcoal brown from the sun and he sports a two-day growth of white beard. Geffen looks at me and smiles but doesn't say hello. He doesn't recognize me. But he recognizes Red and gives her a big kiss. I wonder why David didn't say hello to me. I'm immediately depressed and irritable. It's the reason I never come to affairs like this. Something inevitably happens that puts me in a disagreeable mood. Later I see Geffen peeking at me furtively through a crowd on the terrace.

"Geffen's sneaking looks at me over Carrie Fisher's shoulder," I tell Red. "He's wondering if I noticed he didn't say hello. I hope it really bothers him."

"I like David a lot," says my wife.

"Of course you do. He kissed you."

"You're annoyed because he didn't kiss *you.*"

"I hope this makes him toss and turn all night, although I doubt that it will."

I hear someone behind me say, "Come on, it's not all that complicated. We're talking denial here. Denial's not just a river in Egypt, you know."

Bill Clinton steps onto the terrace and begins making his way through the crowd. I tell my wife, "I remember what I wanted to ask Clinton."

"Good," she says.

"I want to know if he gets elected President will he see to it that the American colony in Saint-Tropez gets Armed Forces Network television programs piped in so we can watch pro football games on Sundays instead of all that European soccer shit."

"Do you think that's something he really wants to be concerned about?"

"It better be."

"Then you go ahead and ask him, honey."

A man with a horrible tie steps in front of me, lifts a glass of champagne off a silver tray for another man, takes one for himself and says, "Clark's the only guy I know who's happy with T-bills at three fucking percent."

The Democratic candidate for President of the United States is standing directly in front of me. He reaches his hand out to shake mine. I shake it and say, "Governor Clinton, good luck."

"Thank you."

"I was wondering, Governor, if it would be possible . . ."

"Thank you," he says again, looking over my shoulder, smiling with joy at someone else.

And then he's gone.

"How 'bout that!" I growl to Red. "Can't wait two minutes to hear what I have to say? Who the hell was standing behind me that got him so excited?"

"Nicole Kidman, Tom Cruise's wife," says my wife.

I look at Mrs. Cruise. She's very pretty. I can't help thinking that if my accountant Max Fleishman had been standing behind me we would be enjoying professional football in Saint-Tropez next season.

Red and I are assigned to table #17. I see game show producer and media magnet Mark Goodson and a pretty blond companion sitting at our table. So far they are the only ones there. I panic. I say to Red, "You don't think the Wassermans put all the game show producers at one table, do you?"

"No, dear. I don't think they would do that."

Red's right. The table is filled with campaign contributors, fat cats from all over southern California. An elegantly dressed, handsome man who looks to be in his late fifties is sitting to my left. His date for the evening is an incredibly sexy girl who couldn't be more than nineteen or twenty. They are both tall, both bronzed from the sun. The older man is lazily picking at his food. I hear him tell the sexy girl, "I read somewhere that a prompt man was a lonely man."

"And," adds the girl, "if a man or woman takes forever to eat their food he or she has sexual problems."

"Where did you read that?" snaps the man, alarmed.

"I didn't," says the girl, laughing a wonderful laugh. "I just made it up."

The sun goes down. A full moon rises. An evening chill sets in. The heat lamps are lighted. No one at our table seems to notice. They're too busy chatting. A large man sitting across from me announces to one and all that he's from Reno, Nevada, and that he's in real estate.

I whisper to my wife, "I guess he thinks all of us at this table are sitting on the edge of our chairs dying to know where he's from and what he does for a living."

My wife shushes me and returns to chatting with Mr. Goodson, who is sitting on her immediate right. My wife apparently likes the game show maven. She's not only talking to him with enthusiasm but she's patting his hand. Mr. Goodson's hands are covered with large brown liver spots.

But then, so are mine.

"Can I have your attention," says the real estate baron from Reno, tapping a glass with a spoon. When everyone at our table quiets down, he says, "I have a funny Hollywood-type story to tell you all. It's a true story, I might add. I think you'll find this story interesting, and quite amusing. Last night I was having dinner at Chasen's with an old friend of mine and his new wife. The wife gets up to go to the ladies' room and while she's gone my friend says to me . . ."

My mind wanders.

I can't help recalling how excited we always get when there's a full moon in Saint-Tropez. If the sky is clear the moon will light up the sea and make it look like a sunny afternoon. When we know it's going to be a cloudless sky and the moon is going to be round and as bright as a spotlight, a bunch of us will change whatever plans we had, head for the dock, and climb aboard *Bam Bam*. With the sun just setting behind the hills, a warm breeze in our face, and classical music filling our ears, we'll glide across the sea in the *Bammer* toward Port Grammount, drinking wine, talking, laughing, having fun, happy we're alive and together in such a pleasant place. I'll steer *Bam Bam* up the inland waterway that leads to a wonderful Moroccan restaurant . . .

"Time to go," says my wife.

The Clinton For President party's over.

There's a rush for the vans to take us back to the street and our cars. What begins as an orderly line quickly disintegrates into a rowdy crowd. The very important people want to go home now, this minute. They push ahead of each other, jamming important elbows into important ribs, trying to get into the next van. Red and I pass up the bedlam and walk down the driveway to the street. It's a madhouse there, too. Everybody is yelling at Chuckie of Chuckie's Parking Concession. All the people with clout want their black four-door BMWs or black four-door Mercedeses right now. They are not used to waiting. Every time a black four-door BMW or Mercedes arrives fifteen people with clout run to claim it.

A couple are arguing right in front of us. They speak to each other as though they're in their own living room. I hear him say to her, "We're not getting a divorce because you committed adultery, Mavis. We're getting a divorce because you *bragged* about it."

Our GMC Cyclone Truck arrives.

Nobody runs to claim it.

That night I can't sleep. Around two in the morning I give up, get out of bed and go to the kitchen. Red waddles in while I'm eating a peanut-butter-and-jelly sandwich.

"I can't sleep because I don't want to do television like I thought I did," I say before she asks me why I can't sleep.

"I'm hungry," she replies.

"I tossed and turned in a cold sweat ever since we turned the lights out."

"Why?" asks Red, her head hidden inside the refrigerator.

"Just thinking about going back into the studio, auditioning contestants again, and big-toothed game show hosts. The thought actually made me nauseous."

"Did you take two Tums?" she asks, coming to the kitchen table with jars of peanut butter and jelly, a quart of milk, and a loaf of Wonder Bread under her arm.

"And if the show's a hit," I add, "I'll have to do it for years and years. I'll die thinking up game show questions. What a revolting way to go."

Red sits down beside me and makes herself a peanut-butter-and-jelly sandwich. The carefully coiffed hairdo she prepared for the fund-raiser some hours ago is now all messed up and in her eyes. I like it better this way. The beautiful powder-blue dress that had Perrier spilled all over it minutes after we arrived has been replaced by a kelly-green Philadelphia Eagles football jersey with white letters saying R. Cunningham stitched on the back. I think she's so cute I feel like a high school kid with a crush.

I tell her she looks pretty and I love her.

"The dress is fine," she says, my words of endearment going right over her head. "The stain's all gone."

"Yeah? Good." I take a bite of my sandwich. "Anhoeverl daewgame . . ."

"Finish chewing."

I swallow. "And whoever I do a new game show for is going to want to change things. Not only that, there's always going to be some third-string bureaucrat from the network or the syndicator attached to my ass, hanging around my office all day, seeing to it that I do things the way his boss wants me to do it. That's what goes on these days. It's a new business out there. Who needs it?"

"Yeah, who needs it?" repeats my wife.

"You should always do what you want to do, not what you think you ought to do."

"That's deep," says my wife.

"I overheard someone say that at the party tonight."

We sit quietly for a moment.

"Anyway, I'm not doing what I want to do. I'm doing what I think I ought to do. Just look at the way I went to the MCA meeting. I walked into Shelly Schwab's office like I had a death wish. In the old days I would have never gone to a buyer like that, trying to sell a show so unprepared. I wasn't looking for a sale. I was looking to get crucified. I wanted to embarrass myself so badly I would never have the desire to try selling game shows again. At this stage of my life the one thing I don't need is self-inflicted pain."

"Absolument, mon mari."

"Not me, that's for sure."

"Mais bien sûr."

"Like I said, who needs that shit?"

"Yeah, who needs that shit."

"Are you making fun of me?"

"*Moi?*"

"Come on, Red, this is serious."

"So what are you trying to tell me, *mon petit poulet?*" she asks. "As if I didn't know. *Alors. Est-ce que vous voulez me dire quelque chose?*"

"What's with all the French?"

"Practicing," replies my wife, and takes another bite of her sandwich.

PART IV

Everything comes from the immense and eternal law of fatality.

—*Seneca*

CHAPTER FORTY-THREE

It's three o'clock in the morning. I'm dozing. I can hear distant thunder. Which means I better get out of bed as quickly as possible so that I can leap about the house unplugging every appliance I don't want destroyed by the lightning that's bound to follow. I sit on the edge of my bed trying to wake up. This is no easy matter. We were out very late last night. It was our first night back in Saint-Tropez. We celebrated our homecoming with friends at Restaurant Nano. I ate like I was going to the electric chair in the morning. I knew I would suffer later. Now it's later and I'm suffering. If I ask my wife what to do she'll tell me to take two Tums.

But before I do anything I must get up, put on my slippers and unplug my TV sets, fax machine, computer, and printer. Anything I don't unplug I leave at their own peril. Lightning has been known to come down chimneys and whisk around the room scaring the inhabitants half to death and blowing up every appliance in sight. Mind you, lightning coming down your chimney's rare. What isn't rare is lightning blowing up anything that's plugged into a socket without bothering to come inside.

Wouldn't you'd think French scientists and engineers would have discovered ways by now to protect its citizens' television sets and fax machines? How about just copying what we do in the USA? My friend Dominique Lapierre, a professional Frenchman if ever there was one, gets all riled up when I say that. He huffs and puffs and snorts and fumes, barely controlling his temper long enough to babble, "Well, goddamn it, you had a power blackout in New York that lasted two days, so what the hell are *you* talking about?" First of all, it didn't last two days. Secondly, it was an aberration that happened once. Once in two hundred years, not every other day.

I hear the thunder again.

I look around my bedroom. Usually I can see our VCR and TV sets' digital clocks blinking in the night. Since the power is always going out, digital clocks are constantly blinking all over our house. All over the south of France, for that matter. You know why I can't see the blinking lights tonight? Because last night before I went to bed I covered them with Red's sweat socks and my Jockey shorts. Everybody in this part of the country covers their twinkling digital clocks with sweat socks, bras, and Jockey shorts. I hear the more fastidious French use crocheted doilies, but that's not the point. The point is, it's 1992 for Christ sake.

"We're back," I mutter irritably to myself.

"Are you all right?" mumbles my wife, mostly asleep.

"We're definitely back in France," I growl, hearing the thunder coming closer. "It's three in the morning and I have to go unplug. It pisses me off that in this day and age I still have to do this."

"Take two Tums," says my wife.

The next night the mayor of Saint-Tropez comes to our little house in the port for dinner.

I'm glad. My wife and I want to talk to him. We want him to change his mind and give us permission to rehang a small balcony outside the second floor of our house. We already have two large French doors in my studio that were made to open out to the balcony. We even have the balcony. It's nothing elaborate. Just a simple wrought-iron thing we had made, maybe three feet wide and five feet long. When the balcony arrived, workmen fastened it to our house. After the platform was secure I stepped onto it and waved to an elderly couple standing in Place Willard Person. Less than an hour later, several neighbors filed complaints with the mayor saying we were "destroying the old-world charm of the neighborhood." No one bothered to point out that there were five similar balconies on houses surrounding Place Willard Person. Those balconies were there before, they didn't count, whined the Old Port Tropeziens. Our balcony was new, an eyesore. They demanded the blight be removed. The mayor agreed. His office informed me to get rid of it. The problem, said the mayor, was strictly aesthetics. Nothing personal.

"That's what I'm going to tell the mayor when he comes tonight for dinner," I say to my wife.

"What are you going to tell him?"

"I'm going to tell him to take my balcony and stick it up his esthetic ass."

"You do that, honey," she says, and walks away shaking her head. I wonder if my wife's shaking her head at the mayor or me.

So the mayor comes. We have a nice dinner. We talk about everything but the balcony. My wife is nervous. She's waiting for the argument. But I don't argue. I'm the perfect host.

We all have after-dinner drinks in the living room. This is the first time the mayor's been to our renovated home. I ask him if he would like a quick tour. He says he would like that very much. I take the mayor to the third floor and work my way down. I start with our bedroom and bathroom, each with their own fireplaces, our small dressing room, the spectacular views from our windows. Then we go down to the second floor. I show the mayor my office and its adjoining cozy bathroom, also with its own fireplace. I open the large French doors that overlook the little square below. The mayor steps out onto the balcony. Since the mayor forced me to take the balcony down, it is not there. Before I can remind him of that, the mayor falls two flights to the cement below. By the time it takes me to get downstairs and outside to the mayor, he's dead.

"That's why I need a balcony!" I yell at his corpse furiously. "So accidents like this won't happen!"

CHAPTER FORTY-FOUR

"Wake up," says my wife, gently shaking me. "You're having a bad dream."

I sit up and clear the cobwebs out of my head. I tell Red what my dream was about.

She says that's kind of a great idea.

That night the mayor really comes to our house for dinner.

Mayor Spada is thin and wiry and as I mentioned before is never without his coat and tie.

The mayor of Saint-Tropez is a controversial guy. He makes a lot of the locals angry, particularly the working class. He issues bizarre edicts that prohibit new house and hotel construction, digging new swimming pools, putting up new balconies, things like that. Yet other Tropeziens insist he's protecting the integrity and property value of the port; preventing Saint-Tropez from becoming the Las Vegas of the Riviera. I can't make up my mind if he's doing a good job or a bad one, or if he's right or wrong. Yet I like him. The mayor cannot speak English. And he talks very fast. I have difficulty understanding what he says, like now, when he's insisting I never gave him a *Bam Bam* jacket.

He's right. I never did.

Giving the mayor of Saint-Tropez a *Bam Bam* jacket is fraught with political danger. It could ruin my standing with the mostly laboring *boule* players of the Place des Lices. *Bam Bam* jackets symbolize a certain honor and comradeship that cross all xenophobic boundaries in this little seaport. But maybe not where the mayor's concerned. Sometimes I wonder why I ever bothered with *Bam Bam* jackets in the first place.

One of the first things I did after I got my boat *Bam Bam* was order half a dozen boat jackets. They were for Red and me, my instructor Patrick Mercurio, his brother Jean François, and his sister Teetee.

The *Bam Bam* jackets are navy-blue and made of thick nylon. They zip up the front, have long sleeves, and big button-down pockets. Over the jacket's heart are crossed American and French flags. On the opposite side is a crescent-shaped red-and-black fireman's patch that says Saint-Tropez. Under the patch is a yellow caricature of Woodstock from the Peanuts comic strip. On the back of the windbreaker is a duplicate of that Saint-Tropez fireman's patch and Woodstock, only this one takes up the entire area like the Hell's Angel emblem on a Harley Davidson motorcycle jacket. I had one extra *Bam Bam* jacket from the original half dozen. I gave it to Henri Bruni.

That started it.

Henri was appreciative and wore his *Bam Bam* jacket with pride; possibly because of what it meant or possibly because it featured the Saint-Tropez fireman's patch and looked great. In any case, I was both surprised and touched by the fact that the jacket never left his body. I also noticed how all the other locals envied Henri and coveted a *Bam Bam* jacket. So I ordered a dozen more from New York. When they arrived, I passed them out covertly to those who, like Henri, had befriended me. It was my way of showing appreciation. Getting them to the deserving, however, was a bit tricky. I would often slip someone his jacket by putting it in a paper shopping bag and handing it to him on a dark street. Sometimes I would hang the jacket on the knob of a chair in the Gorille while he or she was having their morning coffee. Other times I would leave a jacket hooked on a lamppost in the park, go to the person I was presenting it to, and say, "Your *Bam Bam* jacket's over there on that pole." Once, while driving home, I forced a motorcyclist off the road to give him his jacket. At first my friend was so frightened and furious he was going to punch me in the mouth. But when he saw what I had under my arm, he kissed me on both cheeks.

Soon I had to order a dozen more.

Then two dozen more.

Bam Bam jackets became an institution. They were mentioned in Paris *Vogue*. The article said: "You're not in, not a real Tropezien unless you have a *Bam Bam* jacket." Today there are almost two hundred *Bam Bam* jackets in Saint-Tropez. In the fall, when the weather turns chilly, *Bam Bam* jackets appear all over the place like wildflowers. "Chuck's Army" is how the locals refer to them.

"You see, you see," says the mayor in his machine-gun way of speaking, "you never ever gave me a *Bam Bam* jacket. Everyone in town has one but me. Am I not good enough for Chuck's Army?"

I avoid answering his question. Instead I ask the mayor and his wife if they would like to take a quick tour of our remodeled house. The mayor says he would love to.

Red drops her coffee cup.

The tour is uneventful.

The dinner is uneventful, too, except for my wife's repeated gaff. The mayor's daughter's name is Anastasia. Red insists on calling her Anesthesia. I can't correct her. She's sitting too far away.

At the end of the evening, as the mayor prepares to leave, he asks if I would be so kind as to attend a dinner he is giving for some purpose I don't quite understand. The Ultimate Cooking Machine is summoned from the kitchen to translate.

She says, "I fink the mayor wants you to go to a dinner to christen the new Chamber of Commerce hall."

My wife, who is standing behind the mayor, rolls her eyes in supplication. She's begging me not to accept the dinner invitation. She knows the evening will be a crushing bore.

Teetee says, "The mayor wants you to know the dinner is in your honor."

"In my honor?"

"Yes, I fink so. It's to fank you for saving the trees of the Place Des Lices."

The mayor's nodding his head vigorously, taking a chance that it's the proper time to do so. Then he talks some more.

"The mayor says," continues Teetee, "that your name was never mentioned in any of the newspaper articles or on the radio because that's what you said you wanted. But the mayor says everybody knows it was you who saved the trees. He says it's a small town and word gets around. So now he wants to honor you properly."

"Tell the mayor that's very nice of him and I'm flattered, but I'd rather not have a dinner in my honor. The town should use the money they will spend on the dinner for something better."

Teetee tells the mayor this.

The mayor slaps the sides of his thighs with his hands in disappointment. He says something to Teetee. She tells me, "The mayor fought you would say that."

The mayor and his wife are leaving. There's a lot of kissing cheeks and shaking hands between the mayor and me, and the mayor's wife and Red, and me and the mayor's wife, and Red and the mayor. As they walk away, the mayor turns and says to me, "If you ever think of a way we can repay your kindness for saving the trees of the Place des Lices, please let me know."

"How about letting me put my balcony up," I suggest.

"Absolutely not," says the mayor.

It is the last Sunday in October.

In a few weeks it will be too cold to play *boule* comfortably. We will all have to wear heavy sweaters and jackets, which makes throwing and getting down into a crouch uncomfortable. Before the winter weather sets in, Le Championnat de Boule—the traditional championship of the year—takes place. It's the tournament they call The Big One. I've never been asked to participate in a small tournament, let alone The Big One. So when a couple of the guys approach me to play with them, I think they're kidding me. Particularly since the guys—Gerard and Loulou—are two of the best *boule* players in Saint-Tropez. I laugh at their joke. But way down deep I'm angry. I sense Gerard and Loulou are teasing me, like: Don't you wish we were serious? But they are serious; they're not teasing me at all. They want me to be their third man.

Cynically I consider the possibility that maybe Gerard and Loulou are fishing for invitations to be my guests at the World Cup soccer finals in Los Angeles in 1994. Or perhaps the boys are trying in their own way to thank me for saving the trees in the park? Or maybe they simply think I'm good enough to be their partner. Whatever the reason, I'm their choice and I accept.

Le Championnat de Boule is next Saturday at noon. I have exactly one week to get in shape. If I practiced hard before, I practice obsessively now. Every morning at sunrise I'm out on the Place des Lices playing on all the different sections of the park. I am trying to get used to the terrains; soft ground, hard ground, rocky ground, lumpy ground, flat ground. I place the little wooden *cochonnet* in tough-to-reach locations and roll my *boule* balls as best I can. Most of the time I do well. But there are still those occasions when my throws are pathetic. Consistency is not my forte. I tend to be distracted. More often than not I'm straining to hear what people are saying on the sidelines. Or trying to catch a glimpse of the expressions on my teammates' faces. Or I'm looking around to see if Red's watching. Often she's nowhere to be seen. That's because when I'm playing in an important match, Red and Teetee hide behind the crowds at one of the outdoor cafés that circle the square. They sit there waiting for news from friends, nervously moving their silverware around.

Saturday finally arrives.

It's high noon and The Big One begins. Thirty-four three-man teams have paid their ten-dollar entrance fees and are assembled on the Place des Lices. One game determines a winner. The loser is eliminated. Our first game is against a team that appears easy to beat. They just don't look like good *boule* players. And they're not. We breeze through that match. And the next one. And the one after that. We win the fourth match, but it's close, 13–11. The victory puts us in the semifinals. Thirty of the thirty-four teams have been eliminated. The crowds of people who have been watching all the matches now converge on the last two. Red and Teetee are sitting at The Café Renaissance drinking Perrier and playing with their silverware.

Our semifinal match is tough. Midway through the game I'm absolutely convinced we're going to lose. The other team is winning 10–5. They're doing everything right and suddenly Gerard and Loulou are doing everything wrong. And then escargot!—we begin to crawl forward slowly but surely, like snails. We fight our way back to 12–11. They need one point to win and we need two. And then Gerard surprises everybody including himself by making a miraculous shot. We have the two points we need to go to the finals! The finals, with me in it. An American from South Philadelphia. As Teetee would say, "Ummm-believable."

Now there's just one game and one crowd.

It's the biggest crowd I've ever seen watch a *boule* game on the

Place des Lices. Red and Teetee have moved to yet another restaurant, and are nervously playing with new sets of silverware. Henri Bruni is running messages to them, a sort of human wireless bringing the girls updates every five or ten minutes. When the final game begins it's after five o'clock in the evening. Gerard, Loulou, and I have been competing since noon. The sun has set. We're playing by lamplight. It doesn't matter. My adrenaline's pumping away and I'm not the least bit cold or tired.

The team we must beat to win the championship has three of my best friends playing on it: Louis Ugo, Dede With The Beard and, George, a retired schoolteacher whom everyone calls The Professor. He's called the Professor because he's always lecturing you on how you could have made a better shot.

Someone says there's a lot of money riding on this game. I can see a bunch of locals furiously placing bets. I suppose we're the underdogs, mainly because of me.

It's an extremely close game. I won't bore you with all the gruesome details. Suffice it to say it all comes down to Dede With The Beard and guess who? Me! The score is 12–12. Dede and I each have one ball left. It's Dede's turn. His roll is excellent. It passes all the other balls and ends up roughly two inches from the wooden *cochonnet*. It's my turn. I will have the last throw of the game. If I roll my ball closer to the *cochonnet* than Dede's, we will win the championship. If I don't, we'll lose. It's as awful as that. That's what Henri tells Red and Teetee sitting at the café.

They say, "Oh my God," in unison.

Gerard tells me to relax and take my time. Loulou says it's only a game. He doesn't mean it, but it's a nice try. I nod, grab my *boule* ball, and go to the circle. I shake my arm to relax it, take a deep breath, and look at Henri. He smiles back at me. I shouldn't be looking at Henri. I should be concentrating. I should be remembering what Teetee told me. She said, "Fink before you shoot."

So I fink.

And then I shoot.

CHAPTER FORTY-FIVE

It's early the next morning and I am out on *Bam Bam*.

I'm heading into one of those perfect Saint-Tropez sunrises. The *Bammer* and I have the sea all to ourselves. The water's flat and green. It resembles the top of a pool table. I'm steering *Bam Bam* in huge figure eights as though my boat and I were in the center of an enormous ice-skating rink. After about a dozen eights, I turn out to sea. When I'm miles and miles away, when land is no longer in sight, I turn off *Bam Bam*'s engines and let the monster drift. I climb onto the back cushions of the boat, prop my head against a pillow facing the morning sun, and review the last toss of yesterday's championship *boule* game.

I had the shot. It was mine to win or lose. Sure, it was a tough shot, but what did I expect? It was a championship. Gerard coughed and told me to relax and take my time. Loulou gave his usual nervous laugh and tried his best to calm me down. I nodded, grabbed my *boule* ball, and went to the circle. I shook my arm a little to relax it, took a deep breath, crouched, aimed, and rolled my ball toward the *cochonnet*. I put a little spin on it and watched the ball curve around the others, stopping alongside Dede's. But closer to the *cochonnet* than his.

We won!

Gerard, Loulou, and I are the *boule* champions of Saint-Tropez for 1992.

The three of us shook hands and looked at each other affectionately. We each received fifty dollars and a free team photograph. (My picture hangs above my computer at Très Cher.) Reviewing yesterday's championship match still gives me a thrill. I stand up in the back of *Bam Bam*, throw my arms over my head like Rocky and yell, "I finally got their respect!" And I did.

Still, there must be something to that old saying: You better watch out what you wish for. You may get it. For years that's all I wished for, to play in a championship *boule* game with The Big Boys. I never even dreamed of being on the winning team. Now that I've done both, I've discovered I really don't care that much about *boule* anymore. I'd much rather spend my writing breaks in the afternoon sitting on a bench with Henri, Janot, Loulou, and the others, licking ice-cream cones and yelling, *"Court!"*—Short!—when the others make lousy shots.

Like they used to do to me.

It's the afternoon after the championship *boule* match and I'm driving in my Citroën Deux Cheveaux to the Place des Lices to meet the boys.

In case you're not familiar with a Citroën Deux Cheveaux, it's one of those funny-looking little French cars that resemble Volks-wagens, only uglier. The Citroën Deux Cheveaux—also known as the Douche Bag, or simply the Bag—literally means two horses, or two horsepower, which isn't very much. The car takes forever to climb a modest hill, but climb it, it will. You just have to be patient. A Citroën Deux Cheveaux will go straight up Everest— right to the summit—if you want it to. They're that dependable. You either love Douche Bags or hate them. I happen to love them.

Anyway, I'm driving my Bag into town, taking a shortcut along a thin, winding road that passes the soccer stadium. Actually the sta-dium isn't a stadium at all, but rather an ill-kept field surrounded by cement seats a couple of rows high. Sitting on that cement's a real treat. The locals have the nerve to call this monstrosity The Coli-seum.

So I'm taking my time, which is all I can do in a Citroën Deux Cheveaux, bopping along, listening to my radio, nearing a blind curve, of which there are many on this unfortunate road. Suddenly a white, banged-up Peugeot is coming in the opposite direction. The Peugeot's barreling around the curve at full speed. The driver of the Peugeot is evidently late for something or other, gambling there's no one coming in the other direction. Regrettably I'm coming in the other direction. We both jam on our car brakes. I stop. But he doesn't.

We hit head-on.

CHAPTER FORTY-SIX

I am sitting in the emergency room of the Saint-Tropez General Hospital. It's quiet and clean, and empty. Nothing like the frenzied emergency rooms in American hospitals. A pleasant nurse has just given me permission to leave. I've telephoned Red and asked her to please come fetch me. I sit in a chair waiting for her with my head held back. There are hunks of paper towel stuffed up the nostrils of my broken nose to absorb the bleeding. I am holding two ice bags; one against my nose and fat upper lip and one against the back of my neck, trying to soothe the whiplash. A third ice bag is strapped to my right knee, the one that banged into the dashboard.

To get my mind off my throbbing nose, neck, and knee, I try to think of happier times. I ponder my early days as a page at Rockefeller Center in New York; single, carefree, without responsibilities. I recall the Camelot years of my company when we knew the *Dating Game* was a hit, followed by the *Newlywed Game*, followed by the . . . Or the halcyon, crazy years of the *Gong Show*, coupled with the fun I had producing the *$1.98 Beauty Show*.

The $1.98 Beauty Show; one of my most favorite creations.

And my last.

The $1.98 Beauty Show was named for the amount of money the winner received.

The show's cast included a host, a model, and three celebrity judges. The celebrity judges were some of the biggest names in show business. These judges were quite unusual in that they never judged anything. In fact, they never spoke. Ostensibly they were supposed to pick a winner. But my staff and I picked the winner. The three celebrity judges simply smiled when they were introduced, cheerfully accepted our mentioning their latest book, movie, or record, and then sat for the rest of the half hour entertaining themselves as best they could: doodling on pads of paper, keeping make-believe scores, pretending to be thinking who the winner might be. The judges never questioned their bizarre roles on the program. Neither did the television authorities, nor the public.

Since we refused to formulate any criteria for *$1.98 Beauty Show* candidates, the girls were a mixed bag. Some were pretty with blah personalities while others were plain but great to talk to. They were young and old, thin and fat, tall and short. Along with the judges not judging, I had a difficult time explaining why I called my program a beauty show.

Maybe that was the point.

Anyway, the program would begin by introducing the day's aspirants for the title of Miss $1.98 Beauty Queen. This was followed by the talent segment: each girl performing a song, a dance, reciting poetry, rendering a dramatic reading. During the last third of the program each contestant would take a turn down the runway in a bathing suit. The winner would be chosen for "her talent, poise, and personality." When our flamboyant host, Rip Taylor, announced the winning girl, if she didn't scream loud enough or jump in the air with unabashed excitement, we'd pick another winner. Our final choice would promenade once again down the red velvet runway holding her very own bouquet of dead vegetables while Rip sang a horrendous parody of "There She Goes, Miss America." The show was rather successful. It was a staple in barrooms and prisons across the country.

Along with the ridiculousness of *The $1.98 Beauty Show*—and the fun we had producing it—was the tempting availability of the better looking $1.98 beauties. True, I was living with Red at the time but rationalized my extracurricular activities by repeating to myself: "All's fair in love and war, until one is married. Then fidelity is paramount."

I loved Red desperately, but in those happy-go-lucky years dodging the marital bullet was my mission in life. This calling was the result of my conviction that the supportive, agreeable, and pretty single female once married stopped being a girlfriend at once and became a wife: a strict, ill-tempered, semihag with curlers in her hair and a wart that appeared on the end of her nose the morning following the nuptials. So convinced was I of all the above, that when it came to avoiding wedlock, I strived to be the best. Toward this end, I invented the marriage license gambit.

The MLG was employed when I sensed my back was to the wall. The occasion would require me suggesting Red and I obtain a marriage license and promising to marry before the license expired. This would entail going to a doctor for blood tests, taking the tests to City Hall so a clerk could confirm we were free of any communicable diseases, and receiving in return a license that was valid for thirty days. For some reason or other the license always expired before we made it to the altar. I would suggest getting another, which meant another month of freedom. New York was better. A New York license allowed ninety days of freedom, which I acquired when our third Los Angeles license lapsed.

Now I sensed these ninety days might be my last. One was the fact that Red and I had taken so many blood tests, our arms looked like a junkie's. I doubted if Red would take another. A second reason was my conviction that it was only a matter of time before Red would see the Marriage License Gambit for what it was: a monumental stall. Sooner, rather than later, she would put her foot down. As it turned out, both rationales were wrong. My downfall was occasioned by Red unexpectedly dropping by the television studio one afternoon and catching me and a $1.98 Beauty Show cutie in the lady's dressing room.

The Redhead, more angry than hurt, turned and slammed the dressing-room door behind her. I chased the Redhead into the parking lot and begged her to forgive me. I said, "Listen, the way I look at it, all's fair in love and war, until you get married."

"That's not the way I look at it," she said over her shoulder, still walking to her car.

"Then after you're married," I said, trying to catch up, "there's absolutely no more fooling around. When you're married you're faithful to each other like storks. That's it. When you're—"

"Don't say it!" Red snapped turning around, holding up her hand, her palm in my face. "Don't mention that word again."

"What word?"

"Marriage."

* * *

A week later I convinced the Redhead to go with me to New York to see a Ranger hockey game.

Red was giving me one last chance, knowing as I did that our New York marriage license was still valid. Regrettably, I mused, my days of freedom seemed to be drawing to a close. It was only a matter of time before I'd become a stork. We boarded the plane to New York suffering mixed emotions.

On the plane Red became ill.

Her birth control device had caused an infection she was unaware of. The infection had turned to peritonitis. During the flight, the peritonitis exploded much the same as a ruptured appendix. The eruption sent poisons all through Red's body. As soon as we arrived in New York, I rushed Red to Mount Sinai Hospital. While she lay in agony on a gurney waiting for a doctor, I suddenly sensed the frightening possibility of losing her. I knew then I would marry Red the first day she could go to City Hall. I told her that. She smiled, her face creased with pain, and whispered, "I won't hold you to it. You're under a lot of pressure."

Red almost died.

I sat by her bed in Mount Sinai Hospital for two weeks. I sat by her bed at the Wyndham Hotel for two more. Then one morning I helped Red out of the Wyndham and into a limousine. I had bought an audio cassette of the Beatles singing, "I'm Getting Married In The Morning" and played it as we drove to City Hall. We got there just in time. We had three hours left of our New York marriage license. A nice councilman named David Dinkins pulled us out of a long line of applicants and signed our affidavit. An hour later my business manager and his wife arranged to have us married at their apartment. During the ceremony I peeked at Red. She had never looked more radiant.

Afterward, we went to the Russian Tea Room and ate blinis and caviar. Then Red turned gray and faded. I took her back to the Wyndham, and bed. That night, before going to sleep, I set my alarm. I wanted to wake up in the morning before Red to see if there was a wart on the end of her nose. The next morning when I looked, she was as beautiful as the night before.

Red arrives at the emergency room in Saint-Tropez to pick me up. I give her a frail smile.

She is ashen.

With all the ice bags and bloody swabs up my nose, I look much worse then I am. I tell Red I'm fine and not to worry. "Just a broken nose, a fat lip, a little whiplash, and a banged-up knee."

"Very funny," she says, not amused.

On the drive back to Très Cher I look at Red's face. She's prettier now than she ever was. I think once again of my wife on that Mount Sinai Hospital gurney waiting for the doctor.

"Remember when I took you to the hospital in New York after our infamous plane ride?"

"Yes."

"Remember when you were lying on that gurney and I asked you to marry me?"

"Yes."

"Remember what you said to me?"

"Yes."

"You said you wouldn't hold me to it because I was under too much pressure."

"I told you I remembered what I said. Anyway, I was delirious."

"I'm glad we got married," I say, and give my wife a look brimming with love.

"You're a goddamn careless, lousy driver because your mind is always millions of miles away, and nothing you say will ever change that fact."

"I'm not a careless driver," I growl. Sometimes redheads are impossible.

CHAPTER FORTY-SEVEN

"You're limping?" asks Henri under the ice-cream vendor's umbrella. "What happened to your nose?"

"I had a car accident."

"Bad accident?"

"There is no more front on the front of my Douche Bag."

"No front?"

"The car begins at the windshield."

"Where's the Bag now?"

"*C'est mort.* They towed it away to the car cemetery. I'll miss it."

"Are you okay?"

"I broke my nose and my knee hit the dashboard, but not too hard."

Henri says I look like a short Jean Paul Belmondo. He hands me my ice-cream cone. It's his treat. The cone is coconut sherbet. It's delicious.

"They will fix your Douche Bag," he tells me. "They are always fixing them. French mechanics are good at it. You'll see. They will make it look like new."

"Fat chance," I mutter.

The expression doesn't translate well in French. Henri thinks I said he's fat and wonders why I said that.

The two of us walk to the Place des Lice and find an empty green bench. We sit down and make ourselves comfortable. Janot the retired mailman and Dede the baker join us, along with a few others.

Dede says to me, "I read in the newspaper that you're playing in a big concert in Marseilles next weekend."

Dede the baker is talking about Chuck Berry. A lot of the locals confuse me with the legendary rock and roller.

"Yeah," I tell Dede, "it's going to be a big concert."

"Is it sold out?"

"I don't think so. I think there are still some tickets available."

"Maybe my wife and I will go."

"If you do, come backstage after the performance and say hello."

Some of the guys wander off to play *boule*. Not me. I'm happy sitting on the green bench pretending I'm Chuck Berry. Personally I'd rather be talking about the 49ers-Giants game that'll take place at the Meadowlands this Sunday, but it's tough to find a Tropezienne wise in the ways of the National Football League. I learned back in Los Angeles when I was trying to sell my television show that life's a compromise; you can never be everything you want to be, nor can you be everywhere at the same time. Nothing brilliant about those observations, just useful to your overall state of well-being if you accept them. Oddly enough, the only one who would have remotely cared about the San Francisco-New York Giants football game is Little Janot DeBartello whose alleged uncle Ed owns the 49ers. But Little Janot died yesterday.

And so did Victor Talbert. He died yesterday, too. Remember the old man who crossed the Place des Lices early one Sunday morning while I was trying to practice *boule?* I was having a tough time getting the *boule* ball to stay at the top of the hill near the *cochonnet* without it rolling down. The old man walked up to me, bent over, and marked the ground with his finger. He never said a word, just made an X in the dirt. I threw my *boule* ball, hit the X, it rolled up the hill and stayed there, right next to the *cochonnet*. That was Victor Talbert. He owned a candy store in town. The news of his passing makes me sad.

"You always are saying nothing ever changes in Saint-Tropez," Dede the butcher says to me. "Now Victor's son runs the candy store. See? Things change."

"The storms are over," says Janot the Retired Mailman. "Soon it will be too cold for ice cream."

He's right. There have been powerful rainstorms. There always are in the Mediterranean when winter approaches. Suddenly the clouds turn black and the winds violent. Lightning fills the sky. Rain falls in sheets for days and then abruptly stops. The storms sail away as suddenly as they came. The clouds part and the sun shines through. Afterward there's a nip in the air.

"I'm glad it's getting too cold for ice cream," I tell Loulou. "Now I can save all that money I spend treating you."

Loulou laughs his nervous laugh.

"Tell us a story about Hollywood," says Henri.

I tell Henri he sounds like a six-year-old.

Henri shrugs.

Janot asks if something's bothering me.

Dede wonders if my writing is going poorly.

George the professor says I look tired. I should stay in bed longer in the morning.

"He's not getting his biscuit," says Loulou, inserting his right index finger into the hole of his left clenched fist and pushing the finger back and forth.

I agree to tell Henri, and the others, a story about Hollywood.

"Good," says Henri.

Everybody moves in closer to hear the story better. A few other locals from a nearby bench come over. These Frenchmen love to be told stories about Hollywood. And me? All of a sudden I'm a bard. Just what I wanted to be all my life, a goddamn bard.

"What's the story about?" asks Henri.

I have to think for a minute, and then I decide. "It's about the time an evil television critic named John P. Grissom pretended to be a contestant on the *Dating Game.*"

"That sounds like a good one," says Henri. "Make it long."

CHAPTER FORTY-EIGHT

I can't believe it.

The *Gong Show Movie* is playing in Saint-Tropez! In the little movie house on the Place des Lices. I am amazed the picture is still in circulation let alone playing in the south of France.

The *Gong Show Movie* was my second effort to enter the motion picture business. The results of this quest were as debilitating as my adventures with El Cordobés. Only this time I didn't recover as quickly.

It was 1980.

I was tired of television and wanted to try something else. I had two choices. One was to go on tour with the Gong Show band. Since the program was off the air, the musicians were free to travel. The Gong Show band had some of the best studio musicians in Hollywood. It was my idea to call ourselves the Hollywood Cowboys and travel around the country playing country and western music. We would begin our journey at a modest country and western bar in Yuma, Arizona. We'd work our way east playing small clubs across the United States until we were ready for the Big Three: The Lone Star Cafe in New York, Gilleys in Dallas, and the Palomino Club in Los Angeles. I would film our cross-country tour with the hopes of making an Academy Award-winning documentary. I chartered Linda Ronstadt's tour bus and hired roadies to take care of our equipment. It was all set.

And then I changed my mind.

I decided to go with my other choice: to make a movie for Universal Studios based on the *Gong Show*. I ignored warnings that movies of hit television shows never succeeded, that the public was averse to paying money for something it was used to receiving for free. I dreamed the opposite.

We started out fine. I hired my friend Robert Downey, Sr., to help write the script with me, and direct the picture. The two of us created a funny story line. I booked a cast of relatively unknown but talented actors and actresses. We had a good crew and found wonderful locations. We started shooting the picture feeling confident we were on to something good. Things were going well. And then my evil ego reared its awful head.

I told Downey I wanted to direct. He shook my hand and said, "Good luck." I played the lead. I had Red star as my love interest. I wrote the music and, worse, midway through the picture rewrote the script. I wanted to add meaning and truth to the movie. Instead of the slapstick comedy it started out being, I made the picture into a creature neither funny nor serious.

The studio tested the picture one evening in a movie house on Thirty-second Street in Manhattan. I had never created anything an audience paid hard-earned cash to see. Everything I ever produced the public could watch for free. Now, sitting in a packed theater at a "sneak preview," I suffered the most violent anxiety I ever experienced in my life. I thought my heart would pound itself right out of my chest. When the picture began, I slouched as deep down into my seat as I could get. At the beginning, the audience laughed. But by the middle—at the exact point where I took over writing and directing—I sensed we were turning a calamitous corner. And then when members of the audience started walking out of the theater, I wanted to crawl under my seat and die. I waited until the theater was empty before leaving.

Universal went ahead and released the *Gong Show Movie* in theaters around the country. Red and I attended the first day at a cinema on Second Avenue in New York City. The usher took my tickets and said, "You two ain't gonna last."

That night my wife and I watched the eleven o'clock news in our Plaza Hotel suite, courtesy of Universal Pictures. We were told there would be a review of the *Gong Show Movie* sometime during the program. It came at the very end of the show. The TV critic raised up a garbage pail lid in one hand and a mallet in the other. He said, "What do I give the *Gong Show Movie?* I give it this!" He whacked the garbage pail lid with his mallet. I could hear the hollow laugh of a cameraman in the background.

Red and I returned to Los Angeles. I spent 1981 sitting in a lawn chair on the stoop of my hideaway apartment/office at Charleville and Rodeo. I watched the man next door walk his ancient mother around the block every morning at ten. I noted the United Parcel truck go by at ten-thirty and the Federal Express truck at eleven. I saw the William Morris Agency executives take their lunchtime promenade at noon and the secretaries returning to their offices with their paper bags of food at one. I observed the bare-chested retired businessman walk his doberman every afternoon at four. I wondered how people could live such pathetically regimented lives; every day at the exact time the mother, the deliveries, the promenade, the lunch bags, the dog. Every single day. Then one afternoon I thought to myself: They must be saying the same thing about me. How can that poor man fritter his life away sitting on his stoop from sunup to sundown? I put my lawn chair away and went back to work.

For the next five years I did what I had to do to make my company salable. In December of 1986 I sold Barris Industries.

Early the following year Red and I moved to France.

EPILOGUE

It's December.

By now all the pretty young girls and handsome playboys are long gone from Saint-Tropez. They've taken the hustle-bustle, the noise, the color, and the action with them. The cosmopolitan jet-setters are gone, too, returning to their big city town houses and duplex apartments in other parts of the world. The only movie house is closed. Soon the local entrepreneurs will disappear to hunt in Senegal, sunbathe in the Caribbean, visit various Disney parks. They'll leave behind their restaurants and boutiques; the windows boarded or crisscrossed with masking tape to protect them against the blustery winter winds.

True, the weather can be beautiful in December, but it usually isn't. Instead of being sunny and crystal clear as it is in spring and summer, it's more likely to be windy, rainy, and cold. Those who stay here usually find December, January, and February depressing.

Not me.

I'm just the opposite.

I feel as though I finally got my town back. I love Saint-Tropez best after everyone goes away. My season begins in November when the gates of the pay public parking lots go up and ends in April when they come back down again.

But everyone returns to Saint-Tropez for Christmas: the wives, the pretty young people, the jet-setters, the local restaurateurs, and shop owners. Everybody comes back because Christmas is really special here.

It's about five o'clock in the late afternoon of Christmas Eve.

It was a cold, gray morning today with a mistral blowing in from across the bay. But to everyone's delight the sun popped out at noon. What little sunlight that remains now is leaving a thin orange crown over the distant mountains to the west. We're all reminded of the saying: Red sky at night, Sailor's delight. Red sky in the morning, Sailors take warning. Everyone is pleased with the possibility of a nice day tomorrow. But what is even more pleasing is the imminent arrival of Papa Nöel.

Papa Nöel—Santa Claus to us Americans—comes to Saint-Tropez in a little red tugboat which, at this very moment, is chugging through the entrance to the port. Santa's heading for the dock opposite the town's two favorite bars, the Gorille and the Senequier. That's where most of the children of this village are standing. The kids, like everyone else, are bundled up in heavy coats and scarves. Though they can't see Santa, they whoop and holler and wave their hands in the general direction of his red tugboat. Papa Nöel's tug is a cheerful little thing. It has red and green lights strung from mast to mast and bright white sparklers sizzling on sticks at each end.

"Listen to that," I tell my wife, "they're playing the theme music from *Rocky* on the speakers! Not 'Jingle Bells' or 'Santa Claus Is Coming To Town' but the theme from *Rocky!* That's so like the French. Can't stand America but love everything American."

My wife ignores me. She's heard all this before. She knows I only half mean what I say and that I say it because I feel required to. Just like the French find it necessary to look down their noses at anything American. Right now my Red's more concerned with the occasion; delighting in the festivities, in the feeling of genuine goodwill, in the children's glee and awe at the approaching tugboat and Papa Nöel.

"Santa's coming closer!" says my wife, as excited as the kids.

We can see him now, fat and jolly like he's supposed to be, waving and going, "Ho ho ho!" I must admit, it's much nicer this way than standing in a long line at Saks Fifth Avenue or Bloomingdale's; the store's suffocatingly hot, your overcoat, suit coat, and scarf unbuttoned and unwrapped, hanging on you as though you were a coat tree, waiting for some skinny-ass Santa Claus with bourbon-soaked eyes to push your kid on and off his knees as fast as he can as if his lap were a conveyor belt.

That's not the way it is here. Here it's gentle and tranquil, festive and happy. Hundreds of little lights have been strung from store to store and restaurant to restaurant. Big bright electric stars hang from the curved arches that connect buildings throughout the town. The shops are busy but there's no rush; no shrieking for salesclerks, no sharp elbows in your sides from fellow customers, no pickpocket's hand in your wallet pocket. Here it's civilized, but then, Europe is civilized. New York is more exciting at Christmas—football, hockey and basketball, new movies and shows opening, ballet and opera performances—but one thing it isn't and that's civilized. And Manhattan doesn't have a quaint Christmas train rolling through town during the last three weeks of the year. The brightly colored make-believe train is pulled by a make-believe steam engine driven by one of the town's garbage men. The funny-looking locomotive tows six miniature railroad cars filled with squealing children, their parents strolling nearby so the kids feel safe.

Meanwhile, Santa's tugboat has arrived at the dock. The children queue up to discuss serious matters with Papa Nöel, who is really the town priest. I stand in line, too. Soon it's my turn. Papa Nöel seems confused. His eyes, peering out from a mass of white eyebrows and beard, look to my sides and behind me for a child.

"It's just me, Papa Nöel," I tell Santa in my piss-poor French. "I want something for Christmas, too. Can an adult ask you for something?"

Papa Nöel's eyes reveal his discomfort. "Yes, I suppose so," he says.

"What I want for Christmas, Papa Nöel, is the answer to a question."

"Yes? What is the question?"

"Why, Papa Nöel?"

"Why what?"

"Why am I here?"

"Why are you here?" repeats Papa Nöel.

"Yes."

There's a pregnant pause.

Then Papa Nöel says, "Because you want to be."

"That's it?"

"That's it."

"What kind of an answer is that? That's sort of like: Why? Because."

"I don't care. I still say you're here because you want to be. You like it here. You like living here. You enjoy the life this simple village has to offer."

The little boy behind me is impatient. He's bumping the back of my legs accidentally but not accidentally.

"Then why am I sucking up to people?"

"Why are you what?"

"Why am I always being so obsequious to the locals?"

"Because you like Tropeziens and you want them to like you back."

"Then why do I keep verbally bashing the French? Why am I so angry at you guys?"

"You are not angry at us. You are angry at you. Because you don't like being obsequious. It's not your nature. And you know what, Chuck?"

"What, Father?"

"You don't have to be. You don't have to give out *Bam Bam* jackets and baseball hats. Everybody likes you just the way you are."

"You think so?"

"Absolutely. You just have to learn French. It's a disgrace you haven't learned to speak fluently by now."

"I know."

"And speaking of *Bam Bam* jackets, where the hell's mine?"

"I didn't think priests could wear that kind of stuff."

The little boy behind me is tugging on the back of my coat with two hands.

I tell the little boy I'm almost finished, and then say to Papa Noël, "You're right, Father. I'm here because I want to be here. I wonder why I didn't think of that?"

"It's too obvious."

"Yes, I guess it is. Well, thanks for the advice, Papa Noël. I appreciate it."

"Don't mention it. What time do we play *boule* tomorrow?"

"Three-thirty. Don't be late, Father. It gets dark early now."

"Please don't forget my *Bam Bam* jacket."

"I won't."

An hour later Red and I are walking home to our little house in the port.

Willie's following us. Willie is a nine-month-old yellow labrador.

He's Buddy's nephew. Willie's a handsome pup, just like his uncle was, and just as goofy. As we walk, we pass under the window of the mean old widow. She's leaning out, as usual, with her mean old dog right beside her.

"*Joyeux Nöel,*" I say to the wizened crone on general principles, not expecting so much as a nod in return.

"*Joyeux Nöel to you,*" she answers.

My legs almost buckle.

The old lady asks, "Aren't you l'Americain who saved the trees? You are a very nice man to have done that."

"Thank you."

"Your husband," she tells my wife, "is a very nice man. He says hello to me every morning."

Red smiles.

The old lady says, "Have a merry Christmas," and waves her wrinkled little hand.

We wave back and walk away.

I say to Red, "I don't believe it."

"She likes you," says Red.

"All this time I thought she hated me."

"You always told me she was a mean old fart. You're the mean old fart, if you ask me."

"She even smiled."

"I saw her," says my wife. "She definitely smiled."

"I even think her goddamn dog smiled."

"You're right. I think the dog definitely smiled."

Red slings her arm around my neck and we walk toward our little house by the sea.

INDEX

ABC (American Broadcasting
    Company):
    Barris as employee of, 22–25, 27–31,
        202 204
    Dating Game and, 32–36, 47–54, 59–
        64
    How's Your Mother-in-Law? and, 85,
        99–103
    Mama Cass And Friends and, 178
    People Poker and, 202–204
    Treasure Hunt and, 184–185
    see also *Newlywed Game*
ABC Films, 92
ABC Sports, 31
Allard, Michael, 197–201, 212
Amazon, 78
American Bandstand (TV show), 27–29
Americans:
    French views of, 13, 20, 57
    as tourists, 15–17, 45–47
Anitol, 144
Ariel (fish seller), 45
Armani, Walter (The Ostrich), 21–24,
    29
Ashby, Hal, 68
auditions:
    of bimbos, 229
    for *Gong Show*, 142, 147
    of mothers, 227, 230–231
autographs, 142, 143

babies, 80, 144
bakeries, 39–40
balconies, 266–267, 271
Bam Bam (Riga speedboat), 106–118,
    210, 258, 274
    as birthday gift, 106–107
    crash of, 108–111
    fishing on, 177–178, 187
    Gigi's ashes dropped from, 191–192
    naming of, 111
    racing instruction and, 106–108
    sale of, 112–113, 118
    Ted Kennedy and, 111–117
Bam Bam jackets, 268–270, 291
Banks, Gene, 78
Barbour, John, 136–137
Barisa (housekeeper), 167, 168
Barris, Chuck:
    at ABC, 22–25, 27–31, 202–204
    ambition of, 23
    anxiety of, 38
    appearance of, 19, 89
    asthma attacks of, 141
    book tours of, 169–170
    at Clinton For President fund-raiser,
        253–259
    companies of, see Barris Industries;
        Chuck Barris Productions
    correspondence romance of, 170–
        173
    in crashes, 97–98, 108–111, 134,
        275–276, 282
    depressions of, 20–21, 33
    drug experiences of, 68–70, 179–180
    as Duke of Daytime, 29–30, 202
    education of, 25
    fame of, 141 143
    father of, 25, 26
    firings by, 83
    firings of, 25, 27, 29
    French as spoken by, 17, 19, 41, 55,
        88, 174, 212
    as game-show packager, 32–37,
        46–47, 68, 70, 83, 124–128, 170–
        173, 226–244; see also *specific
        shows*
    as *Gong Show* host, 137, 141–153
    homesickness of, 213, 244
    janitorial job of, 25
    marriage feared by, 278–280
    marriage of, 18–19, 279–281
    money earned by, 29, 46–47, 84, 238
    mother of, 25, 26, 29, 32
    motorcycle accident of, 134
    in move to south of France, 11, 17,
        38, 287
    in NBC management training
        program, 26–27
    power of, 84

racing instruction of, 106–108
in Saint-Tropez, 15–21, 37–48, 55–
　58, 106–108, 119–121, 154–158,
　164–169, 174–178, 191–201, 206–
　213
sexual behavior of, 26, 27, 94–95
sister of, 26, 29, 56–57
sixtieth birthday of, 106, 107
sleep problems of, 21
songwriting of, 24–25, 29
speaking ability lost by, 248–249
stepfather's financing of, 32–33
strangers' recognition of, 15–16, 45–
　47
Barris, Red (wife), 11, 152, 210, 253–
　261, 277–281
　Barris's first meeting with, 18–19
　Barris's sixtieth birthday and, 106,
　　107
　Bastille Day and, 104, 111–112,
　　115–116
　at Bistro Gardens, 219–224
　at Clinton for President fund-raiser,
　　253–259
　French as spoken by, 209, 260–261
　in *Gong Show Movie,* 286
　at Laconda Veneta, 224–226
　marriage of, 18–19, 279–281
　name change of, 19
　Owens's visit and, 165–168
　in Saint-Tropez, 18, 20–21, 38–39,
　　56, 65, 66, 193, 195–197, 206–213,
　　266, 268, 270–273, 277, 280–281,
　　289, 292
　surgeries of, 206–209, 280
　Wyndham Hotel and, 245, 246
Barris Industries, 85–87
　board of directors meetings of, 85,
　　87
　NBC investigation of, 125–128
　Parent Game and, 124–127
　sale of, 287
　stockholders' meeting of, 85–86
baseball, 20, 41
　World Series and, 164–165
Bastille Day, 104–106, 111–117

Baum, Martin, 92
Becker, Jefferson, 146
Belknap, USS, 165
Benitez, Manuel, *see* El Cordobés
Bercovici, Julian, 27–28
Berry, Chuck, 282–283
betting, on horses, 156–158, 251, 252
Big Boys, The, 15, 19–20, 37, 66–67
Big Janot, 41–42, 45
Big Nose, 143
Bimbos (proposed TV show), 228–229
Binfado, Simone, 165, 166
Bistro Gardens, 218–224
blackmail, St. Valentine Day's
　　Massacre and, 52–53
Blenzig, Charlie, 57
boars, wild, 211–213
boats, 37, 41–42, 104–118
　speed limits for, 174–175
　yachts, 104–106, 111, 113–117
　see also Bam Bam
Boix, Dede, 45, 283, 284
Bolin, Lyn, 121–122, 124, 132–133
Bonard, Dede, 39–40, 45, 282–283
Bonard, Madam, 39–40, 283
book tours, 169–170
Bortin, David, 29, 32–33
Boston Red Sox, 41, 42
boule, 15–21, 37, 45, 66–67, 156, 174,
　　175, 210, 271–275, 283
bread, 40
Brill, Charlie, 150
Brisbane, 78
Bruni, Emilie, 18, 88, 98
Bruni, Henri, 17–19, 67, 88, 98, 155–
　　158, 273, 284
　Bam Bam jacket of, 269
　Barris game shows and, 47–48, 120–
　　121
　betting of, 156–158
　Buddy's death and, 210–211
　car accident and, 282
　Mama Cass and, 177–178, 182
Bruni, Josette, 47–48, 120, 156
Buddy (dog), 167, 168, 209–211

death of, 210–213
bullfights, 91, 95–96
bums, 134–136
Burnett, Pearl, 144
business, French way of, 199, 200, 212

Café Des Arts, 67–68
Cahill, Danny, 217–218, 247, 251, 252
"California Dreaming" (song), 177
California Pizza, 228
Cannes, 104–106
Cannon, Freddie, 24–25
Carruthers, Bill, 120, 130
Cassavetes, John, 246, 247, 252
CBP Stompers, 80
CBS (Columbia Broadcasting System), 23, 83, 241
    Mothers and, 232–235
censors, Gong Show and, 147–148
champagne, 115–116, 191
Championnat de Boule, Le, 271–275
chaperons, for Dating Game, 77–79
Charlie (Mothers problem case), 231
Chez Frederick, 104, 111, 112
chimpanzees, on Dating Game, 119–120
chocolate cake, of Mama Cass, 179
Christmas, in Saint-Tropez, 288–292
Chuck Barris Productions, 79 85
    description of staff of, 79–80
    Friday meetings of, 80–81, 83
    success of, 83–85
cigarettes, 42–43
Citroën Deux Cheveaux (Douche Bag), 275–276, 282
Clark, Dick, 27–29, 143
Cleveland, Ohio, 169–170
Clinton, Bill, 253, 255–257
Clinton for President fund-raiser, 253–259
cochonnet, 16–17, 156, 272, 273, 283
coffee, 40–41, 47, 156
Collins, Larry, 88–90, 111–114, 169
    Mayor Spada and, 174–176
Collins, Nadia, 90, 111–112, 169

Columbia Broadcasting System, see CBS
Como, Perry, 147
Comorre, Jimmy, 79
ComTex, 242–243
Cop Out (game show), 170–173
Córdoba, 95–96
Corrigan, Paul, 202, 204–205
costume party, Barris thrown out of, 82–83
Crazy Solena (caretaker), 167, 168
Cronkite, Walter, 147

Dating Game (game show), 32–36, 47–54
    chaperons for, 77–79
    dirty talk on, 34–35
    on French television, 47–48
    Grissom and, 59–64, 284
    host of, see Lange, Jim
    lawsuits and, 78
    Marquis Chimps on, 119–120
    nighttime, 73–79, 83
    rating codes for, 50 51
    "rigging" charges and, 127
    St. Valentine's Day Massacre and, 48–54
    souvenirs from, 125–126
    staff writers for, 127–128
    travel to romantic cities as prizes for, 77–79
David, Madeline, 124, 133, 136, 137
Davis, Clifton, 144
death threats, 144
DeBartolo, Edward, 42, 283
DeBartolo, Little Janot, 42, 43, 45, 283
Debin, Jonathan, 50–51
Dede With The Beard, 273, 274
Dejonge, Trixie, 78
Del Capri Motel, 24
Dexter, Colin, 191
Dinkins, David, 280
doctors, French, 206–209, 212
dog acts, 145, 150
dogs, 291–292
    of Verdi, 193–195

see also Buddy
Donen, Stanley, 226
Douche Bag (Citroën Deux Cheveaux),
    275–276, 282
Downey, Laura, 252
Downey, Robert (The Prince), 246–
    249, 251, 252, 286
Dream Girls (game show), 83
Dropp, Beatrice (Call Me Honey),
    129–132
Dropp, Raymond C., 129–132
Dupee, Paul, 109

Edwards, Geoff, 147, 184–187
El Cordobés (Manuel Benitez), 89–97,
    285
    fiancées of, 92, 93
    film demands of, 92–93, 96
    flying of, 96–98
    as The Maestro, 90, 91, 92
Elhart Reform School, 144
Elliot, Cass (Mama Cass), 177–182
    chocolate cake spiked by, 179
Eubanks, Bob, 133, 134, 135, 147
Euro-Bumpkins, 44–45, 47
Euro-Trash, 44, 45, 47

fainting, 101, 188–190
Falk, Peter, 246, 247, 252
Family Game (game show), 83
Fat Phillipe, 67–68
Federal Bureau of Investigation (FBI),
    36
Federal Communications Commission
    (FCC), 27–29
Ferra, Christina, 227, 228, 230, 231
Fifi La Mass, 150
fireworks, 104–106
Fisher, Carrie, 256
flagpole construction, 166
Flotsam, Ivy, 184–191
    fainting of, 188–190
flying, 96–98
Fochet, H., 208
football, 42, 283

Forster, E. M., 18
Franco, Francisco, 98
Frank, Harriet, 92
Frank, Reuvan, 27, 75
Franke, Annie, 161
French language, 212
    Barris's problems with, 17, 19, 41,
    55, 88, 174, 212
    Red's problems with, 209
French people, 56–57
    Americans as viewed by, 13, 20, 57
    coffee drinking of, 41, 47, 156
    grammatical familiarity and, 42
    holier-than-thou attitudes of, 212
    hugging and kissing of, 42
    rudeness of, 57
    sense of humor of, 20, 39–40
    smoking of, 42–43
    teeth of, 67
    "tsking" by, 199
    see also specific people

Gallin, Sandy, 255
games, *see* sports and games
game shows:
    Barris as packager of, 32–37, 46–47,
    68, 70, 83, 124–128, 170–173,
    226–244
    hosts for, 133–137, 147
    scandals over, 125
    see also specific game shows
Garcia, Cherry, 64
Garvey, Steve, 144
Gazzara, Ben, 246, 247, 252
Geffen, David, 256
Gene Gene The Dancing Machine
    (Gene Patton), 145, 148, 152
George (The Professor), 273, 284
Gerard (*boule* player), 271–274
Germany, *Gong Show* in, 48, 120–121
Gigi (retired fisherman), 67–68, 183
    cremation of, 191
Goldberg, Leonard, 32–34, 73–78
Goldberg, Ruth, 58–62, 85, 87, 163
    Travers and, 180–181

Gong Show, 121–124, 133–137, 141–
     153
  bad acts on, 9–11, 121, 122
  band for, 285
  Barris as host of, 137, 141–153
  Barris's confusion about motivation
     for antics on, 152–153
  censors and, 147–148
  dog acts on, 145, 150
  first host selected for, 136–137
  in Germany, 48, 120–121
  impromptu auditions for, 142
  insults and, 142–143
  live run-through of, 122
  lunatic fringe and, 143–144
  network employees on, 145–146
  reruns of, 48, 120–121
  success of, 141, 148
Gong Show Movie, 98, 285–287
Goodson, Mark, 257, 258
Gorbachev, Mikhail, 229
Gorille, 17, 40–43, 47, 155–158, 219
  Gigi's death at, 183, 191
Gotterer, David, 84
Gottlieb, Larry, 179
Grant, Budd, 124–126, 241
Graves, Theresa, 172
Grimes, Tammy, 73
Crissom, John P. (The Exterminator),
     58–64, 120, 284
  marriage of, 63–64
Guber, Peter, 255

Hardy, Thomas, 139
hashish, 179–180
Herrera, Roger, 196
Holland, Ed (Father Ed), 145–147
Hollywood, Calif.:
  Barris in, 23, 24, 29–30, 33–34, 232–
     242
  clout in, 237–238
Hollywood General Hospital, 134–135
Holy Mother of the Vines, 194–195,
     197
Hope, Bob, 129

horse races, betting on, 156–158, 251,
     252
hospitals, French, 206–209, 277, 280–
     281
hosts, game show, 133–137, 147
house guests, 165–168
How's Your Mother-In-Law? (game
     show), 85, 99–103
Huyck, Willard, 228

jackets, *Bam Bam*, 268–270, 291
Janot the ex-mailman, 67–68, 155–156,
     282, 283, 284
Jean Yves, 45
Just, Ward, 215

Kampala, 78
Kata Kinabala, nudity in, 78
Katz, Gloria, 228
Katzenberg, Jeffrey, 255
Kelly, Grace, 27
Kennedy, John F., 111
Kennedy, Robert F., 111
Kennedy, Ted, 106, 111 117
  sexual behavior of, 114, 115, 117
Kidman, Nicole, 257
King, Michael, 237–240
King Brothers Company, 237–240
Kirby, Linda, 144
Klebenoff, Mrs., 136–137
Kurdistan, 79
Kuvakas, Ronnie, 60

Laconda Veneta, 224–226
Lange, Jim, 63, 133–134, 147
Lanigan, John, 27
Lapierre, Dominique, 88–91, 169, 226,
     265
L'ascale, 90
Las Vegas, Nev., 30–31
Late Night Something (proposed talk
     show), 250–252
lawn specialists, in France, 197–199
lawsuits, *Dating Game* and, 78
Lazar, Irving (Swifty), 88–89
Lee, Brenda, 28

Lennon, John, 144
Letterman, David, 150
Lies, Danny, 146
Life, 79–80
limousines, 217–218, 247
Loulou (electrician), 19–20, 156, 271–274, 284
love affairs, ending of, 172
Lucien (*boule* player), 57
Lupere, Joseph, 193–194, 197
Lupere, Josette, 193–194, 197

MCA Entertainment, 244–252
McEwan, Ian, 38
Mad Janot (caretaker), 167, 168
Madrid, 91
Maison Très Cher, 209–213, 265–268, 270–271
  improvement of grounds of, 197–201
  purchase of, 197
  wild boar incident at, 211–213
"making whoopee," 71–72
Málaga, 96–97
Mama Cass Television Program, The (TV special), 178–181
Mamas and Papas, 177
M&M's, 119–120
Marianna (Louis Ugo's girlfriend), 45
marijuana, 68–70
Marquis Chimps, 119–120
marriage:
  Barris's fear of, 278–280
  Dating Game and, 49–54, 63–64
Matson, Mary, 161
Medavoy, Mike, 92–95
Mercurio, Cathy, 66
Mercurio, Jean François, 66, 110–111
Mercurio, Moineau, 109, 110–111, 113, 195
Mercurio, Patrick, 106–108, 110–117
Mercurio, Tita (Teetee the Ultimate Cooking Machine), 65–67, 167
  Mayor Spada and, 270–271
  Red's health problems and, 206–209
  The Big One and, 272, 273
Mercurio Yacht Company, 117–118

Metzger, Mike, 78
Mexico City, 93–95
Miller, John, 237
Mims, Peter, 146
"Mr. Businessman" (song), 68
Mitchell, Joni, 180
Mobley, Joe, 165, 168
Mobley, Mary, 165, 168
monkeys:
  masturbating, 120
  organ grinder's, 119
  overfrequent exposure of, 136–137
Moreu, Jean Claude, 67–68
Moreu, Jean François, 67–68
Morgan, Jaye P., 136–137, 144, 148, 150, 152
Mothers (proposed TV show), 226–228, 230–235
  attempted sale of, 231–235, 237–244, 247
  origin of idea for, 226
  "problem" audition for, 230–231
mothers-in-law, 99–103
motorcycle accidents, 134, 211
Mount Sinai Hospital, 280, 281
movies, 88–98
  El Cordobés and, 89–98
  Gong Show Movie, 98, 285–287
Muerello, Louise, 144
Mulholland, Robert P., 10–11
music:
  American Bandstand and, 27–29
  on *Gong Show*, 136–137, 143–145
  Gong Show band and, 285
  songwriting and, 24–25, 29
  Travers and, 180–181
music payola scandals, 25, 27

NBC (National Broadcasting Company), 9–11, 23, 241
  Barris as page for, 26
  Barris in management training program of, 26–27
  Mothers and, 237
  Parent Game and, 124–126

Standards and Practices Department
of, 148
see also Gong Show
NBC Evening News, 27
Newlywed Game (game show), 70–75
host of, *see* Eubanks, Bob
nighttime, 73–75, 83
"whoopee" euphemisms on, 71–72
prizes for, 72, 74, 75
Newman, Paul, 92, 96
New Yorker, 154
nurse incident, 209, 212

Obsession (yacht), 111, 113–117
Ogiens, Mike, 81–83
$1.98 Beauty Show (TV show), 277–279
Operation Entertainment (TV show), 129–132
Or I'll Dress You In Mourning (Collins and Lapierre), film rights to, 88–98
Orloff, Thelma, 239
Owens, Monika, 165, 167, 168
Owens, William A., 165–168

"Palisades Park" (song), 24–25, 29
Papa Nöel, 289–291
Parent Game (game show), 124–127
Paris, George, 240–241
Patton, Gene (Gene Gene The Dancing Machine), 145, 148, 152
People Poker (game show), 202–204
Perth, Rod, 232–237
show ideas pitched to, 235–236
Peters, Jon, 255–256
Peterson, Michael, 13
Philadelphia, Pa., 46
Barris in, 26, 27, 28
Philadelphia Spectrum, 152
pipe specialists, in France, 199–201
piranhas, 78
Place des Lices, 98, 119, 159, 282–285
boule in, 15–19, 156, 174, 175, 210, 271–274, 283
trees of, 174–176, 270–271, 292

Playboy, 230–231
Plaza Hotel, 173
policewomen, on *People Poker*, 203, 204
Popsicle Twins, 9–11, 148
prizes:
for *Dating Game*, 76–79
for *Newlywed Game*, 72, 74, 75
for *Treasure Hunt*, 184, 186–187, 190
prostitutes:
Dating Game and, 54, 62–64
dentures of, 64
on *People Poker*, 203, 204

Radio Corporation of America, 26
Radio Nice, 90
Ramatuelle, 193, 194
Ravitch, Irving, 92
Reubens, Paul (Pee Wee Herman), 143
reviews:
of *Dating Game*, 64, 120, 134
German, 120–121
of *Gong Show Movie*, 286 287
by Grissom, 64, 120
Reynolds, Burt, 61, 172
Ritt, Marty, 92
Roberts, Bobby, 178
rock and roll, 24–25, 29, 68
rodeos, 30–31
Ronnie (Bistro Gardens waiter), 219
Ronnie (Laconda Veneta waiter), 225
Rosen, Mort, 242
Ruiz, Paco, 91–95, 97
Rydell, Bobby, 24

Saborine, Diane, 146
Ste. Maxime, 56, 67
St. Patrick's Cathedral, 85
Saint-Tropez, 15–21, 37–48, 55–58, 65–68, 89–90, 98, 119–121, 154–158, 164–169, 174–178, 191–201, 206–213, 258, 265–277, 280–285
Armed Forces Network TV for, 256–257
Bam Bam jackets in, 268–270, 291

bar-restaurants in, 17, 40–43, 47, 155–158
Barris's disinfatuation with, 212–213
Barris's first visit to, 154–155
Barris's homesickness for, 244
Barris's houses in, 193–201; *see also* Maison Très Cher
boule games in, 15–21, 37, 45, 66–67, 156, 174, 175, 210, 271–275
December in, 288–292
described, 15, 249–250
mornings in, 37–48, 155
movie theater in, 88, 285
Owens's visit to, 165–168
tourists in, 15–17, 41–42, 44–47
see also Place des Lices; *specific people*
Saint-Tropez General Hospital, 277, 280–281
St. Valentine's Day Massacre, 48–54
San Francisco Forty Niners, 42, 283
satellite television dish, 164–165
Savage, Dick, 144
scandals:
game show, 125
music payola, 25, 27
Schiff-Dupee, Lizbeth, 109–110
Schwab, Shelly, 245–252, 260
Sebastian, John, 180
Selleck, Tom, 61
Seneca, 263
Senequier, 40, 47
Seville, 91
sex, sexual behavior:
of Barris, 26, 27, 94–95
of Cass Elliot, 181–182
Dating Game and, 34–36
of grandmothers, 231
Popsicle Twins and, 9–11, 148
of "sisters," 92, 94–95
of Ted Kennedy, 114, 115, 117
Shepherd, Dick, 88, 92–93
Shmul, Harry, 46–47
Siegel, Willard, 220–224, 242–243
Sistine Chapel, 79
60 Minutes (TV show), 159, 189–191

smoking, 42–43
Snider, Ed, 66
Snider, Myrna (Yahoo), 114
Snot Nose (Perth's assistant), 234, 235, 236
Soncini, Bruno, 67–68
Spada, Anastasia, 270
Spada, Mayor, 174–176, 266–268, 270
Spain, Barris in, 90–92, 95–98
sprinkler system, 198–199
"Star Spangled Banner, The," 166, 168
Staub, Rusty, 106, 116–117
Steak Pit, 181
stock market, 85–87
Strickland, Loretta, 75–77, 135, 162, 173, 236
Mothers and, 232, 233, 237, 240–241, 247
strip tease, 43–44, 45
Sullivan, Ed, 147
Sweet Doris (housekeeper), 167, 168
Swinging Seminarians, 150

Talbert, Victor, 283
taxis, French, 57
Taylor, Rip, 278
Three's a Crowd (game show), 85, 159–163
Thurber, Susanne, 29, 30
Tijuana, *Dating Game* marriage in, 53–54
Todd, Mike, 86
tourists, 41–42
American, 15–17, 45–47
Bam Bam and, 117
Euro-Bumpkins, 44–45, 47
Euro-Trash, 44, 45, 47
Travers, Mary, 180–181
Treasure Hunt (game show), 183–191
described, 184
Edwards as host of, 147, 184–187
prizes for, 184, 186–187, 190
Tremont, Dede, 45
Tricia (airline stewardess), 82, 83
"tsking," art of, 199

Ugo, Louis, 19–20, 45, 273
unicyclist act, 148–152
unions, *Gong Show* and, 146
Universal Studios, 285–286
Unknown Comic, 143

Vaccaro, Kimberly, 230–231
Vaccaro, Raquel, 230–231
Valenti, Jack, 92
Valentine's Day, *Dating Game* and, 48–54
Van Doren, Charles, 125
Vane, Ed, 49–50, 52, 53
    How's Your Mother-in-Law? and, 99–103
    Three's a Crowd and, 162
Variety, 202, 204–205
Vendela, 255
Verdi, Giancarlo, 193–195, 197
Vert, Reverend, 145
Villobos, 90–91
Vogue, 269–270

Volcheck, Florence, 102–103

waiters:
    American, 219, 221–222, 224–225, 254
    French, 57, 155
Wallace, Mike, 159, 189–191
Wasserman, Lew, 253, 254, 257
Wasserman, Mrs. Lew, 254, 257
Weinbach, Mort, 25, 29
"whoopee session," 71–72
widow of Saint-Tropez, 39, 55, 155, 292
Williams, Andy, 147
Willie (dog), 291–292
World Series, 164–165
Wyndham Hotel, 245–246, 280

yachts, 104–106
    Obsession, 111, 113–117
You And Me, Babe (Barris), 169–171